Transforming
Introductory
Psychology

Transforming Introductory Psychology

Expert Advice on Teacher Training, Course Design, and Student Success

edited by

Regan A. R. Gurung
& Garth Neufeld

 AMERICAN PSYCHOLOGICAL ASSOCIATION

Published by
American Psychological Association
750 First Street, NE
Washington, DC 20002
https://www.apa.org

Order Department
https://www.apa.org/pubs/books
order@apa.org

In the U.K., Europe, Africa, and the Middle East, copies may be ordered from Eurospan
https://www.eurospanbookstore.com/apa
info@eurospangroup.com

Typeset in Charter and Interstate by Circle Graphics, Inc., Reisterstown, MD

Printer: Gasch Printing, Odenton, MD
Cover Designer: Mark Karis, Frederick, MD

Library of Congress Cataloging-in-Publication Data

Names: Gurung, Regan A. R., editor. | Neufeld, Garth, editor.
Title: Transforming introductory psychology : expert advice on teacher training,
    course design, and student success / edited by Regan A.R. Gurung and Garth Neufeld.
Description: Washington : American Psychological Association, 2022. |
    Includes bibliographical references and index.
Identifiers: LCCN 2021002156 (print) | LCCN 2021002157 (ebook) |
    ISBN 9781433834721 (paperback) | ISBN 9781433837289 (ebook)
Subjects: LCSH: Psychology—Study and teaching (Higher)
Classification: LCC BF77 .T736 2022 (print) | LCC BF77 (ebook) |
    DDC 150.76—dc23
LC record available at https://lccn.loc.gov/2021002156
LC ebook record available at https://lccn.loc.gov/2021002157

https://doi.org/10.1037/0000260-000

Printed in the United States of America

10 9 8 7 6 5 4 3 2 1

Contents

Contributors

William S. Altman, PhD, SUNY Broome Community College, Binghamton, NY, United States

Melissa J. Beers, PhD, Ohio State University, Columbus, OH, United States

Guy A. Boysen, PhD, McKendree University, Lebanon, IL, United States

Karen Brakke, PhD, Spelman College, Atlanta, GA, United States

Michael Cassens, MA, Irvine Valley College, Irvine, CA, United States

Stephen L. Chew, PhD, Samford University, Birmingham, AL, United States

Dana S. Dunn, PhD, Moravian College, Bethlehem, PA, United States

Angela Farris-Watkins, PhD, Spelman College, Atlanta, GA, United States

Juanchella Grooms Francis, PhD, Spelman College, Atlanta, GA, United States

Sue Frantz, MA, Highline College, Renton, WA, United States

Regan A. R. Gurung, PhD, Oregon State University, Corvallis, OR, United States

Jane S. Halonen, PhD, University of West Florida, Milton, FL, United States

Elizabeth Yost Hammer, PhD, Xavier University of Louisiana, New Orleans, LA, United States

Bridgette Martin Hard, PhD, Duke University, Durham, NC, United States

Erin E. Hardin, PhD, University of Tennessee, Knoxville, TN, United States

Shani N. Harris, PhD, Spelman College, Atlanta, GA, United States

Danae L. Hudson, PhD, Missouri State University, Springfield, MO, United States

R. Eric Landrum, PhD, Boise State University, Boise, ID, United States

Kai M. McCormack, PhD, Spelman College, Atlanta, GA, United States

Benjamin Mis, PhD, Irvine Valley College, Irvine, CA, United States

Robin Musselman, EdD, Lehigh Carbon Community College, Schnecksville, PA, United States

Karen Z. Naufel, PhD, Georgia Southern University, Statesboro, GA, United States

Garth Neufeld, MA, Cascadia College, Bothell, WA, United States

Aaron S. Richmond, PhD, Metropolitan State University of Denver, Denver, CO, United States

Jerry Rudmann, PhD, Irvine Valley College, Irvine, CA, United States

Yemmy Taylor, PhD, Irvine Valley College, Irvine, CA, United States

Jennifer L. W. Thompson, PhD, University of Maryland Global Campus, Adelphi, MD, United States

Jordan D. Troisi, PhD, Colby College, Waterville, ME, United States

Kari Tucker, PhD, Irvine Valley College, Irvine, CA, United States

Kristin H. Whitlock, MEd, Davis High School, Kaysville, UT, United States

Katherine Wickes, PhD, Blinn College, Bryan, TX, United States

Preface

We both remember our early years of teaching introductory psychology. Assigned to teach the course for the first time, we were stunned by the overwhelming amount of content in a 500-page textbook that we were to somehow help our students learn while only being one step ahead. We recall how vulnerable it felt to be teaching subtopics of psychology in which we had never taken coursework. It seemed like a Herculean task to put together an effective course when we had little-to-no training in teaching or design. There were few places to look and seemingly no sanctioned guidance. How nice it would have been to have a mentor to walk us through those issues, a companion to help us create a meaningful course that would engage our students and open their eyes to the wonder and benefit of psychology.

This book—a compilation of recommendations curated and developed by the members of the American Psychological Association's (APA) Introductory Psychology Initiative (IPI; APA, 2020)—can be that friendly mentor for teachers of introductory psychology. We are hopeful that this collaborative effort by 22 veteran teachers and scholars of introductory psychology will be a valuable resource to the thousands of instructors who teach this course to hundreds of thousands of students each term.

The IPI builds on the contributions from two APA Board of Educational Affairs (BEA) working groups focused on introductory psychology (e.g., the BEA Working Group on Strengthening the Common Core of the Introductory Psychology Course and the BEA Working Group on Assessing Introductory

Psychology), as well as the 2016 APA Summit on National Assessment of Psychology. Each task force presented a set of key recommendations for future work on introductory psychology (APA, 2014, 2017), and a major article on the topic was published in an *American Psychologist* special issue (Gurung et al., 2016).

The IPI convened in December 2017, and during 2018, ten members of the IPI steering committee lead four working groups in a multistep recommendations process. In 2019, APA hosted a Summit on Introductory Psychology. The group conducted a national survey of instructors, the IPI Introductory Psychology Census (Richmond et al., 2021), as well as other data collection endeavors. The group reviewed existing research, gathered missing data, and consulted with stakeholders and instructors of introductory psychology from diverse backgrounds. Early versions of the recommendations were pilot tested in 2019 and 2020 at a wide variety of academic institutions. The feedback received from the pilots led to the final recommendations contained in this book.

We are grateful to our dream team of collaborators who made up the IPI. They are the heavy lifters of this work and need special kudos; these individuals include the following (listed by working group): *Student Learning Outcomes & Assessment*—Cochairs Jennifer L. W. Thompson (University of Maryland Global Campus) and Kristin H. Whitlock (Davis High School), Sue Frantz (Highline College), Jane S. Halonen (University of West Florida), and R. Eric Landrum (Boise State University). *Course Models and Design*—Cochairs Bridgette Martin Hard (Duke University) and Dana S. Dunn (Moravian College), Danae L. Hudson (Missouri State University), Robin Musselman (Lehigh Carbon Community College), and Aaron S. Richmond (Metropolitan State University of Denver). *Teacher Training and Development*—Cochairs William S. Altman (SUNY Broome Community College) and Melissa J. Beers (The Ohio State University), Erin E. Hardin (University of Tennessee), Jordan D. Troisi (Colby College), and Elizabeth Yost Hammer (Xavier University of Louisiana). *Student Success & Transformation*—Cochairs Katherine Wickes (Blinn College) and Stephen L. Chew (Samford University), Guy A. Boysen (McKendree University), Karen Z. Naufel (Georgia Southern University), and Jerry Rudmann (Irvine Valley College).

We are also grateful to our APA liaisons: Martha Boenau, who worked closely with us throughout the nearly 4-year process, and Robin Hailstorks, Catherine Grus, Jaime Diaz-Granados, and everyone else on the APA BEA who have so strongly supported the work. Finally, we are grateful to the hundreds of instructors of Introductory Psychology who participated and contributed by completing surveys and pilot-testing recommendations. This book would not be possible without you.

Finally, to every teacher who believes in the ability of this course to transform students' lives in positive ways, this book is for you.

—Regan A. R. Gurung and Garth Neufeld
Cochairs, APA IPI

REFERENCES

American Psychological Association. (2017). *Assessment of outcomes of the introductory course in psychology.* https://www.apa.org/ed/precollege/undergrad/index.aspx

American Psychological Association. (2020). *The APA Introductory Psychology Initiative.* https://www.apa.org/ed/precollege/undergrad/introductory-psychology-initiative

American Psychological Association, Board of Educational Affairs. (2014). *Strengthening the common core of the introductory psychology course.* https://www.apa.org/ed/governance/bea/intro-psych-report.pdf

Gurung, R. A. R., Hackathorn, J., Enns, C., Frantz, S., Cacioppo, J. T., Loop, T., & Freeman, J. (2016). Strengthening introductory psychology: A new model for teaching intro psych. *American Psychologist, 71*(2), 112–124. https://doi.org/10.1037/a0040012

Richmond, A. S., Boysen, G. A., Hudson, D. L., Gurung, R. A. R., Naufel, K. Z., Neufeld, G., Landrum, R. E., Dunn, D. S., & Beers, M. (2021). The Introductory Psychology Census: A national study. *Scholarship of Teaching and Learning in Psychology.* Advance online publication. https://doi.org/10.1037/stl0000277

Transforming
Introductory
Psychology

INTRODUCTION

The Introductory Psychology Initiative

REGAN A. R. GURUNG AND GARTH NEUFELD

Between 1.2 and 1.6 million undergraduate students take introductory psychology each year (Gurung et al., 2016). The course is featured in nearly every psychology program (Norcross et al., 2016), and it is now a part of other disciplinary plans, such as medicine (Mitchell et al., 2016). How should it be taught? How should learning in the course be assessed?

Given the numbers of students who take the course and its role in presenting the discipline, in 2017 the American Psychological Association's (APA's) Board of Educational Affairs (BEA) formed a working group at the recommendation of the Committee on Associate and Baccalaureate Education. This group, the Introductory Psychology Initiative (IPI; APA, 2020), took a long, focused look at the introductory course given the ramifications that course learning outcomes, assessment, and design could have for learning, general education, the major, and the public face of psychology. The group conducted extensive research, developed a set of recommendations based on that research, and then pilot tested those recommendations.

This book presents the APA IPI's final recommendations surrounding four major areas: Student Learning Outcomes and Assessments, Course Models and Design, Teacher Training and Development, and Student Success

https://doi.org/10.1037/0000260-001
Transforming Introductory Psychology: Expert Advice on Teacher Training, Course Design, and Student Success, R. A. R. Gurung and G. Neufeld (Editors)

and Transformation. This volume is a "must-read" for every department and every faculty member teaching the course; department chairs will have a major interest in these recommendations, and the relevance of these four components make this book essential to anyone teaching the class. The recommendations provided stand to aid more than 17,000 instructors who teach the course and nearly 4,200 colleges and universities; they are relevant to sections of the MCAT (Medical College Admission Test), high school psychology classes, and even how the College Board modifies the Advanced Placement psychology exam.

This book is divided into two main parts. Part I covers the major efforts of the IPI. After making the case as to why introductory psychology is deserving of such attention, chapters tackle major parts of the course, including learning outcomes, assessment, course design, teacher training, and deliverable skills. For quick reference, each of these subsequent chapters begins by offering a list of IPI recommendations. The chapter authors then weave together research and expertise to make the case for these recommendations.

The first chapter positions the current work in the context of a history of research on the introductory course. It also provides an overview of how the course has been used in different disciplines and highlights general pedagogical research on the topic. In particular, it focuses on the different contexts in which the course has been taught (e.g., universities, community colleges, high schools) and highlights some of the various purposes it serves. This is followed by a second chapter outlining the key elements of course design, particularly the use of backward design. Chapter 2 nicely highlights some basic evidence-informed practices that are important for course design in general but also to keep in mind when planning to teach introductory psychology specifically.

The third chapter focuses on student learning outcomes (SLOs) and is followed by a chapter on assessment. The goal here is to create an overarching framework to suggest to instructors how to address curricular goals. First, Chapter 3 provides the context for a focus on assessment and discusses the importance of SLOs in the introductory psychology course. Next, it articulates the most useful outcomes and provides a new set of SLOs for the introductory psychology course. Chapter 4 then helps readers craft assessments that can be used to evaluate indicators that are aligned with SLOs. In addition, it reviews what constitutes good assessment and what is absolutely needed when assessing for reporting purposes. Sample assessments for SLOs are provided for readers to use directly or as a foundation on which to model their own assessments.

Chapter 5 examines the approaches used and the challenges faced by instructors who teach introductory psychology. It takes into account both varying class size and institutional type (e.g., public, private, research 1 [R1], liberal arts, comprehensive university, 2-year colleges), as well as how each affects course design and delivery. The goal of this chapter is to educate and support instructors in how to effectively implement recommended SLOs and assessment guidelines by sharing various approaches to teaching the course and providing techniques and guidance for the challenges that may arise in an introductory psychology classroom.

The sixth chapter focuses on student skills and transformation, compiling best practices and empirical work on which study techniques are most successful (e.g., quizzing, spaced practice) and which indicators (e.g., retention, recruitment to the major) can and should be used to convey the value and utility of introductory psychology to administrators and external constituents (e.g., state boards, taxpayers).

The final chapter in Part I reviews the existing support and training for instructors who teach introductory psychology and identifies training needs. It presents various teacher training models and support for teachers in differing contexts while distinguishing content-agnostic versus content-specific training models. Specifically, it elucidates what training is general to good teaching and what is particular to introductory psychology.

In Part II, we present 10 short chapters as context studies at various institution types, reporting on and modeling what has been done and what can be done to implement the recommendations from Part I. The authors, primarily members of the APA IPI team, invite readers into the different contexts in which the introductory psychology course is taught. Because funding, students, facilities, requirements, and a host of other factors differ across types of school, each author first describes their type of school in detail. Schools vary in class sizes, whether the course is taught in one part or two, and in the level of coordination across sections. Through the authors' rich detailing of all these factors, readers will see how introductory psychology varies across public and private colleges and universities, R1 universities, liberal arts colleges, comprehensive universities, 2-year colleges, and psychology in the high school. Authors then directly address how the IPI recommendations will be implemented at each institution.

We believe that this book will transform the way you teach introductory psychology and that it may very well change how you look at teaching in general. For new instructors, this book can act as the companion and mentor that so many of us never had when we first started teaching the course. Although we have stopped short of making this work prescriptive, the members of the IPI have labored diligently to present recommendations that reflect the best and most current research in teaching and learning, specifically as it relates to this course. In the end, this book is for you and for your students. With a fundamental belief that this course can make our lives and our world better, we want to give students the best chance to understand the value of psychology and its transformative power. We thank you for your role in bringing this to fruition.

REFERENCES

American Psychological Association. (2020). *The APA Introductory Psychology Initiative.* https://www.apa.org/ed/precollege/undergrad/introductory-psychology-initiative

Gurung, R. A. R., Hackathorn, J., Enns, C., Frantz, S., Cacioppo, J. T., Loop, T., & Freeman, J. E. (2016). Strengthening introductory psychology: A new model for teaching the introductory course. *American Psychologist, 71*(2), 112–124. https://doi.org/10.1037/a0040012

Mitchell, K., Lewis, R. S., Satterfield, J., & Hong, B. A. (2016). The new Medical College Admission Test: Implications for teaching psychology. *American Psychologist, 71*(2), 125–135. https://doi.org/10.1037/a0039975

Norcross, J. C., Hailstorks, R., Aiken, L. S., Pfund, R. A., Stamm, K. E., & Christidis, P. (2016). Undergraduate study in psychology: Curriculum and assessment. *American Psychologist, 71*(2), 89–101. https://doi.org/10.1037/a0040095

PART I

INTRODUCTORY
PSYCHOLOGY
INITIATIVE
RECOMMENDATIONS

1

WHY INTRODUCTORY PSYCHOLOGY?

STEPHEN L. CHEW, KAREN Z. NAUFEL, GUY A. BOYSEN, KATHERINE WICKES, AND JERRY RUDMANN

Psychology [is] the study of the mind and behavior. [A] diverse scientific discipline comprising several major branches of research as well as several subareas of research and applied psychology.

(*APA Dictionary of Psychology*; American Psychological Association, n.d.)

This near-standard definition of psychology appears at the beginning of most introductory psychology courses. Although this wording accurately defines psychology, it does not encapsulate the full importance of an introductory psychology course. In the process of studying about the mind and behavior, students also gain insight into their own habits, thoughts and feelings, and interactions with others. Students who complete a well-planned, effective introductory psychology course should leave with the knowledge and skills to better manage their academic endeavors, promote well-being in their personal lives, and improve society.

Introductory psychology can be taught in a way that inspires students to draw connections from course content to the knowledge and skills necessary for success. Yet this value is sometimes lost in the push to deliver breadth of

https://doi.org/10.1037/0000260-002

Transforming Introductory Psychology: Expert Advice on Teacher Training, Course Design, and Student Success, R. A. R. Gurung and G. Neufeld (Editors)

coverage and amount of content. Similarly, because introductory psychology is a course taken by students outside of psychology as part of their general education, students may treat it as a requirement to check off rather than an opportunity to gain knowledge and skills directly relevant to their personal, academic, and professional goals. If taught well, introductory psychology has the unique potential to enhance the academic and career success of students. It can promote critical thinking and scientific literacy, which are essential to make better, more informed decisions. This book makes the case for the value of introductory psychology and the importance of teaching it well.

AN ESSENTIAL COURSE

Introductory psychology is already one of the most popular courses for students to take (Gurung et al., 2016). It is also the most popular course taken to fulfill general education requirements for social sciences (Adelman, 2004). If the course is already so popular, then why should psychology teachers worry about improving it? We believe that introductory psychology has yet to realize its full potential for improving the academic and career success of the students who take it. By describing the specific advantages that can be gained by taking introductory psychology, we will show why it is an essential course for student success and why instructors and institutions should invest the effort to ensure the course is taught well.

First, introductory psychology is the only course that teaches important knowledge and skills for academic success as part of its subject matter. An obvious example is study skills, such as how to focus attention, how to develop good study habits, and how to study for optimal long-term learning. Students can learn about self-regulation of emotions and behavior, dealing with stress and anxiety, the importance of healthy sleep habits, and the importance of ethical practices when dealing with others. Much of the content of introductory psychology is directly relevant to academic success, and because many students take it early in their coursework, it is timely as well. Wang (2017) pointed out that early college success can foster the academic momentum needed for successful degree completion, especially for first-generation college students, students with poor college preparation, and community college students intending to transfer to 4-year colleges. We feel the knowledge that can be gained in a well-taught introductory psychology course can play an integral role in promoting academic momentum.

Second, introductory psychology introduces many skills necessary for work and career success. Naufel et al. (2019) showed that many of the skills most desired by employers can be addressed in introductory psychology. The development of skills is a key Introductory Psychology Initiative (American Psychological Association [APA], 2020) recommendation, as expanded on in Chapter 2.

Third, introductory psychology is uniquely interdisciplinary. Psychology focuses on how individuals think and act and on all the influences that shape individuals. Virtually all other social sciences focus primarily on the behavior of groups. Boyack et al. (2005) scaled the similarity and relatedness of scientific disciplines. Psychology stood apart from the cluster of other social sciences, forming its own unique hub (Cacioppo, 2007). Psychology is more deeply connected with other scientific fields, especially the life sciences. To learn psychology is to learn about the interplay of many other scientific fields.

Fourth, introductory psychology is suited to help students develop scientific literacy and critical thinking skills. Research supports the potential of introductory psychology to improve skills related to critical thinking (Lawson & Brown, 2018; Wentworth & Whitmarsh, 2017) and scientific reasoning (Becker-Blease et al., 2019; Stevens et al., 2016).

A POPULAR COURSE

Introductory psychology is among the most popular courses taken by undergraduate students. Gurung et al. (2016) reported that an estimated 1.2 million to 1.6 million students take the course each year in the United States, making it the second most popular college course in the nation. What explains the high enrollment in the course? There are multiple reasons, some having to do with curriculum requirements and some having to do with a genuine inherent interest in psychology. We start by discussing why introductory psychology is required in many programs.

A Popular Required Course

One obvious explanation for the popularity of introductory psychology is its status as a required course in 94% of the undergraduate psychology degree programs in the United States (Norcross et al., 2016). Thus, introductory psychology serves as the foundational course for one of the most popular majors in the United States (Clay, 2017). Furthermore, introductory psychology is typically required for more advanced psychology courses. If students wish to earn a psychology minor, or even take other popular psychology electives such as abnormal or social psychology, then they must begin with introductory psychology.

Many preprofessional programs and other disciplines require introductory psychology in recognition of the need to incorporate psychology-based knowledge and skills into their own curriculum's structure. Such programs include health professions, teacher education, and business. The Association of American Medical Colleges (n.d.), for example, includes human behavior as a core science competency for students beginning medical school. Consequently, the Medical College Admissions Test (MCAT) began including a section emphasizing psychology, behavioral science, statistics, and research design with 20% of the MCAT containing questions relating to these areas (Hong, 2012). Other health care fields have noted the importance of having a psychology foundation in the general core of their curriculum. Nursing programs in several countries require psychology as part of their curriculum, and many have noted that a strong psychological foundation is essential to providing quality care to patients (de Vries & Timmins, 2012). Dental programs worldwide have also noted the importance of psychology within the curriculum (McGoldrick & Pine, 1999; Murthy et al., 2017), with behavioral science being a required component in the dental undergraduate curriculum in the United Kingdom (Pine & McGoldrick, 2000). This once again shows that introductory psychology can play a prominent role in shaping the education of psychology majors and nonmajors alike.

A Popular General Education Course for the Liberal Arts

Educators see introductory psychology as a way to expose students to social science theories and methods, but they also see it as a valuable course for promoting liberal arts thinking and values (Gray, 2008). The course plays an important role as a service course in the general education curricula of most colleges and universities (APA, 2017). Eighty percent of introductory psychology instructors report that the course is part of their institution's general education program (Richmond et al., 2021).

The most common type of general education program is the core distribution model (Brint et al., 2009). Within the core distribution model, students take a set number of credits from an intellectual core to ensure breadth of education. Across institutions, the social sciences are a standard part of the general education core, along with the humanities and natural sciences (Brint et al., 2009; Warner & Koeppel, 2009). To cite the two largest university systems in the country as examples, introductory psychology fulfills a social science requirement in the general education programs of both the California State University (n.d.) and the State University of New York (n.d.). Distribution models inherently offer students choices in course selection, but introductory psychology is the most popular option among social sciences (Adelman, 2004). As such, it is one of the most common general education courses in the United States.

Psychologists have long recognized the importance of psychology to general education (Costin, 1982; Harper, 1954) because psychology has the potential to foster liberal arts skills. Development of liberal arts skills includes outcomes such as critical thinking, effective communication, ethical reasoning, quantitative literacy, information literacy, effective collaboration, and intercultural competence (American Association of Colleges and Universities, n.d.). Extensive overlap exists between these liberal arts skills and the goals of a psychology education. High-quality programs in psychology have learning outcomes that include writing, speaking, research, collaboration, and information literacy (Dunn et al., 2007). In addition, the concept of psychological literacy largely reflects the development of liberal arts skills (McGovern et al., 2010). Specifically, psychological literacy includes abilities such as communicating effectively, solving problems scientifically, acting ethically, and respecting diversity.

The *APA Guidelines for the Undergraduate Psychology Major* (APA, 2013) defines what students should be able to do after a foundational level of psychology education. At this most basic level, psychology students should develop the knowledge and skills necessary to think critically, communicate effectively, recognize human diversity, and contribute to collaborative work (APA, 2013). Moreover, APA's proposed common core for introductory psychology includes the scientific method, diversity, and ethics (APA, 2014; Gurung et al., 2016). In fact, educators have argued that introductory psychology should emphasize skills such as scientific reasoning and critical thinking as much as content (Jhangiani & Hardin, 2015), and the majority of introductory psychology instructors report that they directly address skills as part of the course (Richmond et al., 2021). The goal of a general education in the liberal arts is to give students a breadth of intellectual tools that will remain even after domain-specific facts have been forgotten or become obsolete, and the learning outcomes of introductory psychology are consistent with that goal.

Understanding how people perceive, think, act, and respond is useful in most any discipline. In certain disciplines, this connection may be more obvious. For instance, disciplines such as marketing, nursing, and public health often apply psychological theories to promote products, patient care, or wellness, respectively. Even disciplines such as geosciences, physics, and chemistry benefit from psychology. These disciplines use the scientific method, which makes knowing about biases—a psychological construct—particularly important. For instance, experimental bias, first described by Oskar Pfungst in 1907 (Hothersall, 2004), is recognized as an important phenomenon to avoid in physics (Jeng, 2006) and as problematic in the life sciences (Holman et al., 2015). Similarly, the confirmation bias, or the tendency to seek out answers that confirm rather than disconfirm beliefs, creates obstacles in the validity of forensic anthropology (Nakhaeizadeh et al., 2014). Aspiring inventors and engineers may wish to know about hindsight bias, as many patent decisions seem influenced by it (Mandel, 2006). Geologists, too, recognize the need to understand cognitive biases in making decisions from data collected via robotic mechanisms (Wagner et al., 2004). To summarize, biases are present in any scientific discipline. Awareness of such biases, as taught in introductory psychology, could both reduce their likelihood and enhance the quality of science.

Research supports the potential of introductory psychology to improve skills related to critical thinking (Lawson & Brown, 2018; Wentworth & Whitmarsh, 2017), ethical behavior (Landrum et al., 2019), scientific reasoning (Becker-Blease et al., 2019; Stevens et al., 2016), diversity (Nordstrom, 2015), ethics (Fisher & Kuther, 1997), and communication (Fallahi et al., 2006; Madigan & Brosamer, 1990). Despite evidence that introductory psychology can lead to skill development, such outcomes require teachers and programs to set liberal arts skills as learning objectives for the course. Analysis of learning objectives listed on introductory psychology syllabi illustrate that goals related to the liberal arts are far from universal (Homa et al., 2013). Although 67% of syllabi listed goals related to research methods and 52% listed goals related to critical thinking, no other goal was listed on more than 26% of syllabi. The absence of liberal arts goals on many syllabi suggests that there is room to expand and unify the common core of introductory psychology as it relates to general education. Overall, introductory psychology is a core component of general education curricula across institutions, and this makes it a prime opportunity for the field to teach students a psychological approach to liberal arts skills.

A Popular Course, Required or Otherwise

The fact that introductory psychology fulfills a general education requirement for social science and is required for a variety of majors still cannot completely explain its popularity. There is a vast interest in how people, including ourselves, think, feel, and behave. The interest exists even before students get to college. About 312,000 students took the Advanced Placement (AP) Psychology exam in 2019, making it the sixth most popular AP exam to take and the most popular AP course among science, technology, engineering, and mathematics fields (College Board, 2019).

Finally, many students simply take introductory psychology out of curiosity, making it a popular elective course. Harackiewicz et al. (2008) found that introductory psychology students enter the course with a high interest in learning about the field. Interestingly, Yu et al. (2020) found that most students who majored in psychology had no intention to do so when arriving at college. Alternatively, the majority of students who entered college as psychology majors but who had no prior exposure to psychology in high school were more likely to change majors. Presumably, the introductory psychology course played a role in stimulating or dampening their interest.

In sum, introductory psychology is popular for many reasons. It is required for psychology majors, but many constituencies outside of psychology also recognize its importance and value. Preprofessional fields such as health, education, and engineering have explicitly noted that knowledge of psychology is vital to the success of their students. Educators see the value of introductory psychology in promoting liberal arts values and critical thinking, specifically from the perspective of the social sciences.

A TRANSFORMATIVE COURSE

A well-planned introductory psychology course can further students' success and positive transformation. The combination of content and format can be structured in a way that promotes academic success beyond the introductory psychology course, and career and life success beyond college.

Effective Study Skills

Introductory psychology can promote student academic success in a variety of ways. Students may face challenges in studying effectively. They must overcome erroneous beliefs—some even shared by professors—about study strategies, such as the effectiveness of rereading the textbook without engagement or recopying notes (Morehead et al., 2016). When students rely on such strategies, regardless of discipline, their academic performance tends to be lower. Unfortunately, students may carry ineffective habits to graduate school, resulting in poorer performance on tests and tasks. As examples, some graduate students in education (Onwuegbuzie et al., 2001), medicine (McNulty et al., 2012), and pharmacy (Persky & Hudson, 2016) continue to use ineffective study strategies that can harm their performance. Beyond academic performance, there is a danger if professionals are only superficially learning information. If they only memorize facts for the short

(handwritten annotation) ⤷difference b/w studying for a test in a non-major class + being motivated to learn on-the-job

term, then they may not recall necessary information when caring for people in the future.

However, introductory psychology may provide the answer to these study skill woes. Memory is a psychological process that is one of the most commonly taught subjects in introductory psychology (Miller & Gentile, 1998; Richmond et al., 2021). The memory discussion could, therefore, incorporate known study strategies that promote long-term retention of material, such as deep processing, self-generation, self-testing, and distributed learning (Hartwig & Dunlosky, 2012). Most introductory psychology instructors report covering study skills explicitly in the course (Richmond et al., 2021). As evidence for the impact of this coverage, seniors who previously took introductory psychology often recalled topics related to memory and study skills as being beneficial to their college career (Hard et al., 2019). To help teachers integrate study skills as part of their discussion of memory and attention, a study skills module is included in the supplementary materials of this book. The module includes a lesson plan, presentation slides, resources, activities, and assessments.

Academic Momentum

Academic momentum is a collection of academic behaviors and efforts that students exhibit that moves them toward academic success (Wang, 2017). These behaviors include taking a sufficient number of challenging courses, using effective study behaviors and strategies, and completing the courses successfully. In an exhaustive review of the academic success literature, Wang (2017) pointed out two main factors not typically emphasized when considering the momentum of community college students: course factors and motivational attributes. Regarding course factors, instructional design and delivery must clearly link the course content to concrete applications (Wang et al., 2017). In addition to course factors, motivational attributes and beliefs contribute to the forward progress of degree completion by community college students (Adelman, 1999, 2006; Tinto, 2013). Students who lack the motivation needed to persevere when they encounter barriers and setbacks have difficulty maintaining sufficient motivation. Sufficient academic momentum in the first year of college is strongly related to later academic achievement and outcomes.

Because introductory psychology is required to fulfill program or general education requirements and students often take it early in their academic careers, it is well positioned to contribute to the greater academic motivation and perseverance of a significant portion of college students. This potential contribution is especially true for transfer-oriented students attending a community college, first-generation students, and students with poor academic preparation for college (Wang, 2017). Incorporating self-regulation skills and evidence-based learning strategies into introductory psychology can contribute to academic momentum.

Career and Work Skills

Introductory psychology provides the opportunity to cultivate workforce-ready skills. APA's Committee on Associate and Baccalaureate Education (CABE) recently convened a working group to identify workforce-related skills produced by undergraduate coursework in psychology. The working group conducted a comprehensive, systematic study of skills desired by today's employers (Naufel et al., 2019). Employers want students to be well versed in a multitude of essential skills: Communication, respect, adaptability, integrity, positive attitude, professionalism, responsibility, collaboration, teamwork, leadership, time management, and work ethic are among the top skills (O'Donnell, 2018; Petrone, 2019; Robles, 2012). The working group identified 17 skills embedded within five domains. These skills reflect labels employers often use when inviting applicants with a psychology BA to apply for position openings. CABE's working group members concluded that undergraduate psychology programs teach these skills to their majors. Naufel et al. (2019) recommended that undergraduate psychology teachers should emphasize how students learn these workforce-ready skills within the psychology curriculum, becoming what they refer to as "the skillful psychology student." Coincidentally, the 17 skills align well with APA's (2013) *Undergraduate Guidelines*. Moreover, psychology can teach these skills in ways that other disciplines do not (Naufel et al., 2019).

Introductory psychology provides an opportunity for students to first learn about the psychological underpinnings of career and work skills. Many workforce-ready skills are already incorporated into introductory psychology. Project management, for example, is a skill often desired by employers. Introductory psychology courses that included a semester-long project predicted the likelihood that students reported successfully engaging in project management their senior year (Hard et al., 2019). Other skills are also included in psychology. In a content analysis of two popular open educational resource texts, Kolman et al. (2020) found that both texts frequently covered topics related to group work, inclusivity, attention, decisions, critical thinking, communication, adaptability, and self-regulation. Similarly, nearly all the subskills associated with the skills were at least mentioned in the two textbooks; however, the authors noted that the mere mention of a skill does not ensure that students will acquire or exhibit that skill.

Introductory psychology students have the opportunity to learn how psychology uniquely contributes to workplace effectiveness. If students aspire to excel in their chosen profession, then they would be well advised to hone their skills and knowledge of psychology. We recommend emphasizing these unique contributions to career success in introductory psychology.

Placing more emphasis on workplace skills and applications of psychology will help counteract comments by misguided critics who claim the bachelor's degree has no job or career usefulness (e.g., Halonen, 2013, 2019; Naufel et al., 2019). Because introductory psychology may be the only formal exposure to psychology received by nonmajors, a skills-embedded course can enlighten many students about psychology's value. Because the majority of psychology majors (75%) enter the workforce upon completion of the baccalaureate degree (APA Center for Workforce Studies, 2017), introductory psychology is our opportunity to initiate their career preparation.

An examination of APA's Skillful Psychology Student finds that most "soft skill" attributes mentioned in the popular media (e.g., O'Donnell, 2018; Robles, 2012; Shaberg, 2019) appear within APA's Skillful Psychology Student skill domains. The discipline of psychology can clearly claim coownership of soft skills. Naufel et al. (2019) noted that the belief that an undergraduate degree in psychology does not prepare students for diverse and meaningful careers is both common and inaccurate. Introductory psychology should address this misconception, both to reassure students who are interested in pursuing a psychology degree and to provide a more accurate understanding of psychology for students in general.

Scientific Literacy

Introductory psychology can improve overall scientific literacy. Scientific literacy is not about knowing scientific facts but about being able to distinguish between evidence and belief, understand the role of theory, and appreciate the value of controlled research methods. Macias (2019) found that introductory psychology students scored higher in a test of scientific literacy than students who had taken other science courses and students who had not taken any science courses. Introductory psychology textbooks devote considerable space to scientific methods (Macias & Macias, 2018), and analysis of teachers' learning goals for introductory psychology indicates that they also emphasize the scientific basis of psychology (Homa et al., 2013; Miller & Gentile, 1998).

Scientific literacy is a form of critical thinking, knowing how to evaluate the strength of evidence for a belief, being aware of cognitive biases that can cause faulty reasoning, and appraising the relative strength of alternative responses. Critical thinking can improve decision making and problem solving, leading to fewer errors. Teachers can craft assignments for introductory psychology that are both informative and that promote critical thinking (e.g., Blessing & Blessing, 2010).

In summary, introductory psychology is well positioned to contribute to the greater academic and career success of many college students. Introductory psychology can improve study skills, provide academic momentum, enhance critical thinking, and help develop career and workplace skills. Such aids to academic and career success are helpful to all students, but especially to transfer-oriented students attending a community college, first-generation students, and students with poor academic preparation for college. Because of the open-access model in place at public community colleges, introductory psychology has the potential to contribute significantly to college-wide and national efforts to increase academic success as measured by student success metrics such as grade point average, transfer, and degree completion. The course has the potential to become a significant contributor to academic success and the nation's college completion agenda (McPhail, 2011), but only if introductory psychology is designed to include strategies that promote academic and career success.

REALIZING ITS POTENTIAL

Introductory psychology is an immensely popular course required by many majors, and it has the potential to be transformative to the students who take it, but such transformation is neither automatic nor inevitable. Students, particularly nonmajors, may struggle to see the pertinence of the course to their career goals. The importance of psychology for nursing education can be traced back to textbooks in the 1920s, but nursing educators still debate the best way to teach psychology to nursing students to highlight its relevance (de Vries & Timmins, 2012). Dental school faculty understand the role of psychology for dentistry, but students often fail to understand why they must take such courses (Neville & Waylen, 2016). Furthermore, many students may not be aware of how they can pursue their interests through psychology. Students interested in health may not know about health psychology, students interested in engineering may not know about engineering psychology and human factors, students interested in neuroscience may not know about behavioral neuroscience, and so on.

The public at large may also struggle in seeing the pervasive value of taking introductory psychology. Lilienfeld (2012) and Ferguson (2015) described popular public misconceptions and cynicism toward psychological science. They highlighted how some of the public misperceptions about psychology are due to self-inflicted mistakes by psychologists such as inflating the importance of small effects, oversimplifying complex ones, and overlooking the importance of replication. Naufel and Richmond (2017) conducted a national survey to assess how the public perceived psychology. The good news was that psychology was valued overall for its contributions to society and its ability to address real-world problems. There was, however, room for improvement. Respondents tended to see other sciences as more important than psychology. When asked in what professions psychology was most useful, respondents viewed psychology as most valuable to organizations whose missions pertained to promoting mental wellness, education, and health. Respondents, however, were less apt to see the value of psychology in domains such as engineering, physics, and meteorology. Respondents who reported having taken psychology courses did rate the value of psychology significantly higher than respondents who had not taken psychology, but the difference was not striking, and there was no significant difference between the two groups when rating the value of psychology in professional domains. Introductory psychology is an opportunity to shape a more positive view of the value of psychology as a science and as an important factor in professional success (Landrum et al., 2019).

Merely covering content in introductory psychology does not guarantee that students will see the significance of information, retain the information for the long term, or apply it appropriately in relevant situations (Bernstein, 2017). Teachers must be intentional about designing their introductory psychology courses to fulfill these goals. For example, Hudson et al. (2014) showed that a careful and thorough redesign of introductory psychology, incorporating cognitive principles of learning and evidence-based pedagogy, could result in significant improvements in academic performance and successful course completion in a large introductory psychology course. Introductory psychology instructors should feel empowered in knowing that they can meet the call to make their courses meaningful and memorable.

To summarize, introductory psychology equips students with a foundational framework of knowledge for understanding psychology, but it has the potential to do much more. It can also equip students with knowledge that augments liberal arts values and skills and promote academic and career success, even if it is the only psychology course a student ever takes. To do so, however, takes intentional planning and design on how to teach introductory psychology for optimal impact. The purpose of the Introductory Psychology Initiative was to initiate such an effort, the results of which are described in the chapters ahead.

REFERENCES

Adelman, C. (1999). *Answers in the toolbox: Academic intensity, attendance patterns, and bachelor's degree attainment.* U.S. Department of Education. https://www2. ed.gov/pubs/Toolbox/toolbox.html

Adelman, C. (2004). *The empirical curriculum: Changes in postsecondary course-taking, 1972–2000.* U.S. Department of Education. https://www2.ed.gov/rschstat/ research/pubs/empircurr/empircurric.pdf

Adelman, C. (2006). *The toolbox revisited: Paths to degree completion from high school through college.* U.S. Department of Education. https://eric.ed.gov/?id=ED490195

American Association of Colleges and Universities. (n.d.). *Essential learning outcomes.* https://www.aacu.org/essential-learning-outcomes

American Psychological Association. (n.d.). Psychology. In *APA dictionary of psychology.* Retrieved March 16, 2021, from https://dictionary.apa.org/psychology

American Psychological Association. (2013). *APA guidelines for the undergraduate psychology major: Version 2.0.* https://www.apa.org/ed/precollege/about/psymajor-guidelines.pdf

American Psychological Association. (2014). *Strengthening the common core of the introductory psychology course.* http://www.apa.org/ed/governance/bea/intro-psych-report.pdf

American Psychological Association. (2017). *Assessment of outcomes of the introductory course in psychology.* https://www.apa.org/ed/precollege/assessment-outcomes.pdf

American Psychological Association. (2020). *The APA Introductory Psychology Initiative.* https://www.apa.org/ed/precollege/undergrad/introductory-psychology-initiative

American Psychological Association Center for Workforce Studies. (2017). *Degree pathways from a bachelor's degree in psychology: A snapshot in 2017.* https://www. apa.org/workforce/data-tools/degrees-pathways

Association of American Medical Colleges. (n.d.). *The core competencies for entering medical students.* https://students-residents.aamc.org/applying-medical-school/ article/core-competencies/

Becker-Blease, K., Stevens, C., Witkow, M. R., & Almuaybid, A. (2019). Teaching modules boost scientific reasoning skills in small and large lecture introductory psychology classrooms. *Scholarship of Teaching and Learning in Psychology.* Advance online publication. https://doi.org/10.1037/stl0000173

Bernstein, D. A. (2017). Bye-bye intro: A proposal for transforming introductory psychology. *Scholarship of Teaching and Learning in Psychology, 3*(3), 191–197. https://doi.org/10.1037/stl0000093

Blessing, S. B., & Blessing, J. S. (2010). PsychBusters: A means of fostering critical thinking in the introductory course. *Teaching of Psychology, 37*(3), 178–182. https://doi.org/10.1080/00986283.2010.488540

Boyack, K. W., Klavans, R., & Börner, K. (2005). Mapping the backbone of science. *Scientometrics, 64*(3), 351–374. https://doi.org/10.1007/s11192-005-0255-6

Brint, S., Proctor, K., Murphy, S. P., Turk-Bicakci, L., & Hanneman, R. A. (2009). General education models: Continuity and change in the US undergraduate curriculum, 1975–2000. *The Journal of Higher Education, 80*(6), 605–642. https://doi.org/ 10.1080/00221546.2009.11779037

Cacioppo, J. (2007, September). Psychology is a hub science. *Association for Psychological Science: Observer*. https://www.psychologicalscience.org/observer/psychology-is-a-hub-science

California State University. (n.d.). *Academic policies*. https://www2.calstate.edu/csu-system/administration/academic-and-student-affairs/academic-programs-innovations-and-faculty-development/Pages/academic-policies.aspx

Clay, R. A. (2017, November). Trend report: Psychology is more popular than ever. *Monitor on Psychology*, *48*(10). http://www.apa.org/monitor/2017/11/trends-popular

College Board. (2019). *AP program participation and performance data 2019*. https://research.collegeboard.org/programs/ap/data/participation/ap-2019

Costin, F. (1982). Some thoughts on general education and the teaching of undergraduate psychology. *Teaching of Psychology*, *9*(1), 26–28. https://doi.org/10.1207/s15328023top0901_7

de Vries, J. M., & Timmins, F. (2012). Psychology teaching in nursing education: A review of and reflection on approaches, issues, and contemporary practice. *Nurse Education in Practice*, *12*(6), 316–321. https://doi.org/10.1016/j.nepr.2012.03.007

Dunn, D. S., McCarthy, M. A., Baker, S., Halonen, J. S., & Hill, G. W., IV. (2007). Quality benchmarks in undergraduate psychology programs. *American Psychologist*, *62*(7), 650–670. https://doi.org/10.1037/0003-066X.62.7.650

Fallahi, C. R., Wood, R. M., Austad, C. S., & Fallahi, H. (2006). A program for improving undergraduate psychology students' basic writing skills. *Teaching of Psychology*, *33*(3), 171–175. https://doi.org/10.1207/s15328023top3303_3

Ferguson, C. J. (2015). "Everybody knows psychology is not a real science": Public perceptions of psychology and how we can improve our relationship with policymakers, the scientific community, and the general public. *American Psychologist*, *70*(6), 527–542. https://doi.org/10.1037/a0039405

Fisher, C. B., & Kuther, T. L. (1997). Integrating research ethics into the introductory psychology course curriculum. *Teaching of Psychology*, *24*(3), 172–175. https://doi.org/10.1207/s15328023top2403_4

Gray, P. (2008). The value of Psychology 101 in liberal arts education: A psychocentric theory of the university. *APS Observer*, *21*(9). https://www.psychologicalscience.org/observer/the-value-of-psychology-101-in-liberal-arts-education-a-psychocentric-theory-of-the-university

Gurung, R. A. R., Hackathorn, J., Enns, C., Frantz, S., Cacioppo, J. T., Loop, T., & Freeman, J. E. (2016). Strengthening introductory psychology: A new model for teaching the introductory course. *American Psychologist*, *71*(2), 112–124. https://doi.org/10.1037/a0040012

Halonen, J. (2013). The worthies vs. the great unwashed: Overcoming psychology's tier problem. *Eye on Psi Chi*, *17*(2), 10–12. https://doi.org/10.24839/1092-0803.Eye17.2.10

Halonen, J. (2019, March). Rewarding psychology degree jobs. *The Best Schools*. https://thebestschools.org/careers/psychology-degree-jobs/

Harackiewicz, J. M., Durik, A. M., Barron, K. E., Linnenbrink-Garcia, L., & Tauer, J. M. (2008). The role of achievement goals in the development of interest: Reciprocal relations between achievement goals, interest, and performance. *Journal of Educational Psychology*, *100*(1), 105–122. https://doi.org/10.1037/0022-0663.100.1.105

Hard, B. M., Brady, S. T., & Lovett, J. M. (2019). What do students remember about introductory psychology, years later? *Scholarship of Teaching and Learning in Psychology, 5*(1), 61–74. https://doi.org/10.1037/stl0000136

Harper, R. S. (1954). The Knox conference on the relation of psychology to general education. *American Psychologist, 9*(12), 803–804. https://doi.org/10.1037/h0057909

Hartwig, M. K., & Dunlosky, J. (2012). Study strategies of college students: Are self-testing and scheduling related to achievement? *Psychonomic Bulletin & Review, 19*(1), 126–134. https://doi.org/10.3758/s13423-011-0181-y

Holman, L., Head, M. L., Lanfear, R., & Jennions, M. D. (2015). Evidence of experimental bias in the life sciences: Why we need blind data recording. *PLOS Biology, 13*(7), e1002190. https://doi.org/10.1371/journal.pbio.1002190

Homa, N., Hackathorn, J., Brown, C. M., Garczynski, A., Solomon, E. D., Tennial, R., Stanborn, U. A., & Gurung, R. A. R. (2013). An analysis of learning objectives and content coverage in introductory psychology syllabi. *Teaching of Psychology, 40*(3), 169–174. https://doi.org/10.1177/0098628313487456

Hong, B. (2012, August). The teaching of psychology and the new MCAT: The MCAT will now include emphasis on psychology, behavioral science, statistics and research design. *Psychology Teacher Network: American Psychological Association.* https://www.apa.org/ed/precollege/ptn/2012/08/mcat

Hothersall, D. (2004). *History of psychology.* McGraw-Hill Education.

Hudson, D. L., Whisenhunt, B. L., Shoptaugh, C. F., Rost, A. D., & Fondren-Happel, R. N. (2014). Redesigning a large enrollment course: The impact on academic performance, course completion and student perceptions in introductory psychology. *Psychology Learning & Teaching, 13*(2), 107–119. https://doi.org/10.2304/plat.2014.13.2.107

Jeng, M. (2006). A selected history of expectation bias in physics. *American Journal of Physics, 74*(7), 578–583. https://doi.org/10.1119/1.2186333

Jhangiani, R. S., & Hardin, E. E. (2015). Skill development in introductory psychology. *Scholarship of Teaching and Learning in Psychology, 1*(4), 362–376. https://doi.org/10.1037/stl0000049

Kolman, J., Bowie, J., Henderson, D., & Naufel, K. Z. (2020, February 18). *Are introductory psychology students learning about transferrable skills?* [Poster presentation]. Southeastern Teaching of Psychology Annual Conference.

Landrum, R. E., Gurung, R. A. R., & Amsel, E. (2019). The importance of taking psychology: A comparison of three levels of exposure. *Teaching of Psychology, 46*(4), 290–298. https://doi.org/10.1177/0098628319872574

Lawson, T. J., & Brown, M. (2018). Using pseudoscience to improve introductory psychology students' information literacy. *Teaching of Psychology, 45*(3), 220–225. https://doi.org/10.1177/0098628318779259

Lilienfeld, S. O. (2012). Public skepticism of psychology: Why many people perceive the study of human behavior as unscientific. *American Psychologist, 67*(2), 111–129. https://doi.org/10.1037/a0023963

Macias, S., III. (2019). Scientific literacy: It's not just the textbooks. Psychology students score higher, too. *Psychology Teacher Network, 29.* https://www.apa.org/ed/precollege/ptn/2019/05/scientific-literacy

Macias, S., III, & Macias, D. R. (2018). A comparison of introductory science textbooks: A sampling and content analysis for non-discipline-specific scientific concepts. In *SAGE research methods cases: Part 2.* https://dx.doi.org/10.4135/9781526445940

Madigan, R., & Brosamer, J. (1990). Improving the writing skills of students in introductory psychology. *Teaching of Psychology, 17*(1), 27. https://doi.org/10.1207/s15328023top1701_6

Mandel, G. N. (2006). Patently non-obvious: Empirical demonstration that the hindsight bias renders patent decisions irrational. *Ohio State Law Journal, 67*(6), 1391–1463.

McGoldrick, P. M., & Pine, C. (1999). A review of teaching of behavioural sciences in the United Kingdom dental undergraduate curriculum. *British Dental Journal, 186*(11), 576–580. https://doi.org/10.1038/sj.bdj.4800172

McGovern, T. V., Corey, L., Cranney, J., Dixon, W. E., Jr., Holmes, J. D., Kuebli, J. E., Ritchey, K. A., Smith, R. A., & Walker, S. J. (2010). Psychologically literate citizens. In D. F. Halpern (Ed.), *Undergraduate education in psychology: A blueprint for the future of the discipline* (pp. 9–27). American Psychological Association. https://doi.org/10.1037/12063-001

McNulty, J. A., Ensminger, D. C., Hoyt, A. E., Chandrasekhar, A. J., Gruener, G., & Espiritu, B. (2012). Study strategies are associated with performance in Basic Science courses in the medical curriculum. *Journal of Education and Learning, 1*(1), 1–12. https://doi.org/10.5539/jel.v1n1p1

McPhail, C. J. (2011). *The Completion Agenda: A call to action.* American Association of Community Colleges. ERIC. https://files.eric.ed.gov/fulltext/ED532208.pdf

Miller, B., & Gentile, B. F. (1998). Introductory course content and goals. *Teaching of Psychology, 25*(2), 89–96. https://doi.org/10.1207/s15328023top2502_2

Morehead, K., Rhodes, M. G., & DeLozier, S. (2016). Instructor and student knowledge of study strategies. *Memory, 24*(2), 257–271 [erratum at https://doi.org/10.1080/09658211.2015.1028737]. https://doi.org/10.1080/09658211.2014.1001992

Murthy, V., Rajaram, S., Choudhury, S., & Sethuraman, K. R. (2017). Are we training enough of communication skills and patient psychology required in dental practice. *Journal of Clinical and Diagnostic Research: JCDR, 11*(4), ZE01–ZE04. https://doi.org/10.7860/JCDR/2017/24664.9619

Nakhaeizadeh, S., Dror, I. E., & Morgan, R. M. (2014). Cognitive bias in forensic anthropology: Visual assessment of skeletal remains is susceptible to confirmation bias. *Science & Justice, 54*(3), 208–214. https://doi.org/10.1016/j.scijus.2013.11.003

Naufel, K. Z., & Richmond, A. (2017, October 20–21). *Is it Chick-Fil-A or NASA? Public perception of psychology from a national sample* [Conference presentation]. Society for the Teaching of Psychology 2017 Annual Conference on Teaching, San Antonio, TX, United States.

Naufel, K. Z., Spencer, S. M., Appleby, D. C., Richmond, A. S., Rudmann, J., Van Kirk, J., Young, J., Carducci, B. J., & Hettich, P. (2019, March). The skillful psychology student: How to empower students with workforce-ready skills by teaching psychology. Connecting the dots for students on the occupational skills acquired through psychology. *Psychology Teacher Network, 29*(1). https://www.apa.org/ed/precollege/ptn/2019/03/workforce-ready-skills

Neville, P., & Waylen, A. (2016). That "mushy boxed fog feeling": Dental students' evaluations of the social and behavioural sciences in dental education. *MedEdPublish, 5*(3), 58–64. https://doi.org/10.15694/mep.2016.000144

Norcross, J. C., Hailstorks, R., Aiken, L. S., Pfund, R. A., Stamm, K. E., & Christidis, P. (2016). Undergraduate study in psychology: Curriculum and assessment. *American Psychologist, 71*(2), 89–101. https://doi.org/10.1037/a0040095

Nordstrom, A. H. (2015). The Voices Project: Reducing White students' racism in Introduction to Psychology. *Teaching of Psychology, 42*(1), 43–50. https://doi.org/10.1177/0098628314562524

O'Donnell, R. O. (2018, March). Employers' top training priority for 2018? Soft skills. *HRDIVE.* https://www.hrdive.com/news/employers-top-training-priority-for-2018-soft-skills/518637

Onwuegbuzie, A. J., Slate, J. R., & Schwartz, R. A. (2001). Role of study skills in graduate-level educational research courses. *The Journal of Educational Research, 94*(4), 238–246. https://doi.org/10.1080/00220670109598757

Persky, A. M., & Hudson, S. (2016). A snapshot of student study strategies across a professional pharmacy curriculum: Are students using evidence-based practice? *Currents in Pharmacy Teaching & Learning, 8*(2), 141–147. https://doi.org/10.1016/j.cptl.2015.12.010

Petrone, P. (2019, January). The skills companies need most in 2019—and how to learn them. *LinkedIn: The Learning Blog.* https://learning.linkedin.com/blog/top-skills/the-skills-companies-need-most-in-2019--and-how-to-learn-them

Pine, C. M., & McGoldrick, P. M. (2000). Application of behavioural sciences teaching by UK dental undergraduates. *European Journal of Dental Education, 4*(2), 49–56. https://doi.org/10.1034/j.1600-0579.2000.040201.x

Richmond, A. S., Boysen, G. A., Hudson, D. L., Gurung, R. A. R., Naufel, K. Z., Neufeld, G., Landrum, R. E., Dunn, D. S., & Beers, M. (2021). The Introductory Psychology Census: A national study. *Scholarship of Teaching and Learning in Psychology.* Advance online publication. https://doi.org/10.1037/stl0000277

Robles, M. M. (2012). Executive perceptions of the top 10 soft skills needed in today's workplace. *Business Communication Quarterly, 75*(4), 453–465. https://doi.org/10.1177/1080569912460400

Shaberg, K. (2019). *Teaching soft skills in workforce programs: Findings from WorkAdvance providers.* American Enterprise Institute. https://eric.ed.gov/?id=ED602408

State University of New York. (n.d.). *SUNY general education requirement (SUNY-GER).* https://system.suny.edu/academic-affairs/acaproplan/general-education/

Stevens, C., Witkow, M. R., & Smelt, B. (2016). Strengthening scientific reasoning skills in introductory psychology: Evidence from community college and liberal arts classrooms. *Scholarship of Teaching and Learning in Psychology, 2*(4), 245–260. https://doi.org/10.1037/stl0000070

Tinto, V. (2013). Issac Newton and student college completion. *Journal of College Student Retention, 15*(1), 1–7. https://doi.org/10.2190/CS.15.1.a

Wagner, J., Thomas, G., Glasgow, J., Anderson, R. C., Cabrol, N., & Grin, E. (2004, September). Error-associated behaviors and error rates for robotic geology. SAGE Publications. *Proceedings of the Human Factors and Ergonomics Society Annual Meeting, 48*(3), 444–447. https://doi.org/10.1177/154193120404800336

Wang, X. (2017). Toward a holistic theoretical model of momentum for community college student success. In M. B. Paulson (Ed.), *Higher education: Handbook of theory and research* (pp. 259–308). Springer Publishing Company. https://doi.org/10.1007/978-3-319-48983-4_6

Wang, X., Lee, S. Y., & Prevost, A. (2017). The role of aspirational experiences and behaviors in cultivating momentum for transfer access in STEM: Variations across gender and race. *Community College Review*, *45*(4), 311–330. https://doi.org/10.1177/0091552117724511

Warner, D. B., & Koeppel, K. (2009). General education requirements: A comparative analysis. *The Journal of General Education*, *58*(4), 241–258. https://doi.org/10.1353/jge.0.0050

Wentworth, D. K., & Whitmarsh, L. (2017). Thinking like a psychologist introductory psychology writing assignments: Encouraging critical thinking and resisting plagiarism. *Teaching of Psychology*, *44*(4), 335–341. https://doi.org/10.1177/0098628317727909

Yu, M. C., Kuncel, N. R., & Sackett, P. R. (2020). Some roads lead to psychology, some lead away: College student characteristics and psychology major choice. *Perspectives on Psychological Science*, *15*(3), 761–777. https://doi.org/10.1177/1745691619898843

2

DESIGNING THE INTRODUCTORY PSYCHOLOGY COURSE

An Evidence-Informed Framework

BRIDGETTE MARTIN HARD, DANA S. DUNN, ROBIN MUSSELMAN, DANAE L. HUDSON, AND AARON S. RICHMOND

KEY RECOMMENDATIONS

1. Adopt backward course design as a guiding framework for designing the introductory psychology course by

    a. identifying the desired results or learning outcomes for the course;

    b. identifying how those results will be assessed, such as with specific course assignments or examinations; and

    c. planning course instruction to ensure that the results are achieved.

2. Create coherence by identifying one or more integrative themes (see Chapter 3) that can serve as a meaningful framework for selecting and organizing course material.

3. Incorporate learning outcomes, assessments, and learning activities that develop relevant skills to support students' current and future goals.

(continues)

https://doi.org/10.1037/0000260-003
Transforming Introductory Psychology: Expert Advice on Teacher Training, Course Design, and Student Success, R. A. R. Gurung and G. Neufeld (Editors)

KEY RECOMMENDATIONS (*Continued*)

4. Encourage students to use effective learning strategies that are rooted in learning science.

5. Promote an inclusive learning environment that welcomes and supports students with diverse backgrounds and interests by providing equal access to course materials, support and resources, diverse representation in course content, and a sense of community.

Educators who elect to teach introductory psychology necessarily face a series of pedagogical decisions. These decisions include determining how best to design this foundational course to ensure that students learn and retain valuable information representing the main topical areas of psychology. The purpose of this chapter is to offer guidance for aligning the course with desired learning outcomes and evidence-based recommendations for structuring the course to maximize student experience and learning. We do not prescribe a single "best" design for the introductory psychology course but highlight key recommendations based on evidence and a thorough review of the relevant literature. There is necessary variability in the way that introductory courses are taught in different teaching contexts because each context comes with particular needs and imposes certain considerations. The goal of the Introductory Psychology Initiative (American Psychological Association, 2020) subcommittee on course models and design was to provide a set of evidence-informed recommendations for course design that will allow any would-be and current instructors to design or update their introductory psychology course effectively.

In this chapter, we offer five broad design recommendations to inform the specific decisions that instructors make as they design their course. We first describe an overall framework for course design that will guide any instructor in designing an introductory psychology course to accomplish the aims for the course laid out in this book. We first advocate the use of backward course design (Wiggins & McTighe, 2005), a tool that allows instructors to anticipate the teaching and learning goals they have in mind for students. With this guiding framework in mind, we then offer four additional design recommendations. For each recommendation, we review the evidence for its importance in teaching practice and offer specific strategies for implementing the recommendation in the introductory psychology course. Later chapters build on these recommendations in the context of introductory psychology. Chapter 3 describes recommended student learning outcomes that should guide course design. Chapter 4 describes specific strategies for assessing those learning outcomes. Chapter 5 provides additional recommendations for navigating specific design considerations and selecting specific instructional strategies to implement. Chapter 6 provides guidance for implementing backward course design in more detail.

RECOMMENDATION 1: USE BACKWARD COURSE DESIGN

A considerable amount of scholarship suggests that successful courses are logically organized to achieve specific goals (e.g., Biggs & Tang, 2007; McKeachie & Svinicki, 2014; Reeves, 2006; Wang et al., 2012). In such courses, the goals of the course are well defined and constructively aligned with the course components, including the course content, the methods for delivering that content, the respective roles that instructors and students will play, the methods of assessing or measuring learning, and the various tasks that learners will be asked to perform (Biggs, 2003; Reeves, 2006). The importance of aligning course components with course goals is best illustrated by imagining a course that lacks this structure.

Consider an instructor whose primary goal is for students to develop their ability to critically analyze psychological research. The instructor presents numerous scientific studies in class each week and hopes that students will learn to see the strengths and limitations found in each one. Yet it is not clear how students will achieve this admirable learning goal without clearer guidance. The instructor presents the studies by lecturing about them, with no class time devoted to allowing students to critique the methods or findings. Furthermore, the instructor designs exams that assess students' ability to recognize the definitions of key terms or relatively minor details of the many scientific studies described in class, not to evaluate them. By the time the course is over and final grades are submitted, the instructor will have little or no evidence that students have developed the desired critical analysis skills. Furthermore, it is unlikely that students can demonstrate such skills given their limited opportunities to practice them. Teaching such a course is similar to a novice runner attempting to race a marathon without a training plan. Even if the runner has a clear image in mind of what crossing the finish line would look and feel like, they will not get there without a training regimen that defines subgoals along the way and an exercise schedule to build skills and stamina.

Courses that are constructively aligned reflect an intentional, thoughtful approach to teaching that helps instructors and students ensure they are meeting their goals. Constructively aligned courses also lead students to approach learning more adaptively. In one study, for example, researchers surveyed students at the beginning and end of the semester regarding their approaches to learning, specifically whether the students adopted *deep* approaches to learning (e.g., "I find most new topics interesting and often spend extra time trying to obtain more information about them"), which enhance information retention, compared with *surface* approaches (e.g., "I only study seriously what's given out in class or in the course outlines because that information will probably be on an exam"). They also analyzed syllabi and conducted semistructured interviews with the faculty members teaching the students' courses. Students in courses with strong evidence of constructive alignment showed a shift toward deeper learning approaches and away from shallow learning approaches across the semester (Wang et al., 2012).

Given the importance of a constructively aligned course, what is required to design one? *Backward course design* is one popular method developed by Wiggins and McTighe (2005), who proposed envisioning the desired results of the course first and then working backwards to create a plan to achieve them. This backward design process can be applied to thinking about the introductory psychology course as a whole, as well as each individual topical unit or class session.

In the first step of backward course design, instructors must identify the desired results of their course (see Figure 2.1). These desired results, or

FIGURE 2.1. Backward Course Design

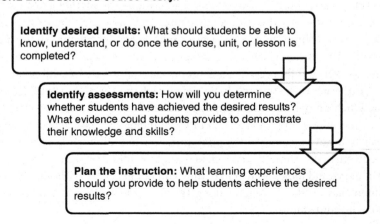

learning objectives, should focus on helping students develop deep knowledge, skills, and the ability to transfer such knowledge and skills to other relevant situations. Instructors can identify desired results by asking themselves what students should be able to know, understand, or do once the course, unit, or lesson is completed. In Chapter 3 of this book, recommended objectives for the introductory course reflect this process. But even with this list in hand, instructors must still reflect on the desired results envisioned for their own course. On the basis of the specific needs or considerations of their institution and students discussed in Chapter 6 and in Part II of this book, instructors may need to prioritize some recommended objectives over others or add new ones to the recommended list.

In the second stage of backward design, instructors should consider how they will determine whether students have achieved the desired results (see Figure 2.1). What evidence could students provide demonstrating their knowledge and skills, as well as the ability to transfer what they have learned to new situations? Answers to this question determine the necessary assessments for the course (see Chapter 4). Some assessments may be formal, graded components of the course, such as exams and assignments. Other assessments may be informal, low-stakes, or even ungraded opportunities for instructors and students to measure what and how well they are learning.

The third and final stage of backward design is to plan the learning experiences and actual instruction tied to course material (see Figure 2.1). The backward design framework evokes a metaphor of the instructor as a coach or personal trainer: With the desired results clearly defined and methods selected for measuring whether results are achieved, instructors now need to define the "training" plan to help students get there. Instructors must define the right balance of sharing knowledge with students while providing them the opportunity to use their knowledge and skills.

Well-designed courses require instructors to be intentional in their approach from start to finish. They also provide instructors with far more valuable information about whether their objectives have been met and what, if anything, can be improved next time. With this overall framework of the constructively aligned introductory psychology course in mind, the sections that follow offer additional recommendations for designing the course, organized around four design characteristics that are summarized in Figure 2.2. We recommend specific ways to design the introductory psychology course to be coherently organized, focused on skill development to support students' current and future goals, firmly rooted in evidence from learning science, and inclusive of diverse backgrounds and interests.

FIGURE 2.2. Design Characteristics of an Effective Introductory Psychology Course

Coherently Organized

Provides a meaningful framework for selecting and organizing course material, such as by using unifying themes that showcase psychology's breadth but also what unites it as a discipline.

Develops Relevant Skills

Develops skills that support students' current and future goals, including cognitive, communication, personal, technological, and social skills.

Characteristics of the Effectively Designed Introductory Psychology Course

Promotes Effective Learning Strategies

Encourages students to use learning strategies that are rooted in the learning sciences, such as elaborative processing, retrieval practice, distributed practice, interleaving, and strategies to improve metacognition.

Promotes Inclusion

Inclusive of diverse backgrounds and interests by providing equal access, support and resources, diverse representation in course content, and a sense of community.

RECOMMENDATION 2: CREATE COHERENCE

One of the most daunting challenges of teaching an introductory psychology course is to wrangle its breadth. Psychology is an expansive discipline. When we wrote this chapter, the American Psychological Association (APA) had 54 divisions representing diverse areas of specialization (and there are well-defined subfields within each area). Psychology also has an expansive impact. As a "hub science," it intersects with other fields, such as medicine, public health, engineering, and education (Boyack et al., 2005). Consequently, instructors risk overwhelming themselves and their students with a seemingly endless list of topics and applications.

A successful introductory psychology course must be designed to be coherent. By *coherent,* we mean that the course design conveys a useful framework for meaningfully organizing and synthesizing carefully selected content material. The course cannot be a list of seemingly unrelated theories, concepts, and findings; it requires conceptual "glue" to hold it all together. The goal of an introductory psychology instructor, then, is to create this conceptual glue so that students can recognize and piece together disparate psychological findings from the different topics in the course (e.g., research methods, sensation and perception, social psychology) into an organized and integrated account about why people think, feel, and act as they do. Such an integrated understanding of human mind and behavior is arguably one of the most important *learning objectives* of the introductory psychology course (see Chapter 3). Beyond specific key terms and findings, students should develop a deeper insight into the human experience that stretches across the subdomains of the field.

To accomplish this, we recommend that instructors define a meaningful framework for the students in the class and periodically remind them how this framework helps them to think about the topics covered in the course. Creating a meaningful framework in introductory psychology allows students to encode findings from psychology into a mental package that can be retained and drawn upon for future use after the course ends. For example, Hard et al. (2019) found that students taking an introductory psychology course that was organized around meaningful "big ideas" retained information about these big ideas several years later.

How to Create Coherence Using Integrative Themes

A straightforward way to create a meaningful framework in introductory psychology is to identify a theme or themes for organizing and integrating the course material. By *integrative theme*, we refer to an organizing idea that recurs by pedagogical design across the 10 to 15 units typically found in introductory psychology or, more specifically, in the textbooks used to teach this ever-expanding course. Integrative themes, then, serve "as a lens or point of view for categorizing and explaining what might be best described as the core topical areas in the discipline" (Dunn, 2018, p. 2).

One suggested student learning outcome (SLO) for the introductory psychology course described in Chapter 3 is to include a set of seven integrative themes that can, individually or together, provide a framework for the course (SLO 3.A–G). Consider, for example, SLO 3.E, the theme: "Our perceptions and biases filter our experiences of the world through an imperfect personal lens." Human perception can guide intuition and reasoning, but the conclusions reached may or may not be valid (i.e., objective); that is, human conclusions about daily life are subjective, as they inhabit people's minds and not the external world. This theme allows educators to explore how and why human experience contains particularly illusory elements and beliefs that nonetheless bolster confidence and guide judgment (see Weiten, 2018). An instructor drawn to this theme would work backward, using the thematic

framework to create targeted assessments and integrate key studies and research findings (e.g., perceptual illusions, the misinformation effect, the fundamental attribution error) into the lectures and class discussions.

The integrative themes proposed as part of the suggested learning outcomes provide a convenient framework for designing the introductory psychology course, but there are other possibilities. Another way to frame findings in psychology is as a tool for human problem-solving. Research findings can be construed as ways to solve daily problems, such as using sensation and perceptual processes both to navigate and come to know the physical and social environment. Memory processes, in turn, allow humans to retain information for future use without relearning the same or similar material each time they encounter it. Social psychological processes (i.e., attribution, person perception) permit people to identify similarities and differences between people, thereby noting whether a target person is apt to be friend or foe and so on (see Hardin, 2018, on thinking like a psychologist, and Silvestri Hunter & Teague, 2018, on infusing scientific thinking into classes). An instructor drawn to the theme of problem solving would, as for any theme, work backward, using the thematic framework to identify key learning outcomes (e.g., what problems can be solved using psychological research from each of the topical units in the course?), create assessments, and select key studies and research findings to introduce in the course. Other thematic approaches include overturning key myths in psychology (e.g., "People only use 10% of their brains"; Bernstein, 2017), skills (Landrum, 2018), and evolution (Lynch, 2018; see Dunn & Hard, 2018, for additional examples).

Selecting Course Content to Fit Within a Coherent, Defining Framework

Having an organizing framework for introductory psychology can prevent students and their instructors from feeling overwhelmed by the breadth of psychology by providing not only conceptual glue between the field's many theories, concepts, and findings but also a means for choosing content more selectively. Rather than trying to cover as much content as possible, instructors can curate content that complements their organizing framework. In fact, we recommend that they limit their content in this way and avoid trying to "teach it all." When limiting content, instructors should still showcase the breadth of psychology by representing the many perspectives (e.g., biological, sociocultural) and levels of analysis (e.g., neural level, cultural level) that psychologists use to understand the mind and behavior. Chapter 3 provides additional guidance on how to limit content selection while adequately representing psychology's breadth.

To summarize, introductory psychology instructors should create coherence in their course by choosing and using an integrative theme or themes for the introductory psychology course that will serve as a memorable framework for students to learn about, reflect on, and recall pertinent material from introductory psychology. Such themes provide instructors with a guide for planning assessments, selecting content, and designing course activities. As the first course in the major grows ever more detailed, instructors as well as students benefit from a clear way to make sense of a large amount of material they must learn (Dunn, 2018). As a guiding principle, then, creating coherence for students can have clear benefits for both teachers and learners.

RECOMMENDATION 3: DEVELOP SKILLS

Recently, APA commissioned a group of scholars from across the United States to develop an evidence-based list of transferable job skills that are derived in psychology. After studying more than 10,000 job ads on *Indeed*, the working group deciphered five skill domains with 17 skills (Naufel et al., 2018, 2019). For a complete description of the list of skills, see https://www.apa.org/careers/resources/guides/transferable-skills.pdf. Additionally, we have devoted an entire chapter to these skills, see Chapter 6.

We recommend that instructors incorporate job skills within their introductory psychology course design. There are several ways to do so. First and foremost, prioritizing job skills as a student learning objective will demonstrate the instructor's commitment to teaching workforce readiness skills in introductory psychology. Moreover, Naufel and colleagues (2019) suggested that instructors incorporate a list of transferable skills into the syllabus and directly explain to students how the course will help them develop skills that employers value. With workplace skills defined in the student learning objectives, instructors can then design assessments and learning activities to measure and train students in these skills. In what follows, you will find a brief introduction to the skills and how they specifically relate to introductory psychology course design.

Cognitive Skills

Job skills clustered around cognitive skills include judgment and decision making, information management, creativity, critical thinking, and analytical thinking (e.g., APA, 2013; Appleby, 2014; Dunn & Halonen, 2020; Landrum & Davis, 2010; Naufel et al., 2018). Instructors interested in developing

cognitive skills may adopt SLOs such as: "Students will demonstrate critical thinking skills through writing" or "Students will compare and contrast competing psychological theories." Assessments to measure these SLOs might include writing assignments in which students critique the design of a hypothetical study or that compare two competing theories in social psychology.

Communication Skills

This skill domain includes oral and written communication (Naufel et al., 2019). A learning outcome related to oral communication might state that students will "demonstrate strong active listening and conversational abilities in both formal and professional environments, as well as aptitude for public speaking and communicating scientific information to diverse audiences" (Naufel et al., 2018). A sample assessment might be a project requiring students to interview adolescents and adults to determine developmental differences in motivation regarding oral presentation skills. Or students may write a description of their experience as a research participant, attend a guest lecture or research talk, or complete an assignment that teaches students how to professionally communicate with their instructors (e.g., write a professional email).

Personal Skills

Personal skills include adaptability, integrity, and self-regulation (Naufel et al., 2018). Sample learning outcomes for such skills might describe how students will demonstrate self-regulation by "managing time and stress by completing assigned tasks with little or no supervision; display initiative and persistence by accepting and completing additional duties in a careful, thorough, and dependable manner" (Naufel et al., 2018). In introductory psychology, personal skills could be assessed by asking students to keep a metacognition log, where they track how they studied, how they performed on an assessment, and how they adjusted their study strategies for the assessment.

Social Skills

Within this skill domain, students are expected to demonstrate collaboration, inclusivity, leadership, management, and service orientation (Naufel et al., 2018). A learning outcome might describe how students will demonstrate *inclusivity skills* by "demonstrating sensitivity to cultural and individual differences and similarities by working effectively with diverse people, respecting and considering divergent opinions, and showing respect for others" (Naufel et al., 2018). To assess such skills in introductory psychology, instructors may have students complete a service learning project. Kretchmar (2001), for example, had students volunteer at daycares, kid camps, hospitals, state psychiatric facilities, and group homes, among other sites. Part of the students' assignment included identifying the developmental, social, clinical, and motivational concepts within their respective service learning placement.

Technological Skills

Finally, technological skills include flexibility and adaptability to new systems and familiarity with hardware and software (Naufel et al., 2018). Most notably, students may demonstrate their familiarity with hardware and software by "demonstrating competency in using various operating systems, programs, and/or coding protocols; troubleshoot technical errors; and use software applications to build and maintain websites, create web-based applications, and perform statistical analyses" (Naufel et al., 2018). For example, in introductory psychology, instructors may have students demonstrate social learning by recording and uploading their social learning demonstration to a private YouTube channel. Or instructors could have students demonstrate their ability to write an APA Style paper using a word-processing program.

RECOMMENDATION 4: PROMOTE EFFECTIVE LEARNING STRATEGIES

A well-designed introductory psychology course includes clearly defined learning objectives (e.g., a chosen theme to enhance meaning, specific skills to develop) and assessments carefully aligned with these intentions for the course. To effectively meet the learning objectives of the course, thoughtful decisions need to be made regarding the specific day-to-day activities associated with the course. How should instructors structure class time to maximize students' ability to meet the learning objectives? Thankfully, there is a rich and vast literature from cognitive and learning science outlining empirically supported strategies and techniques that, when implemented correctly, lead to successful learning (Ambrose et al., 2010; Brown et al., 2014; Roediger & Pyc, 2012). These strategies and techniques can also help students become more effective learners, thus serving a specific recommended learning objective for introductory psychology to help students

"Apply psychological principles to personal growth and other aspects of everyday life (SLO 1.3)," as well as learning objectives related to cognitive skills that instructors may define. Instructors have opportunities to model how these strategies encourage learning by highlighting their presence in the course design. Learning science principles can also be taught explicitly in the course as part of a specific learning objective. Although there are many evidence-based strategies, we focus on five learning strategies that have substantial support and have been replicated by various researchers.

Elaborative Processing

Elaborative processing has come to represent many different ideas and terms, such as elaborative encoding, elaborative rehearsal, and depth of processing. All refer to the general idea that information that is expanded upon in a meaningful way is more likely to be remembered. Anderson and Reder (1979) referred to elaboration as a method of "exercising the reader in thinking about the content" (p. 401). Elaboration of content involves the important processes of constructing meaning, making connections to previously learned material, and finding personal relevance in the content. *Elaborative interrogation* (EI) is a specific method of elaboration that involves asking relevant questions that encourage elaborative processing. Teaching students how to engage in this process as they are reading and studying is an incredibly valuable skill that will change the way they learn. If the text or reading materials include learning objectives as headers, these orienting questions can be used as a starting point for EI. Instructors should encourage students to *actually read* the learning objective before reading the section and then, as they read, to be on the lookout for the answer that reflects the learning objective. After reading, students should be encouraged to return to the learning objective and ask themselves if they can provide the information described in the learning objective. For example, if one of the learning objectives from the learning chapter is "Students will be able to distinguish negative reinforcement from punishment," then students should train themselves to return to this learning objective at the end of the reading and ask, "What is the difference between negative reinforcement and punishment?" Verifying their answer with the information in the text provides important feedback to the student and should assist them in determining if they are prepared to proceed to the next learning objective.

Other important questions students can ask while reading include "How does this information relate to concepts I already understand?" or "How can I relate this information to my life?" Asking specific questions like these, that align with the overall meaning of the course, leads students away from the superficial characteristics of the content and require them to process the information at a deeper level. Information that is deeply processed, self-referenced, and connected to prior knowledge facilitates learning (Ambrose et al., 2010; Craik & Lockhart, 1972).

Retrieval Practice

Elaborative processing is an important strategy to use during the encoding of information. Another equally important process that promotes learning involves retrieving information from memory at some point after the initial exposure to the content. It is expected that between the time of encoding and retrieval, some information will be forgotten. It is the process of pulling the information from memory coupled with the relearning of information that strengthens and consolidates memories (Brown et al., 2014; Endres et al., 2017; Nunes & Karpicke, 2015).

The *testing effect*, which describes the memory advantage caused by answering test-like questions, is one of the most robust scientific findings in cognitive science and education. During the first 30 years of the Association for Psychological Science (APS), Roediger and Karpicke's (2006) article on test-enhanced learning was among the 30 most cited articles in any APS journal (Roediger & Karpicke, 2018). Low-stakes quizzing has been repeatedly demonstrated to lead to improved learning (Ambrose et al., 2010; Dunlosky et al., 2013; Thomas et al., 2018). Instructors should thus implement quizzing as a regular learning activity. This can be accomplished in any course modality (i.e., face-to-face, blended, online) and can take various forms (e.g., online, multiple choice questions, in-class polling questions, short-answer questions generated by the students or instructor). Students can even practice generating their own questions to quiz themselves and one another, although in general, the research has concluded that students benefit most when the practice questions are provided by the instructor, rather than generated by the students (Colliot & Jamet, 2019; Lloyd et al., 2018).

Distributed Practice

More than a century of research has demonstrated the value of repeatedly studying information over time rather than all at once (Benjamin & Tullis, 2010; Cepeda et al., 2009). Designing an effective learning environment is similar to meal planning for children. Most children *know* they should eat vegetables because vegetables are healthy, but left to make their own decisions, vegetables will rarely make it onto their plate. Course planning is similar: Most students know they should not cram but rather space out their practice. And most instructors know that most students, despite this knowledge, will continue to cram before exams. If an instructor's assessments include only a midterm and final, students will be naturally drawn to intensify their studying immediately before the exam. Therefore, students will benefit from a carefully designed syllabus that plans repeated learning activities at regular intervals. Because students tend not to do "optional" assignments, these activities should be worth some points in the course (Twigg, 2013). The assignments do not need to be worth a significant number of points for students to be motivated to complete them. In fact, repeated, low-stakes testing has been found to significantly improve retention and learning (Brame & Biel, 2015; Roediger & Pyc, 2012). As one example, instructors can require regular quizzes that are completed at some time before each exam.

Designing a learning environment with built-in distributed practice is best achieved by spacing out due dates for homework and assignments and by providing a number of assessment opportunities (i.e., exams) as well as regular low-stakes quizzes. Gurung and Burns (2019) found in a multisite study that students performed better on exams when they were required to complete low-stakes quizzes at regular spaced intervals (e.g., every few weeks) rather than all at once (e.g., the night before an exam). This schedule can become complicated if there are also a number of other assignments due for the class, but a thoughtfully created syllabus that creates an environment of distributed practice will inevitably lead to more student learning.

It can also be helpful to understand and teach students some of the neurobiological reasons *why* distributed practice is superior to massed practice. Because memory is a topic discussed in most introductory psychology courses, instructors can seize the opportunity to provide empirical support for their recommendations regarding effective studying. At a biological level, learning is represented in neural networks, or patterns of connection among neurons throughout the brain. Neural networks are created from experiences, and the more students can connect new learning to previous learning and then retrieve that information at a later date, the more likely the memory will be strengthened and learning will occur (Hebb, 1949; Turner & Carriveau, 2010). This process of memory consolidation takes time, which is one reason it is beneficial for students to space out their practice. Sleeping is yet another beneficial activity for encouraging the consolidation of memories (Maingret et al., 2016; Peter-Derex, 2019; Siegel, 2001). Although instructors cannot require their students to sleep the night before an exam, encouraging spaced practice through the course design may reduce the need for students to stay up all night cramming for an exam.

Interleaving

The strategy of interleaving is an effective but counterintuitive idea for most students. Interleaving is a learning strategy that involves alternating between different concepts while studying (Brown et al., 2014; Dunlosky et al., 2013; Kornell et al., 2010). The typical example of interleaving involves learning math skills (Rohrer et al., 2014). Children are often taught, and then practice, specific operations in isolation or in a blocked fashion. They might spend 2 days learning addition followed by 2 days learning and practicing subtraction. On the fifth day, they are given a test that has both addition and subtraction questions interspersed within the same exam. This experience can be unsettling for students because they never had the opportunity to practice switching between operations. An interleaved approach would involve days that included instruction and practice in a variety of operations and skills. In addition to allowing students to practice in a way that is consistent with how most exams are constructed, interleaving capitalizes on the principle of distributed practice to increase overall learning (Foster et al., 2019).

How can interleaving be woven into the design of introductory psychology? A thoughtful approach to course design that emphasizes coherence and meaning often naturally lends itself to interleaving. When presented as an integrated whole, the field of psychology has a common set of theoretical underpinnings that can be continually referred to throughout the course. However, it is often the case that instructors present information from the field in silos according to chapter number. Instructors who want to implement interleaving should be explicit about making connections between the content presented in different chapters and referring back to previously discussed principles and asking students to apply them in a new context.

Instructors can also incorporate interleaving into homework and assignments. Increasingly complex assignments that require the student to use prior knowledge and skills requires a return to previously learned content and thus reinforces that information. For example, most introductory psychology students will be introduced to research methods early in the course. Interleaving these important concepts throughout the course could involve having students critically evaluate classic or new research consistent with the topic of each chapter. Designing a course to include cumulative exams can also encourage studying that capitalizes on interleaving and retrieval practice. It is important to distinguish a cumulative final exam in a course from a cumulative exam course. Cumulative exam courses start with a small exam that becomes progressively larger throughout the course. Therefore, each exam includes the most recently discussed content as well as content from all previous chapters. The course concludes with a cumulative final, but in this case, students have "practiced" taking cumulative exams throughout the entire class. In theory, this strategy should encourage interleaved practice but students often need a reminder to "mix up" their studying.

Metacognition

Are introductory psychology students properly aware of their own thoughts regarding the course material they are reading and studying? In other words, are they thinking about how they are processing and learning the material? Most instructors would be quick to answer "no." The lack of metacognition in introductory psychology students may lead to detrimental academic habits and have negative consequences for academic performance. Gurung et al. (2010) reported that introductory psychology students often use ineffective study strategies, such as highlighting and continual rereading. Moreover, they found that these ineffective study strategies were negatively correlated with course performance. Gurung and colleagues attributed these findings in part to the lack of metacognition in many introductory psychology students. Richmond et al. (2015) also suggested that the lack of metacognitive abilities in introductory psychology students leads to the students' susceptibility in believing in psychological, educational, and neurological myths (e.g., learning styles). In two studies with more than 700 introductory psychology students, Richmond and colleagues found that the actual metacognitive performance of the students (in the form of calibration; when you know your answer or when you do not) was highly predictive of whether the students believed in these myths. If students had high metacognitive abilities, the students were far less likely to believe in the myths. Considering these findings, and as introductory psychology is often one of the first courses that students take, it is imperative that instructors capitalize on opportunities to teach students the concept of metacognition and how to improve their metacognition in their course.

There are several strategies and assignments that instructors may use to teach and improve metacognition. First, Scharff (2017) described a series of assignments to guide students in increasing the effectiveness of their study strategies and goal setting (see Carpenter, 2017). In the first assignment, students describe what they believe it takes to be successful in the class, then write two strategies that they want to work on in the course, and then list three goals that they achieve by using the strategies they choose. In the second assignment, students review the effectiveness of these strategies based on an exam performance, analyze why they did or did not work to achieve their goals, and then develop a plan to modify their strategies to achieve their goals (Carpenter, 2017; Scharff, 2017). For the final assignment, students reflect after a second exam and share and discuss their goals and strategies with other students. Scharff (2017) argued that students make significant changes and gains in the effectiveness of study strategies through these assignments.

Introductory psychology instructors may also use a metacognitive assignment that focuses on both pre- and postexam interventions, such as "exam wrappers," a quick activity in which students examine their performance on a test or exam (Ambrose et al., 2010; McCabe, 2019). McCabe (2019) argued that most exam wrappers are only slightly effective; however, she describes a well-studied method proposed by Chen et al. (2017). Chen and colleagues had students, before an exam, predict what their exam score would be, indicate how motivated they were, indicate how important it was that they achieved their targeted grade, and how confident they were in achieving the grade. Students were also asked about what types of resources they had to help them prepare, exam format (e.g., essay vs. multiple choice), and how they would use these resources to achieve their goal. Students who used this preexam wrapper assignment performed significantly better than students that did not. Thus, instructors may consider using preexam wrappers to improve the metacognition and academic performance of their students although the current literature on exam wrappers is mixed.

Last but not least, Stephen Chew from Samford University has made an incredible series of videos about metacognition titled "How to Get the Most Out of Studying" (see https://www.youtube.com/watch?v=RH95h36NChI). This five-part video series describes metacognition, study strategies (e.g., interleaving), and common misconceptions. Instructors can use these videos in online and face-to-face courses. See also John Dunlosky of Kent State University's discussion of best ways to study (https://youtu.be/Tp6yc96qNWU). We suggest that these videos or an alternative assignment directed at effective study strategies be one of the first assignments in an introductory psychology course. Instructors can use these videos as the basis of a discussion post in online courses or as a reflective assignment completed after Carpenter's (2017) first assignment. There are many ways in which these videos may be used effectively.

RECOMMENDATION 5: PROMOTE INCLUSION

Introductory psychology courses are not only a requirement for the psychology major at most institutions, they are also a popular general education elective taken by more than 1 million undergraduates each year (Gurung et al., 2016). As a result of the course's popularity, it typically serves a diverse array of students who vary in race, gender, age, disability, socio-economic background, political views, and interests and goals. Therefore, instructors must consider how to promote an *inclusive* course environment (see Figure 2.3), by which we mean an environment that embraces student diversity in its many forms and promotes an optimal learning experience for all students (Davis, 2009; Sathy & Hogan, 2019). For education to be transformational, it is critical that it be relevant to the current lives of our students (Gannon, 2020).

Providing Access to Content

Students may enter an introductory psychology course with university or college documented disabilities that require specific accommodations. Universal design for learning is a framework that originated to provide guidelines for how to adapt teaching and learning to accommodate students with disabilities (CAST, 2018). Whether teaching face-to-face or online courses, instructors should consider how students access the course materials and ensure that all course materials are accessible to students. For example, how might a student with a visual impairment access materials that include figures and tables? How might a student with a hearing impairment access a video or podcast that has been assigned?

Students may require very specific accommodations to access course materials based on the nature of their disability, but we recommend that instructors adjust their course materials to be more accessible to a wide range of students, regardless of whether a student with a documented disability is enrolled in their course. Textbooks and other reading materials,

FIGURE 2.3 Features of an Inclusive Course Environment

Inclusive Course Environment			
Accessibility: Course materials are accessible and affordable for all students.	**Support:** The instructor and course materials support learners with various skills and resources.	**Representation:** Course materials reflect and welcome student diversity.	**Community:** Course structure fosters meaningful social connection among course members.

whether from a publisher or a compilation of materials developed through open educational resources, should be accessible to all students. For example, written content should be compatible with screen reading tools that make them accessible to students with visual impairments. If a document is formatted to be accessible to the screen reading tool, then the reader can automatically interpret its format and "read it" appropriately. Graphics and pictures require alternative ("alt") text, which consists of written descriptions that help screen reading tools describe images to visually impaired readers. Digital formats may be favored because they tend to be more flexible than print; however, all formats should be compatible with assistive technologies.

Instructors should also make sure that any documents they produce, such as assignment instructions, are formatted to be accessible to screen reading tools. Additionally, we recommend instructors add captions or accompanying transcripts to video and audio components of their course, which can make them more accessible for hearing-impaired students, as well as for students whose first language was not English. There are multiple sources for assisting instructors with creating accessible documents and files, and many campuses have resources available to assist faculty with this task. Many word processing and presentation programs (e.g., Microsoft Word and PowerPoint) now have accessibility tools built into their platform that can guide instructors in adding alt text, add automated captions, and identify any other potential problems with accessibility. Digital video platforms like YouTube also have automatic captioning programs.

In addition to considering the formats for delivering information, instructors should also consider affordability of course materials. Many students resist purchasing course textbooks due to cost, and this can reduce course persistence and performance (e.g., Florida Virtual Campus, 2016; Jhangiani & Jhangiani, 2017). Instructors should make it easier for students to access course materials even if they cannot afford them. There are many strategies to accomplish this. Some instructors allow students to use older, less expensive editions of a text. Some select textbooks with less expensive digital or loose-leaf versions. Many instructors put textbooks on reserve at a campus library for students to borrow. Others loan their own desk copies to students who need them. Yet others make use of open educational resources (OER) that are entirely free for their students or work with commercial publishers to test new products (which often comes with free access for students). Some research on the use of OER in introductory psychology courses has demonstrated that students do as well or better using OER compared with other types of texts (Hardin et al., 2019; Jhangiani et al., 2018; but see Gurung, 2017, for an exception) and that the use of OER positively influences underrepresented students' likelihood of enrolling in and continuing in the course (Hardin et al., 2019).

Providing Support for All Skill and Resource Levels

Moving from the one-size-fits-all brand of teaching toward a more accessible pedagogy (Rose et al., 2006) requires that we consider the variability of the learner, the context, and the teacher. Disability and the ability to afford materials are two sources of learner variability; yet another is experience with the language that we use to communicate key ideas in the introductory psychology course. Students enrolled in introductory psychology can vary in their proficiency in English. For such students, the use of uncommon vocabulary words on exams and assignments may pose an unnecessary barrier to success. When working with students for whom English is not their first language, instructors should consider whether the student can use a translator during writing and assessments. Hispanic-serving institutions often make transcripts for audio materials, textbook glossaries, and even textbooks available in Spanish.

Even for native English speakers, vocabulary can sometimes pose a barrier to learning. Masland (2018) identified 87 general vocabulary words often used in college classrooms that are not familiar to students. Of course, developing one's vocabulary, both broadly and within a given discipline, can be an important goal of the course. Instructors can increase exposure and familiarity with new words by being sure to introduce more complex words with their meanings or even to provide vocabulary quizzes for words that may be especially common in the discipline.

Another source of learner variability is prior preparation for and experience with college-level work. Teaching inclusively requires instructors to include more explicit directions and structure to their course, with the goal of removing potential barriers to student success. Instructors should strive to transparently and explicitly communicate their expectations for student behavior. Instructors should specify, for example, how students should address them and contact them. They should then continue a pattern of transparent expectations through assignments, exams, and grading, not assuming that students are aware of the often implicit norms of the college classroom. This support is particularly important in the online setting where opportunities for students to ask for and receive clarification are more rare. Other examples of support for students may include various study aids, as appropriate to the level of the learner and the context. Graphic organizers (Hall & Strangman, 2008), reading guides, chapter outlines, and study guides are all means of providing support for students. Research suggests that these sorts of instructional supports benefit all students, but especially those from underrepresented groups (Eddy & Hogan, 2014; Sathy & Hogan, 2019).

Students in introductory psychology may vary in their life circumstances in ways that influence their ability to keep up with the course requirements. Some students may be focused full-time on school, whereas others attend school while holding full-time jobs, family responsibilities, or athletic commitments, for example. A supportive class environment establishes course policies that are fair yet flexible. Policies for missing class or deadlines should be fair and consistently applied but should also acknowledge the many circumstances that students, as human beings, may face. Instructors should get to know the background of their students to help establish these policies fairly. Some instructors allow students to miss a certain number of class periods without penalty, to drop the lowest score on one or more low-stakes assignments, or offer a "free extension" to be used on any one assignment, for any reason. Such policies afford students flexibility if life circumstances prevent them from fully engaging in the course, without needing to disclose those circumstances to the instructor.

Representing Diverse Backgrounds and Experiences

Students enrolled in introductory psychology often come from diverse cultural backgrounds and differ in the extent to which they feel their cultural backgrounds are valued and validated. In predominantly White institutions, White students experience more opportunities than students of color to connect with students and faculty from the same cultural background and are more likely to report feeling that their cultural backgrounds and identities are valued (Museus et al., 2018). These experiences matter because they are a significant predictor of a sense of belonging in college (Johnson et al., 2007; Museus et al., 2017, 2018).

With these findings in mind, instructors should seek ways to diversify course content to represent the diversity of the students in the course, allowing students to see people and ideas that reflect their own experiences and cultural perspectives. Diverse representation is a challenge given that the field of psychology tends to be dominated by researchers and research samples that reflect Western, educated, industrialized, rich, and democratic (WEIRD) populations (Henrich et al., 2010). A first step in creating diverse representation in introductory psychology is to know one's students and understand the diversity of language, culture, gender identification, race, ethnicity, and ability in one's classroom (Davis, 2009; Dunn & Hammer, 2014). A second step is to take a close look at course content, including the researchers and research populations that are featured. Instructors should work to include researchers, historical and contemporary, that represent diversity in gender, race, and ethnicity. They should strive to teach research studies that include populations that reflect the student population rather than solely WEIRD populations. When this is not possible, instructors should directly acknowledge the cultural bias that is inherent in the research and help students understand how it limits the generalizability of findings. Instructors should also consider the images of people in their assigned textbook or that are presented to students in lecture slides to illustrate psychological concepts, as well as the names of fictional people used in examples on exams. As much as possible, instructors should make sure these images and names reflect the multiple cultural backgrounds in their course. Such examples matter to students and can keep them engaged, rather than feeling left out of the course material being discussed (Hockings et al., 2009; Ryan & Deci, 2000).

Instructors should work to ensure that examples used in class or on exams can be understood by students from a range of cultural and socioeconomic backgrounds either by using broader examples or by explaining examples that may be culture-specific. An unexplained reference to an American television show may not make sense to an international student (and in our experience, references that are meaningful to an instructor may not make sense to American students either). For example, an episode of the show *The Office* depicts one character (Jim) classically conditioning another (Dwight) by offering him mints every time his computer reboots. Simply mentioning this example is only appropriate if everyone is familiar with the characters or has seen the relevant episode of *The Office*. Instructors can remedy this situation by simply showing all students the video clip.

Instructors should also be careful not to make assumptions about their students that leave some groups excluded from a discussion. As one example, consider teaching the topic of attachment in a unit on human development. Not all students grew up in a two-parent household, or with heterosexual parents, or even with parents at all. Discussions about attachment in class that refer only to "mothers" and "fathers" may exclude some students but can easily become more inclusive with broader language like "caregivers." Similarly, an instructor's social class or relative affluence, which can manifest itself in speech, behavior, and even examples, can unknowingly confuse or even alienate some students who hail from lower- or working-class households. As an instructor, taking care in what and how material is presented can have a decided influence on student learning (e.g., Markus & Connor, 2014).

Providing a Sense of Community

Many of the previous strategies we've described, such as considering the diversity of the learners and incorporating that diversity into the course, are ultimately expressions of *caring* on the part of the instructor. Creating a safe classroom with caring faculty is consistently important to students (Higbee et al., 2008; Whisenhunt et al., 2019) and is a key ingredient for providing students with a sense of community. By *sense of community*, we mean the experience among members of the class of sharing connectedness and common commitment toward the goals of learning (e.g., Osterman, 2000; Rovai & Lucking, 2003).

There are a number of practical strategies to help instructors achieve a sense of community in their course (Wilson et al., 2012). First, instructors should learn and use student's names. This may be a challenge depending on how many students are enrolled, but even in large classes, teachers can create seating charts that allow them reference to the names of individuals. Some instructors encourage students to share (e.g., post on a course website) audio introductions to themselves to help the instructor and classmates in pronouncing names. When communicating directly with students, through email or in feedback on assignments, instructors can start the communication with the student's name rather than jumping right into the message.

Second, instructors should establish individualized communication with students. A study by Legg and Wilson (2009) demonstrated that a welcoming email sent to individual students before the start of the course improved students' attitudes toward both the instructor and the course. Instructors should consider reaching out to their students throughout the semester, just to check in with them. A few weeks into the term, instructors can begin contacting a certain number of students each week using a personal message to open new doors of communication and help students feel connected with the instructor. With the help of technology, this personalized feedback can even be achieved in very large introductory psychology classes (Whisenhunt et al., 2019). In the face-to-face class, depending on its size, instructors can conduct a similar type of intervention by chatting with individual students informally to ask them how they feel about the class.

Third, instructors should know their students and include them in course content. In addition to making sure to represent the diversity of students in the researchers and examples that they provide in class, instructors should also consider ways to connect their content to students' specific interests and goals. For example, instructors may incorporate examples from their students' favorite television shows to illustrate concepts, or create examples that relate to their specific career goals. Some instructors survey their students at the beginning of the course and then play their favorite music each day before class begins.

Fourth, instructors should encourage students to connect with one another. Students should be encouraged to learn each other's names and to form connections through structured group work or collaborative projects, either during or outside of class time. Instructors can encourage students to form study groups, which provide peer support and opportunities for social interaction. Finally, instructors should ask for feedback on the quality of their classroom community. They should share with students at the start of the course that they intend to create a sense of community and invite students to share their expectations of what that might mean in their learning environment at several points in the term. At the start of the term, instructors might ask students what aspects of a course make them feel valued and included. At midterm, students can be specifically asked if they do feel valued or included in the class and what the instructor can do to improve. Finally, at the end of the semester, instructors can return to the topic by asking students what the instructor did during the semester that demonstrated caring about all students (Sathy & Hogan, 2019).

CONCLUSION

The quality of the course material in introductory psychology can matter little if the design in which it is presented does not match the needs of students. No matter how interesting psychological findings and facts may be, they will not be retained for exams or future use if attention is not paid to the contextual factors of the class and its constituents. Relying on five design recommendations—using backward course design, creating coherence, developing students' skills, using effective learning strategies, and promoting inclusion to achieve community—will help instructors to create an engaging introductory psychology course that can satisfy the needs of psychology majors and minors, premed students, and those students seeking to satisfy a general education requirement, among others.

We recommend that instructors augment their course designs with ideas and concepts found elsewhere in this book, including attending to concrete SLOs tied to introductory psychology (Chapter 3). They should consider crafting outcomes to examine for their own purposes, demonstrating through careful assessment whether learning outcomes have been met (Chapter 4). Chapter 5 details specific instructional methods that can be implemented to achieve the learning outcomes established for the course.

Introductory psychology is already one of the most popular and sought out courses in the undergraduate curriculum. By designing the course effectively from the start, instructors can ensure that students find the course not only memorable but also meaningful and applicable to their futures.

REFERENCES

Ambrose, S. A., Bridges, M. W., DiPietro, M., Lovette, M. C., & Norman, M. K. (2010). *How learning works: Seven research-based principles for smart teaching.* Jossey-Bass.

American Psychological Association. (2013). *APA guidelines for the undergraduate psychology major: Version 2.0.* https://www.apa.org/ed/precollege/about/psymajor-guidelines.pdf

American Psychological Association. (2020). *The APA Introductory Psychology Initiative.* https://www.apa.org/ed/precollege/undergrad/introductory-psychology-initiative

Anderson, J. R., & Reder, L. M. (1979). An elaborative processing explanation of depth of processing. In L. S. Cermak & F. I. M. Craik (Eds.), *Levels of processing in human memory* (pp. 385–404). Lawrence Erlbaum Associates.

Appleby, D. C. (2014). A skills-based academic advising strategy for job-seeking psychology majors. In R. L. Miller & J. G. Irons (Eds.), *Academic advising: A handbook for advisors and students: Volume 1. Models, students, topics, and issues* (pp. 143–156). Society for the Teaching of Psychology, Division 2 of the American Psychological Association.

Benjamin, A. S., & Tullis, J. (2010). What makes distributed practice effective? *Cognitive Psychology, 61*(3), 228–247. https://doi.org/10.1016/j.cogpsych.2010.05.004

Bernstein, D. A. (2017). Bye-bye intro: A proposal for transforming introductory psychology. *Scholarship of Teaching and Learning in Psychology, 3*(3), 191–197. https://doi.org/10.1037/stl0000093

Biggs, J. (2003). Aligning teaching and assessing to course objectives. *Teaching and Learning in Higher Education: New Trends and Innovations, 2,* 13–17.

Biggs, J., & Tang, C. (2007). *Teaching for quality learning at university: What the student does* (3rd ed.). McGraw-Hill.

Boyack, K. W., Klavans, R., & Borerner, K. (2005). Mapping the backbone of science. *Scientometrics, 64*(3), 351–374. https://doi.org/10.1007/s11192-005-0255-6

Brame, C. J., & Biel, R. (2015). Test-enhanced learning: The potential for testing to promote greater learning in undergraduate science courses. *CBE Life Sciences Education, 14*(2), 14, es4. https://doi.org/10.1187/cbe.14-11-0208

Brown, P. C., Roediger, H. L., III, & McDaniel, M. A. (2014). *Make it stick.* Harvard University Press.

Carpenter, D. D. (2017, June 17). Metacognitive reflection assignments in introductory psychology. *Teaching With Metacognition.* https://www.improvewithmetacognition.com/wp-content/uploads/2017/06/Carpenter.TwM_.June2017.pdf

CAST. (2018). *The UDL guidelines.* http://udlguidelines.cast.org/

Cepeda, N. J., Coburn, N., Rohrer, D., Wixted, J. T., Mozer, M. C., & Pashler, H. (2009). Optimizing distributed practice: Theoretical analysis and practical implications. *Experimental Psychology, 56*(4), 236–246. https://doi.org/10.1027/1618-3169.56.4.236

Chen, P., Chavez, O., Ong, D. C., & Gunderson, B. (2017). Strategic resource use for learning: A self-administered intervention that guides self-reflection on effective resource use enhanced academic performance. *Psychological Science, 28*(6), 774–785. https://doi.org/10.1177/0956797617696456

Colliot, T., & Jamet, É. (2019). Asking students to be active learners: The effects of totally or partially self-generating a graphic organizer on students' learning performances. *Instructional Science, 47*(4), 463–480. https://doi.org/10.1007/s11251-019-09488-z

Craik, F. I., & Lockhart, R. S. (1972). Levels of processing: A framework for memory research. *Journal of Verbal Learning and Verbal Behavior, 11*(6), 671–684. https://doi.org/10.1016/S0022-5371(72)80001-X

Davis, B. G. (2009). *Tools for teaching* (2nd ed.). Jossey-Bass.

Dunlosky, J., Rawson, K. A., Marsh, E. J., Nathan, M. J., & Willingham, D. T. (2013). Improving students' learning with effective learning techniques: Promising directions from cognitive and educational psychology. *Psychological Science in the Public Interest, 14*(1), 4–58. https://doi.org/10.1177/1529100612453266

Dunn, D. S. (2018). On the primacy of introductory psychology. In D. S. Dunn & B. M. Hard (Eds.), *Thematic approaches for teaching introductory psychology* (pp. 1–9). Cengage.

Dunn, D. S., & Halonen, J. S. (2020). *The psychology major's companion: Everything you need to know to get where you want to go* (2nd ed.). Worth.

Dunn, D. S., & Hammer, E. D. (2014). On teaching multicultural psychology. In F. T. L. Leong, L. Comas-Díaz, G. C. Nagayama Hall, V. C. McLoyd, & J. E. Trimble (Eds.), *APA handbook of multicultural psychology: Vol. 1. Theory and research* (pp. 43–58). American Psychological Association.

Dunn, D. S., & Hard, B. M. (Eds.). (2018). *Thematic approaches for teaching introductory psychology*. Cengage.

Eddy, S. L., & Hogan, K. A. (2014). Getting under the hood: How and for whom does increasing course structure work? *CBE Life Sciences Education, 13*(3), 453–468. https://doi.org/10.1187/cbe.14-03-0050

Endres, T., Carpenter, S., Martin, A., & Renkl, A. (2017). Enhancing learning by retrieval: Enriching free recall with elaborative prompting. *Learning and Instruction, 49*, 13–20. https://doi.org/10.1016/j.learninstruc.2016.11.010

Florida Virtual Campus. (2016). *2016 student textbook and course materials survey*. https://florida.theorangegrove.org/og/items/3a65c507-2510-42d7-814c-ff-defd394b6c/1/

Foster, N. L., Mueller, M. L., Was, C., Rawson, K. A., & Dunlosky, J. (2019). Why does interleaving improve math learning? The contributions of discriminative contrast and distributed practice. *Memory & Cognition, 47*(6), 1088–1101. https://doi.org/10.3758/s13421-019-00918-4

Gannon, K. M. (2020). *Radical hope: A teaching manifesto*. West Virginia University Press.

Gurung, R. A. R. (2017). Predicting learning: Comparing an open educational resource and standard textbooks. *Scholarship of Teaching and Learning in Psychology, 3*(3), 233–248. https://doi.org/10.1037/stl0000092

Gurung, R. A. R., & Burns, K. (2019). Putting evidence-based claims to the test: A multi-site classroom study of retrieval practice and spaced practice. *Applied Cognitive Psychology, 33*(5), 732–743. https://doi.org/10.1002/acp.3507

Gurung, R. A. R., Hackathorn, J., Enns, C., Frantz, S., Cacioppo, J. T., Loop, T., & Freeman, J. E. (2016). Strengthening introductory psychology: A new model for teaching the introductory course. *American Psychologist, 71*(2), 112–124. https://doi.org/10.1037/a0040012

Gurung, R. A. R., Weidert, J., & Jeske, A. (2010). Focusing on how students study. *The Journal of Scholarship of Teaching and Learning, 10*, 28–35. https://scholarworks.iu.edu/journals/index.php/josotl/article/view/1734

Hall, T., & Strangman, N. (2008). *Graphic organizers.* A report prepared for the National Center on Accessing the General Curriculum. https://www.northernhighlands.org/cms/lib5/NJ01000179/Centricity/Domain/18/Graphic_Organizers_2008.pdf

Hard, B. M., Lovett, J. M., & Brady, S. T. (2019). What do students remember about introductory psychology, years later? *Scholarship of Teaching and Learning in Psychology, 5*(1), 61–74. https://doi.org/10.1037/stl0000136

Hardin, E. E. (2018). Seeing the world like a psychologist. In D. S. Dunn & B. M. Hard (Eds.), *Thematic approaches for teaching introductory psychology* (pp. 187–203). Cengage.

Hardin, E. E., Eschman, B., Spengler, E. S., Grizzell, J. A., Moody, A. T., Ross-Sheehy, S., & Fry, K. M. (2019). What happens when trained graduate student instructors switch to an open textbook? A controlled study of the impact on student learning objectives. *Psychology Learning & Teaching, 18*(1), 48–64. https://doi.org/10.1177/1475725718810909

Hebb, D. O. (1949). *The organization of behavior.* Wiley.

Henrich, J., Heine, S. J., & Norenzayan, A. (2010). The weirdest people in the world? *Behavioral and Brain Sciences, 33*(2–3), 61–83. https://doi.org/10.1017/S0140525X0999152X

Higbee, J. L., Chung, C. J., & Hsu, L. (2008). Enhancing the inclusiveness of first-year courses through universal design. In J. L. Higbee & E. Goff (Eds.), *Pedagogy and student service for institutional transformation: Implementing universal design in higher education* (pp. 61–78). University of Minnesota. https://files.eric.ed.gov/fulltext/ED503835.pdf

Hockings, C., Cooke, S., & Bowl, M. (2009). Learning and teaching in two universities within the context of increasing student diversity—complexity, contradictions and challenges. In M. David (Ed.), *Improving learning by widening participation in higher education* (pp. 95–108). Routledge.

Jhangiani, R. S., Dastur, F. N., Le Grand, R., & Penner, K. (2018). As good or better than commercial textbooks: Students' perceptions and outcomes from using open digital and open print textbooks. *The Canadian Journal for the Scholarship of Teaching and Learning, 9*(1). https://doi.org/10.5206/cjsotl-rcacea.2018.1.5

Jhangiani, R. S., & Jhangiani, S. (2017). Investigating the perceptions, use, and impact of open textbooks: A survey of post-secondary students in British Columbia. *The International Review of Research in Open and Distributed Learning, 18*(4), 172–192. https://doi.org/10.19173/irrodl.v18i4.3012

Johnson, D. R., Soldner, M., Leonard, J. B., Alvarez, P., Inkelas, K. K., Rowan-Kenyon, H. T., & Longerbeam, S. D. (2007). Examining sense of belonging among first-year undergraduates from different racial/ethnic groups. *Journal of College Student Development, 48*(5), 525–542. https://doi.org/10.1353/csd.2007.0054

Kornell, N., Castel, A. D., Eich, T. S., & Bjork, R. A. (2010). Spacing as the friend of both memory and induction in young and older adults. *Psychology and Aging, 25*(2), 498–503. https://doi.org/10.1037/a0017807

Kretchmar, M. D. (2001). Service learning in a general psychology class: Description, preliminary evaluation, and recommendations. *Teaching of Psychology, 28*(1), 5–10. https://doi.org/10.1207/S15328023TOP2801_02

Landrum, R. E. (2018). A skills theme for the introductory psychology course. In D. S. Dunn & B. M. Hard (Eds.), *Thematic approaches for teaching introductory psychology* (pp. 130–139). Cengage.

Landrum, R. E., & Davis, S. F. (2010). *The psychology major: Career options and strategies for success.* Prentice Hall.

Legg, A. M., & Wilson, J. H. (2009). E-mail from professor enhances student motivation and attitudes. *Teaching of Psychology, 36*(3), 205–211. https://doi.org/10.1080/00986280902960034

Lloyd, E. P., Walker, R. J., Metz, M. A., & Diekman, A. B. (2018). Comparing review strategies in the classroom: Self-testing yields more favorable student outcomes relative to question generation. *Teaching of Psychology, 45*(2), 115–123. https://doi.org/10.1177/0098628318762871

Lynch, M. F. (2018). Using evolutionary theory as an overarching theme for understanding psychology. In D. S. Dunn & B. M. Hard (Eds.), *Thematic approaches for teaching introductory psychology* (pp. 113–129). Cengage.

Maingret, N., Girardeau, G., Todorova, R., Goutierre, M., & Zugaro, M. (2016). Hippocampo-cortical coupling mediates memory consolidation during sleep. *Nature Neuroscience, 19*(7), 959–964. https://doi.org/10.1038/nn.4304

Markus, H. R., & Connor, A. (2014). *Clash! How to thrive in a multicultural world.* Plume.

Masland, L. C. (2018, October). *How basic is basic vocabulary? Surprising words our students don't know and what to do about it* [Conference presentation]. Society for the Teaching of Psychology Annual Conference on Teaching, Phoenix, AZ.

McCabe, J. (2019, June). *Wrapping up metacognition: Pre- and post-exam interventions.* https://www.improvewithmetacognition.com/wrapping-up-metacognition/

McKeachie, W. J., & Svinicki, M. (2014). *McKeachie's teaching tips: Strategies, research, and theory for college and university instructors* (14th ed.). Wadsworth.

Museus, S. D., Yi, V., & Saelua, N. (2017). The impact of culturally engaging campus environments on sense of belonging. *The Review of Higher Education, 40*(2), 187–215. https://doi.org/10.1353/rhe.2017.0001

Museus, S. D., Yi, V., & Saelua, N. (2018). How culturally engaging campus environments influence sense of belonging in college: An examination of differences between White students and students of color. *Journal of Diversity in Higher Education, 11*(4), 467–483. https://doi.org/10.1037/dhe0000069

Naufel, K. Z., Appleby, D. C., Young, J., Van Kirk, J. F., Spencer, S. M., Rudmann, J., Zaufel, K. Z., Spencer, S. M., Hettich, P., Carducci, B. J., & Richmond, A. S. (2018). *The skillful psychology student: Prepared for success in the 21st century workplace.* https://www.apa.org/careers/resources/guides/transferable-skills.pdf

Naufel, K. Z., Spencer, S. M., Appleby, D. C., Richmond, A. S., Rudman, J., Van Kirk, J., Young, J., & Carducci, B. (2019, March). The skillful psychology student: How to empower students with workforce-ready skills by teaching psychology. *Psychology*

Teacher Network. https://www.apa.org/ed/precollege/ptn/2019/03/workforce-ready-skills

Nunes, L. D., & Karpicke, J. D. (2015). Retrieval-based learning: Research at the interface between cognitive science and education. *Emerging Trends in the Social and Behavioral Sciences*. Advance online publication. https://doi.org/10.1002/9781118900772.etrds0289

Osterman, K. F. (2000). Students' need for belonging in the school community. *Review of Educational Research, 70*(3), 323–367. https://doi.org/10.3102/00346543070003323

Peter-Derex, L. (2019). Sleep and memory consolidation. *Neurophysiologie Clinique, 49*(3), 197–198. https://doi.org/10.1016/j.neucli.2019.05.046

Reeves, T. C. (2006). How do you know they are learning? The importance of alignment in higher education. *International Journal of Learning Technology, 2*(4), 294–309. https://doi.org/10.1504/IJLT.2006.011336

Richmond, A. S., Rauer, H. M., & Klein, E. (2015). How does metacognition predict beliefs in psychological and educational misconceptions? *The Researcher, 27*(1), 20–24. https://www.nrmera.org/wp-content/uploads/2016/02/Richmond.et_.al_.2015.Vol27.Issue1_.pdf

Roediger, H. L., III, & Karpicke, J. D. (2006). Test-enhanced learning: Taking memory tests improves long-term retention. *Psychological Science, 17*(3), 249–255. https://doi.org/10.1111/j.1467-9280.2006.01693.x

Roediger, H. L., III, & Karpicke, J. D. (2018). Reflections on the resurgence of interest in the testing effect. *Perspectives on Psychological Science, 13*(2), 236–241. https://doi.org/10.1177/1745691617718873

Roediger, H. L., III, & Pyc, M. A. (2012). Inexpensive techniques to improve education: Applying cognitive psychology to enhance educational practice. *Journal of Applied Research in Memory and Cognition, 1*(4), 242–248. https://doi.org/10.1016/j.jarmac.2012.09.002

Rohrer, D., Dedrick, R. F., & Burgess, K. (2014). The benefit of interleaved mathematics practice is not limited to superficially similar kinds of problems. *Psychonomic Bulletin & Review, 21*(5), 1323–1330. https://doi.org/10.3758/s13423-014-0588-3

Rose, D. H., Harbour, W. S., Johnston, C. S., Daley, S. G., & Abarbanell, L. (2006). Universal design for learning in postsecondary education: Reflections on principles and their application. *Journal of Postsecondary Education and Disability, 19*, 135–151.

Rovai, A. P., & Lucking, R. (2003). Sense of community in a higher education television-based distance education program. *Educational Technology Research and Development, 51*(2), 5–16. https://doi.org/10.1007/BF02504523

Ryan, R. M., & Deci, E. L. (2000). Self-determination theory and the facilitation of intrinsic motivation, social development, and well-being. *American Psychologist, 55*(1), 68–78. https://doi.org/10.1037/0003-066X.55.1.68

Sathy, V., & Hogan, K. A. (2019, July 22). Want to reach all of your students? Here's how to make your teaching more inclusive. *The Chronicle of Higher Education*. https://www.chronicle.com/interactives/20190719_inclusive_teaching

Scharff, L. (2017, June 16). Metacognitive reflection assignments in Introductory Psychology. *Improve With Metacognition*. https://www.improvewithmetacognition.com/student_metacognition_development_carpenter/

Siegel, J. M. (2001). The REM sleep-memory consolidation hypothesis. *Science, 294*(5544), 1058–1063. https://doi.org/10.1126/science.1063049

Silvestri Hunter, A., & Teague, S. M. (2018). Infusing scientific thinking into introductory psychology. In D. S. Dunn & B. M. Hard (Eds.), *Thematic approaches for teaching introductory psychology* (pp. 219–237). Cengage.

Thomas, R. C., Weywadt, C. R., Anderson, J. L., Martinez-Papponi, B., & McDaniel, M. A. (2018). Testing encourages transfer between factual and application questions in an online learning environment. *Journal of Applied Research in Memory and Cognition, 7*(2), 252–260. https://doi.org/10.1016/j.jarmac.2018.03.007

Turner, P. M., & Carriveau, R. S. (2010). *Next generation course redesign.* Peter Lang, Inc., International Academic Publishers.

Twigg, C. A. (2013). Improving learning and reducing costs: Outcomes from changing the equation. *Change: The Magazine of Higher Learning, 45*(4), 6–14. https://doi.org/10.1080/00091383.2013.806169

Wang, X., Su, Y., Cheung, S., Wong, E., & Kwong, T. (2012). An exploration of Biggs' constructive alignment in course design and its impact on students' learning approaches. *Assessment & Evaluation in Higher Education, 38*(4), 1–15. https://doi.org/10.1080/02602938.2012.658018

Weiten, W. (2018). The utter subjectivity of human experience. In D. S. Dunn & B. M. Hard (Eds.), *Thematic approaches for teaching introductory psychology* (pp. 93–112). Cengage.

Whisenhunt, B. L., Cathey, C., Visio, M. E., Hudson, D. L., Shoptaugh, C. F., & Rost, A. D. (2019). Strategies to address challenges with large classes: Can we exceed student expectations for large class experiences? *Scholarship of Teaching and Learning in Psychology, 5*(2), 121–127. https://doi.org/10.1037/stl0000135

Wiggins, G. P., & McTighe, J. (2005). *Understanding by design* (2nd ed.). Association for Supervision and Curriculum Development.

Wilson, J. H., Wilson, S. H., & Legg, A. M. (2012). Building rapport in the classroom and student outcomes. In B. M. Schwartz & R. A. R. Gurung (Eds.), *Evidence-based teaching for higher education* (pp. 23–37). American Psychological Association. https://doi.org/10.1037/13745-002

3

MEASURING MEANINGFUL LEARNING IN INTRODUCTORY PSYCHOLOGY

The IPI Student Learning Outcomes

JANE S. HALONEN, JENNIFER L. W. THOMPSON, KRISTIN H. WHITLOCK, R. ERIC LANDRUM, AND SUE FRANTZ

KEY RECOMMENDATIONS

1. Craft the introductory psychology course around desired student learning outcomes based on backward design principles.

2. Adopt student learning outcomes that focus on knowledge, skills, and abilities that students should have at the end of the course.

    a. Psychology content: Identify basic concepts and research findings.

    b. Scientific thinking: Solve problems using psychological methods.

    c. Key themes: Provide examples of psychology's integrative themes.

As a survey course that includes content from a wide range of areas, introductory psychology can be challenging to teach. College instructors who tend to specialize in one area of research may feel apprehensive about teaching outside of their comfort zone. High school instructors, who are primarily trained to teach social studies courses such as history or government,

---

https://doi.org/10.1037/0000260-004
Transforming Introductory Psychology: Expert Advice on Teacher Training, Course Design, and Student Success, R. A. R. Gurung and G. Neufeld (Editors)

may feel inadequately prepared to teach the science of psychology. At all levels of instruction, teachers work with students of diverse backgrounds with different expectations for the course and varying motivation levels.

For many students, their experience in introductory psychology may be their only formal exposure to the science of psychology. During that time, instructors have a limited window of opportunity to produce a positive impact on their students and to present a more diverse human perspective (Boatright-Horowitz et al., 2019). Learning about psychological science can help students improve their personal well-being, develop a better understanding of themselves and others, and increase their ability to think critically. Students may also realize the potential psychological science has to solve some of the most vexing problems we face in society today. Our students are the consumers of psychological science; many will become policy makers, designing programs and enacting legislation for the public at large. The promise of introductory psychology as a high-impact experience can weigh heavily on an instructor, leaving us with two essential questions: Because the course entails a daunting amount of information about psychological science, where and how should we focus? This chapter is dedicated to answering this question.

THE SCOPE OF INTRODUCTORY PSYCHOLOGY

The introductory psychology course represents a complicated ecosystem in the United States; there is no simple one-size-fits-all description of how the course is taught or how it should be taught. The course is ubiquitous at the college level, with 1.2 million to 1.6 million students in the United States enrolled annually (Gurung et al., 2016; Steuer & Ham, 2008). Approximately 99% of psychology departments in U.S. colleges and universities offer introductory courses (Norcross et al., 2016). At this level, many students take introductory psychology to fulfill a general education requirement, and most students enrolled in the course will not major in psychology. For an excellent overview of the challenges of teaching the course, from conceptual misperceptions to learning objectives, organizational tips, the difficulties in teaching students new to college, large classes, and dealing with plagiarism, see Stoloff (2010).

Introductory psychology is a popular elective at the high school level as well. In 2009 (the last year in which these data were collected by the National Center for Education Statistics), approximately 30% of all high school graduates had completed a course in psychology in one format or another (U.S. Department of Education, 2011). According to their recent annual reports, more than 300,000 students completed the Advanced Placement Test in Psychology (College Board, 2019) and more than 21,000 completed the International Baccalaureate Exam in Psychology (International Baccalaureate Organization, 2019). A substantial number of students also complete introductory psychology through dual enrollment in which a local higher education entity provides the course. A well-taught high school course can play an important role in the educational pipeline as many students may be inspired to take more psychology courses as part of their post–high school education.

Sometimes the introductory course is taught within the constraints of one term; sometimes psychology programs at the college level break the course into two courses, differentiating the natural versus the social science foci. Several small sections of a college's introductory course can be taught by different instructors using different course designs in the same semester, or large mega-sections, or a mixture. Similarly, at the high school level, a course can extend for a half year or a full year. When resources allow, sometimes teachers incorporate an accompanying laboratory experience for students. Many teachers focus on active learning strategies and demonstrations; others, driven to size constraints, may rely on the lecture as the primary course activity. The course can be delivered successfully online as well as face-to-face. Some teachers prefer course designs that reflect a particular orientation, such as focusing on misconceptions, critical thinking, social justice, or neuroscience, among other approaches (Dunn & Hard, 2018). We offer these details to underscore that such complexity across courses obviates attempts to design and prescribe the "ideal" introductory psychology course.

Textbook availability and access (including access to technology) also influence course design. The market for introductory psychology textbooks is both vast and potentially profitable, a reality that encourages publishers to seek new and different strategies to engage prospective adopters. Publishers have flooded the contemporary market with options, but the review process that publishers typically use discourages removing old material. Consequently, since new content does not usually displace old content, textbooks verge on encyclopedic and are impossible to cover comprehensively in a one-term course design. This practice leaves educators feeling challenged about what chapters constitute the essential content that should be addressed in the introductory course. Another complication related to textbook selection is the burgeoning production of open educational resources. Although open educational resources can allow instructors to make psychology content accessible at no cost, there is typically more limited guidance for the faculty in the implementation of courses when compared to the instructor manuals and other ancillaries that traditional publishers often provide.

The American Psychological Association (APA) sponsored the Introductory Psychology Initiative (IPI; APA, 2020) in part to address the complexities of delivering an effective introductory course across different contexts. Our IPI subcommittee, Student Learning Outcomes and Assessment, undertook the challenge of helping introductory psychology teachers make well-informed decisions about how to approach introductory psychology's expansive content. This task included identifying what desirable skills students should develop during their course experience and what key themes should linger in their perceptions about psychology long after the course is over. This chapter represents the result of that collaboration.

To that end, we provide some background about the role of student learning outcomes (SLOs) and assessment, specifically as those concepts apply to the introductory psychology course. We begin with a brief discussion of the national push toward SLOs to set the stage for the main purpose of this chapter: to outline an overarching set of SLOs that can be broadly useful for designing and scaffolding the introductory psychology course. Our task force carefully considered what types of content, skills, and values should cut across contexts. We provide a rationale for the selection of specific SLOs and key themes that emerged from those discussions.

THE CONTENT VERSUS SKILLS DEBATE

Historically, for many instructors, the focus of the introductory psychology course has been content. Instructors tended to measure the impact of their courses by concentrating on how much content a student could master. That is, how many chapters could be "covered" and what are the resultant scores on multiple-choice tests? As a consequence, many students spend their time in their courses memorizing definitions of terms. Does this exercise best serve our students? Do we want our students to remember definitions in isolation without making those more substantial connections to other salient ideas or to their world at large? Does this practice give students an accurate understanding of our dynamic and integrative discipline? What is the optimal impact that should transpire in a well-taught introductory psychology course? Questions such as these have given rise to spirited debates about whether the primary emphasis of a course should be on content mastery or perhaps skill development.

The Struggle to Define Core Content

Calls for standards in the introductory psychology course have been heard for decades. Dunn et al. (2010) issued one of these strong appeals:

> Given the ubiquitous relevance of psychology to other majors and fields, most jobs, and the world in general, as well as the many contributions an understanding of psychology can have to personal growth and development, all students need to receive a common core of content. (p. 59)

But debate continues over what should be considered "core," as defined by Dunn et al., representing the most fundamental aspects of the introductory psychology curriculum.

As one might expect, the APA has exercised leadership in helping educators at all levels work effectively to address high-quality psychology curricula. The APA first examined quality concerns related to introductory psychology at the high school level when the organization endorsed the publication of the *National Standards for High School Psychology Curricula* beginning in 1999 (APA, 2011). These standards outlined the key topics and comprehensive learning objectives for 20 content areas. Some have suggested these high school standards be applied to courses at the college level (Smith & Fineburg, 2006). Others have suggested that higher education instructors look to the *APA Guidelines for the Undergraduate Psychology Major: Version 1.0* (APA, 2007) and *Version 2.0* (APA, 2013) for guidance on curricular matters (Dunn et al., 2010; Weiten & Houska, 2015). However, as Weiten and Houska (2015) noted, generalizing introductory psychology objectives from those established for the *psychology major* may not be reasonable. These authors did acknowledge that the emphasis on skills rather than knowledge in the *APA Guidelines* is a welcome development. It appears there is a need for an outcomes resource that is specific to introductory psychology.

Part of the challenge of identifying core content is that psychology itself has become more specialized. Dunn et al. (2010) noted this evolution, as well as the challenge that comes with such specialization, which has produced the impression that the discipline has become fragmented, making it more difficult for students to see psychology as a unified enterprise. In their quest to examine the common core of introductory psychology, the authors of the APA initiative *Strengthening the Common Core of the Introductory Psychology Course* (2014) concluded that textbooks contribute to fragmentation by presenting each content area as distinctly separate from others. Gurung et al. (2016) concurred that "unfortunately, the contemporary Intro Psych course structure does not adequately reflect the current scope of the discipline, which increasingly emphasizes multiple influences, inter-connections, and synthesis" (p. 114).

In response to this concern, the *Common Core* group recommended a "pillar" model to represent a different approach to teaching this course (see Figure 3.1). Like an ancient Greek structure, the base of the building represents the basic need to teach the foundational principles of scientific inquiry. Each pillar of the structure signifies the content of psychology divided into domains (biological, cognitive, developmental, social and personality, and mental and physical health). Allowing for factors such as expertise, student needs, or departmental emphasis, the authors recommended that instructors include at least two topics from each pillar to create a fair representation of the discipline in the beginning course. To represent the integrative nature of contemporary psychology, the model also includes cross-cutting themes (cultural and social diversity, ethics, variations in human functioning, and applications). The Common Core Working Group suggested that instructors "explicitly elevate the importance of the cross-cutting themes . . . [to] ensure that important issues such as diversity and ethics are frequently on the students' radar versus seen as only solitary requirements" (Gurung et al., 2016, p. 117).

The structure's rooftop emphasizes integration across the different content pillars because more will be learned through integration than focusing on the isolated content domains. Gurung et al. (2016) proposed that integrating content across introductory psychology's domains provides opportunity to develop higher-order thinking skills. We note that specific integrative themes were not listed, an element provided by our current recommendations. The authors also urged "for Intro Psych in particular, much work remains. For example, the discipline needs to identify learning goals and outcomes for the Intro Psych course, evaluate the [pillar] model proposed here, [and] develop assessment strategies for the Intro Psych course" (p. 123).

Focusing on Skills

In contrast with a traditional emphasis on covering the content, some scholars have advocated a skills-based approach to introductory psychology (Jhangiani & Hardin, 2015; Watson et al., 1999). Others have also offered actual published teaching modules regarding scientific reasoning skills with accompanying assessment strategies and assessment data (Becker-Blease et al., 2019; Stevens et al., 2016). These developments suggest that the skills focus is becoming more popular. This work parallels the growth of scholarship regarding what psychology majors believe to be important

FIGURE 3.1. Pillar Model

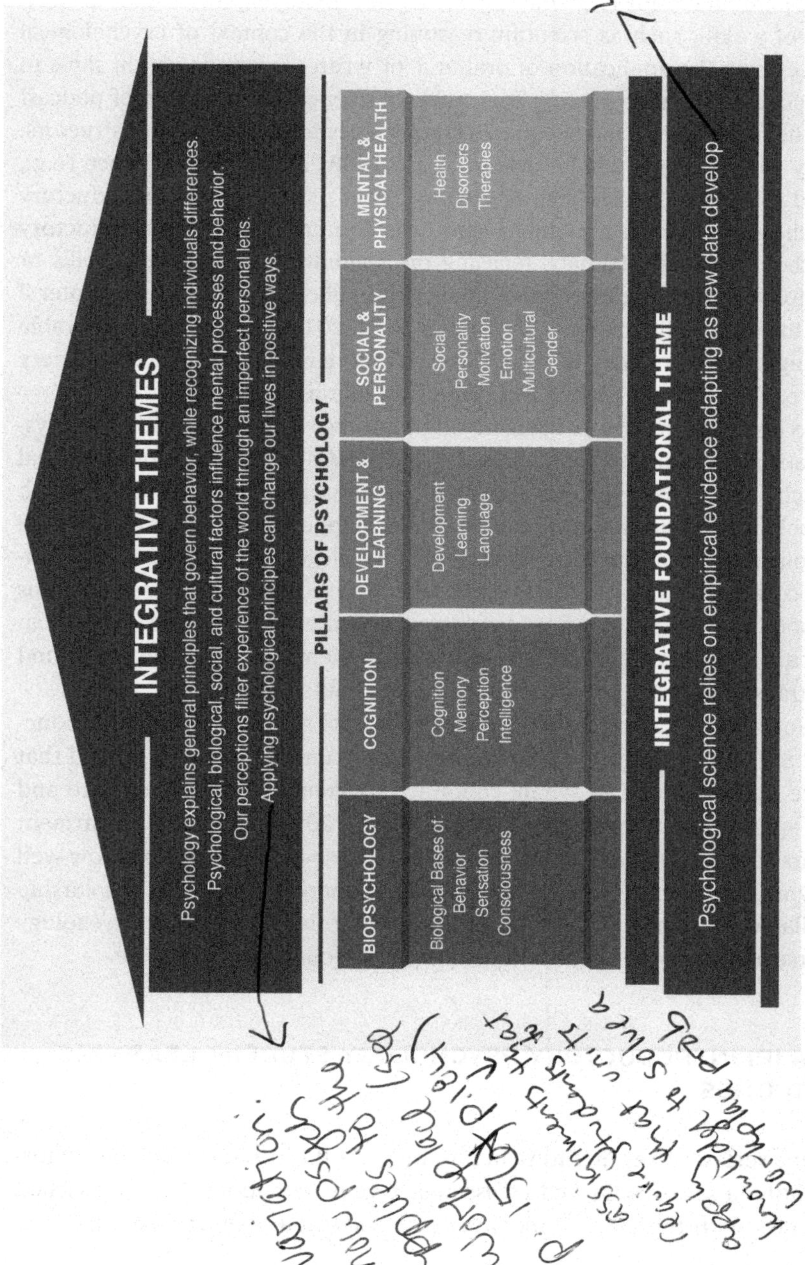

From "Strengthening Introductory Psychology: A New Model for Teaching the Introductory Course," by R. A. R. Gurung, J. Hackathorn, C. Enns, S. Frantz, J. T. Cacioppo, T. Loop, and J. E. Freeman, 2016, *American Psychologist, 71*(2), p. 120 (https://doi.org/10.1037/a0040012). Copyright 2016 by the American Psychological Association.

about the skills they possess (Hund & Bueno, 2015; Miller & Carducci, 2015; Strohmetz et al., 2015).

Instructors typically find it easier to conceptualize assessment strategies that test for the retention of content as compared to the demonstration of a skill, particularly for large enrollment classes. Assessing a student's acquisition of a skill, such as scientific reasoning in the context of psychological concepts or the application of oral and/or written communication skills to translate a scientific concept to a public audience (such as a brief podcast or an infographic), may require training assistance for many instructors. Early (e.g., Greene, 1931; Rickard et al., 1988) and recent evidence (e.g., Hard et al., 2019; Landrum & Gurung, 2013) suggests that introductory psychology students remember very little content from their introductory psychology course. Perhaps focusing on a handful of meaningful skills or reinforcing recurring integrative themes throughout a course (see Chapter 2 and the entire edited volume by Dunn & Hard, 2018) can provide memorable lasting events for students in contrast with more traditional content-mastery approaches. This, of course, is an empirical question.

As discussed in Chapter 2, an important strategy in being organized and systematic about skill development is the use of SLOs as the chief organizational principle of the course. This approach is helpful in many ways. At the high school level, a systematic approach will encourage greater consistency in the various forms that the course takes. At the college level, standardizing content coverage and learning activities can produce consistency across numerous sections on a campus or across distributed campuses. A systematic strategy can also aid in the generation of articulation agreements between institutions and the transferability of introductory psychology course credits.

Homa et al. (2013) examined course syllabi to ascertain how introductory SLOs aligned with APA *Guidelines 1.0* documents and determined that more than 50% of 158 syllabi contained outcomes specific to science and the application of psychology. Pfund et al. (2018) surveyed department chairs about how introductory psychology SLOs were selected and how well they aligned with *Guidelines 2.0*. However, there is very little scholarship available about how SLOs are used concerning the introductory psychology course and no consensus on what appropriate outcomes should be.

APA IPI INTRODUCTORY PSYCHOLOGY STUDENT LEARNING OUTCOMES

After a review of key literature in this area, our IPI working group began formulating a set of SLOs and assessment recommendations. We approached our task with three basic operating principles and assumptions. First, the introductory psychology course exists in many formats and contexts with various stakeholders. Because of this complexity, assessment demands will vary accordingly; therefore, our recommendations must be broadly conceived. Second, we concentrated on what elements should be in common across contexts. Our recommendations should be just as relevant to college as high school instructors, to large lectures as small classes, to face-to-face as digital delivery, and to selective versus open-access settings. Third, we wanted to recognize and honor prior work from other influential documents and stakeholders (e.g., *National Standards for High School Psychology Curricula, APA Guidelines for the Undergraduate Major 2.0*, the *AP Psychology Course and Exam Description*, and the "pillar" model from *Strengthening the Common Core of the Introductory Psychology Course*).

We believe that the recommendations regarding teaching content across the five domains presented in the *Common Core* pillar model can be useful. However, we have purposely focused on identifying the key skills that students should acquire as a result of taking this course, rather than identifying specific content that should be covered. We are not suggesting content is unimportant, but we propose that content provides a foundation for building skills and applying concepts. This stance supports instructors' autonomy in how to make content choices to reach their selected goals. We also believe that a central outcome of an introductory psychology course is a student's ability to recognize and apply the kind of scientific thinking psychologists demonstrate. Additionally, we focused on identifying integrative themes to promote enduring understanding by students that should linger long after the course is over.

[handwritten margin note: *Focus on Skills and content*]

We began with a consideration of the first three skill-based goals in *Guidelines 2.0*, namely, Knowledge Base in Psychology, Scientific Inquiry and Critical Thinking, and Ethical and Social Responsibility in a Diverse World. However, definitions matter in psychological science so we present slightly different terminology to communicate our findings. In our framework the overarching categories or goals constitute *student learning outcomes*. Indicators for these outcomes are designated as *learning objectives*.

This framework reflects Suskie's (2009) recommendation that assessment practices should clearly distinguish learning outcomes and objectives. In her approach to learning outcomes, Suskie described the ultimate goal to be achieved by the course, the end state; learning outcomes "are the knowledge, skills, attitudes, and habits of mind that students take with them from a learning experience" (p. 117). According to Suskie, learning objectives describe more of the details about what the students are to achieve.

In our conceptualization, we highlight three "aspirational" SLOs that involve psychology content, scientific thinking, and key themes along with their related learning objectives. Exhibit 3.1 presents the IPI SLOs and learning

EXHIBIT 3.1. APA IPI Student Learning Outcomes for Introductory Psychology

SLO 1. Psychology Content: Identify basic concepts and research findings.

1.1. Define and explain basic psychological concepts.

1.2. Interpret research findings related to psychological concepts.

1.3. Apply psychological principles to personal growth and other aspects of everyday life.

SLO 2. Scientific Thinking: Solve problems using psychological methods.

2.1. Describe the advantages and limitations of research strategies.

2.2. Evaluate, design, or conduct psychological research.

2.3. Draw logical and objective conclusions about behavior and mental processes from empirical evidence.

2.4. Examine how psychological science can be used to counter unsubstantiated statements, opinions, or beliefs.

SLO 3. Key Themes: Provide examples of psychology's integrative themes.

A. Psychological science relies on empirical evidence and adapts as new data develop.

B. Psychology explains general principles that govern behavior while recognizing individual differences.

C. Psychological, biological, social, and cultural factors influence behavior and mental processes.

D. Psychology values diversity, promotes equity, and fosters inclusion in pursuit of a more just society.

E. Our perceptions and biases filter our experiences of the world through an imperfect personal lens.

F. Applying psychological principles can change our lives, organizations, and communities in positive ways.

G. Ethical principles guide psychology research and practice.

Note. SLO = student learning outcome.

objectives. Our framework specifies learning outcomes with numbers (1, 2, or 3). We detail related learning objectives with numerical designations (e.g., 2.1, 2.2) and themes with alphabetical notations (e.g., A, B, C).

Learning objectives typically have three components (Diamond, 2008; Marzano, 2009): (a) what the learner is to do, usually including an action verb; (b) the conditions under which the action will take place; and (c) the criterion at which the learner's performance is acceptable. Our learning objectives address the first component by providing verb-based indicators of each SLO.

Instructors would then customize the objective to fit their specific courses. Instructions for assignments address the second step, specifying the learning context. Many instructors develop rubrics to communicate the third step to establish acceptable performance levels. Ideally, teachers should address all three aspects of the student learning objective to optimize learning.

We provide an example using the learning objective 3.F from Exhibit 3.1. Step 1 offers a description of the theme: "Applying psychological principles can change our lives, organizations, and communities in positive ways." In Step 2, the instructor designs instructions for an assignment in which the student must generate an error-free infographic that highlights the practical application of one principle from psychology that can be used to benefit an individual's life. In Step 3, the instructor would specify what constitutes successful performance (e.g., use of at least five APA Style citations from peer-reviewed works in an aesthetically appealing graphic). From an accountability standpoint, a performance benchmark may be established to gather data for external purposes. For example, "By the end of this course, 80% of enrolled students will meet specified infographic criteria" establishes a performance benchmark that can help with program data collection or planning teaching improvements.

The incredible complexity of formats and contexts of introductory psychology discouraged our dictating what specific content should be presented in the course, but we endorse the idea that when learning how to master psychology content, mastery should be a course goal. This stance allows for substantial flexibility and academic freedom in how to meet the *psychology content* SLO.

Moreover, we felt compelled to emphasize scientific literacy and critical thinking skills as well as the value of psychological science in our *scientific thinking* SLO. Dunn et al. (2010) maintain that understanding scientific methods is "central to the discipline" (p. 55). Although we do not turn introductory psychology students into psychological scientists, we should give them practice with the methods that psychologists use to solve problems and gain insight into behavior.

Our *key themes* SLO affirms the proposition presented in the *Common Core* pillar model that SLOs should reflect the contemporary nature of the field. As such, we emphasize the integrative themes in psychology, such as ethics and diversity, that recur throughout the discipline to avoid the "silo-like representation of psychology in most textbooks" (Gurung et al., 2016, p. 114). In deciding upon these themes, our group reviewed the work of others who have approached the teaching of introductory psychology in a thematic way, such as Weiten's (2017) "Unifying Themes," Myers and DeWall's (2017) "Four Big Ideas," and Hard's "Big Ideas" (2017). We looked for areas of alignment, and after careful discussion and consideration of feedback from APA members; APA divisions, boards, and committees; and experts in the field, we developed seven broad themes that can be woven throughout the introductory psychology course. A thematic outcome should inspire students to provide several content examples of the theme across different topical domains. Thus, rather than instructors focusing on specific content that must be covered, they can choose the content that best helps them illustrate specific themes. We believe this framework provides instructors with flexibility to teach within a local or institutional/mission-based context while also assisting students to draw memorable connections across different content domains in psychology. For recommendations on how to design an introductory psychology course using organizational themes, please see Chapter 2.

Regardless of the teaching philosophy that undergirds introductory psychology course design, we think these outcomes should fit well with what students should know and be able to do at the conclusion of their course experience. Careful observers will note that the outcomes and objectives are expressed in general terms; we detail the rationale to justify the broad strokes outcomes in the next section. Just as we did not dictate essential content out of respect for teacher autonomy and academic freedom, we also did not endorse or prescribe one preferred course strategy. Instead, we think the outcomes provide a framework that will support teacher creativity in executing interesting and effective courses that reflect both disciplinary values and the unique influences of the introductory psychology teacher. In the next section, we offer the rationale for each learning objective.

OUTCOMES RATIONALES

The selected outcomes concentrate on the most salient aspects of the psychology major: psychology content and thinking like a psychologist, and the themes that pervade any well-taught introductory course. For each element detailed in the outcomes, we provide some examples that illustrate how these can be incorporated into the curriculum plan.

Outcome 1. Psychology Content: Identify Basic Concepts and Research Findings

Traditional assessment strategies focus on how well students learn the content that is communicated within a course. In the content outcome, we should strive to equip students with a reasonable repository of psychological knowledge. The results we describe in the psychology content outcome progress from lower-level concept recognition to higher-level cognitive functions, such as application that should make the course concepts more enduring and useful beyond the end of the course.

Objective 1.1. Define and Explain Basic Psychological Concepts
Becoming familiar with the terminology psychologists use to describe, explain, and predict behavior is a primary objective of any good psychology course. Students should be able to identify the link between the formal concept and the behavior the concept attempts to convey. Explaining the concept may require a bit more depth as students translate the concept into their own words.

Objective 1.2. Interpret Research Findings Related to Psychological Concepts
Empirical research serves as the basis for the evolution of knowledge in psychology. Introductory students should develop some facility to describe the purpose and results of classic research studies and discuss how studies shed light on the concepts they have been studying. For example, the concept of cognitive dissonance is challenging to master, but understanding the details of Festinger and Carlsmith's (1959) original design can bring the concept to life. Students should be able to describe how research enhances our understanding of psychological concepts, and students should also describe potential biases inherent in psychological research due to either the researcher themselves or the lack of generalizability of results because of the population studied.

Objective 1.3. Apply Psychological Principles to Personal Growth and Other Aspects of Everyday Life
Moving beyond recognition and interpretation of concepts, our final objective in our first SLO focuses on the ability of students to see the connection of the concepts they are studying to their own existence. For example, students can appreciate the sensory process of habituation when they explore why the first bite of a good meal seems more satisfying than the bites that follow, thanks to how habituation affects gustation. Similarly, students might embark on a campaign to improve their study habits by being conscientious about getting sleep to consolidate their learning. As students become more engaged in their studies, they may spontaneously observe and report psychological concepts in operation either to enrich class discussion or as part of a formal assessment.

Outcome 2. Scientific Thinking: Solve Problems Using Psychological Methods

Whether a course is taught at the high school, 2-year, or 4-year program level, teaching students to think like psychological scientists is an important goal in introductory courses. The outcomes associated with this outcome help students develop critical thinking skills that focus on psychology as a research-based enterprise. The skills associated with this outcome necessarily involve higher-level cognitive involvement that can be fostered most effectively through active learning strategies. However, we recognize that the degree of involvement is necessarily constrained by course size, access to resources, teaching modality, lab availability, and so forth that would facilitate research activity. Thus, we acknowledge that students may have to glean many of these critical thinking skills through careful evaluation of research methods and results through reading and observation.

Objective 2.1. Describe the Advantages and Limitations of Research Strategies

Students should learn about the various methods psychologists use to generate evidence about behavior. They should explore the intent behind different research strategies (e.g., case studies, surveys, correlational studies, and experiments). The distinction between quantitative and qualitative research can also be a fruitful exploration. Each psychological research strategy has advantages and limitations in producing conclusions about behavior. Therefore, students should recognize that researchers strive to deploy strategies that are the most appropriate for the research question. For example, if we wanted an in-depth psychological profile of a trauma victim, then a case study or a qualitative approach would be preferred. If we wanted to conduct forensic psychology experiments, we might not choose serial killers as participants since there will be too few to assign to different treatment conditions randomly. If we wanted to determine whether a political speech was persuasive, then a survey is the tool of choice, even with the challenges of proper sampling, survey construction, and potential biasing influences.

Objective 2.2. Evaluate, Design, or Conduct Psychological Research

The duration of an introductory course may not provide sufficient time for students to design and conduct their own research. However, many instructors incorporate simple research strategies that students can enact to help them understand both the mechanics and the messiness of behavioral research. For example, students might stage a controlled comparison study in which they attempt to identify variables that increase altruistic acts. Alternatively, students might generate simple surveys to explore how to improve food quality in the student union or cafeteria. Students might try to replicate a classic research study to see if the original results can be duplicated. Along those lines, Psi Chi, the International Honor Society in Psychology, operates a student-focused replication program that can assist faculty who want to give students hands-on experience in executing psychology research. Similarly, the APA Summit on High School Psychology Education published an ebook showcasing lab activities that support this outcome (see https://teachpsych.org/ebooks/promotingpsychscience).

Designing and conducting simple studies not only enlightens students about how research works but also introduces why operational definitions and measurement are so central to problem solving in psychology.

Not all classes can readily engage students directly in research since class size, time, space, and even institutional review board oversight can be constraining factors. However, learning what constitutes high-quality research design can also be accomplished by having students evaluate whether claims from research are legitimate based on the research's design. For example, after students learn about why experiments use control procedures, they can be provided with experimental claims that derive from flawed design. Students learn that controlled comparisons help us rule out alternative explanations for the results of a study. Similarly, a researcher may make inappropriate causal claims from a correlational study, not recognize flawed control procedures, or narrowly select the population so the research findings won't generalize. When students can detect design flaws and describe procedures to correct those problems, they demonstrate rudimentary skills in problem solving through research.

Objective 2.3. Draw Logical and Objective Conclusions About Behavior and Mental Processes From Empirical Evidence

This objective assists students to grasp the scientific foundation of psychology. Students should be able to tease out when conclusions about behavior might not be warranted. They should see the value of seeking empirical support for claims made about behavior and to recognize that the strongest conclusions derive from solid logic and objective procedures. Students should explore the differences between correlated and causal factors in explaining behavior. They should recognize that there may be dangers in generalizing research findings from one study to all humans. One impact of this outcome is encouraging students to seek evidence before coming to conclusions about behavior.

Objective 2.4. Examine How Psychological Science Can Be Used to Counter Unsubstantiated Statements, Opinions, or Beliefs

"Commonsense" knowledge about behavior is rife with beliefs that are likely to collapse under scientific scrutiny. One of the biggest impacts a well-taught introductory course can have is making students more aware of how many of their beliefs may be unsubstantiated. Simply examining a family belief (e.g., "a hat on the bed brings bad luck") may produce a good hypothetical research question in which students can see research principles in action. For example, students have been schooled to think they can only learn efficiently and effectively if the teaching style matches their learning styles. This claim has taken root in teacher training, even though there is no empirical evidence to support that it makes any difference (Willingham et al., 2015). Exploring how a well-designed research study can either corroborate or challenge a belief should contribute to more respect for predictions about behavior that derive from good design. Indeed, many psychology instructors use "challenging misconceptions" as a theme for their own course design.

Outcome 3. Key Themes: Provide Examples of Psychology's Integrative Themes (A–G)

Some themes resonate across different content areas in psychology. This outcome fosters the ability of students to recognize how the values of the discipline of psychology surface across specialized content areas throughout the course. These integrative themes offer the promise of lessons that may be learned and retained far longer than any specific psychology concepts. The outcome is fairly simple and straightforward, and the themes themselves are rich in instructional opportunity. In this section, we explore themes that we hope students would remember long after the course is over. We designate each theme with a letter, but all themes connect to the basic outcome of being able to generate examples capturing the principles that undergird the discipline of psychology.

As discussed in Chapter 2, some psychology teachers have adopted a thematic approach to the whole of the psychology course. For other teachers, the key themes of psychology may be more implicit rather than explicit (for examples of how these themes might be used in various ways, please see Part II of this book). We believe that explicit discussion of themes is likely to generate a greater appreciation of and a memory aid for the discipline's characteristics. Addressing the themes effectively in course design will help students discern the true nature of the discipline and may be instrumental in facilitating choices in the future regarding additional coursework in psychology. To those ends, we discuss the rationale for each theme and offer some examples of how the themes can emerge throughout different content areas of the course.

Theme A. Psychological Science Relies on Empirical Evidence and Adapts as New Data Develop

Persuading students that psychology is a scientific discipline rather than a commonsense enterprise is often a top priority for introductory psychology instructors. Students arrive with many misconceptions about the discipline, such as all psychologists are therapists, and many students struggle to accept psychology as a science. Students should emerge from the course with the conclusion that the true pursuit of psychological knowledge must reflect principles of good science. These characteristics include identifying influential variations, determining operational definitions and measurement, distinguishing correlation versus causation, assessing validity and reliability of findings, and appropriately generalizing the results. The discipline engages in peer review to promote best practices and ensure the most defensible research claims.

New students of psychology are often surprised that the discipline is still evolving. As our research questions expand, the knowledge base in psychology grows. As a consequence, we sometimes find that claims established from early research may no longer be valid or we have become more astute about the limitations of generalizing research findings. Good science practice requires revision of scientific theories and concepts when warranted to produce the best scientific conclusions possible.

Experimental methods and statistics are the content areas in which we introduce research design. However, other content areas easily demonstrate and reinforce this principle. For example, exploring how conceptualizations of memory have changed over time richly illustrates adapting to new and better theories. The controversies that have attended whether subliminal perception produces any real effects on behavior shows the importance of putting ideas to an empirical test and how conclusions may need to be modified as our understanding becomes more sophisticated. Questions regarding the effectiveness of therapy also illustrate important aspects of empirical design and change over time.

Theme B. Psychology Explains General Principles That Govern Behavior While Recognizing Individual Differences

Psychological research focuses on the production of general principles that influence behavior, but the discipline is also invested in exploring how individuals differ from one another. The primary "unit of analysis" in psychology is the individual. Our statistical tools help us determine how to build general principles from looking at patterns of individual responses.

The theme of individual differences emerges throughout the course. In more biologically oriented examples, individuals who experience synesthesia, or super-tasting, can be distinguished from others who biologically don't have these capabilities. Discussions of intelligence testing (e.g., crystallized vs. fluid intelligence) can appropriately highlight individual variation. Personality concepts, such as delay of gratification or sensation seeking, can point out important differences that drive motivation. Developmental psychology is rife with examples about how age can influence individual characteristics (e.g., sleep patterns, risk taking).

Theme C. Psychological, Biological, Social, and Cultural Factors Influence Behavior and Mental Processes

Behavior usually arises from complex causes. Contemporary practice often invokes a "bio-psycho-social/cultural" model to account for all the influences that might come to bear on any specific action. For example, an act of violence might be perpetrated because an environment is unbearably hot, an individual suffers from having poor impulse control, and the social environment might reward acting out with media attention. Knowing that any behavior may be influenced by biological, personal, and contextual factors engenders more thoughtful consideration of complexity before coming to judgment or taking action.

Content areas in the curriculum that particularly highlight the intersection of the biopsychosocial model include health and wellness. For example, drug addiction has clear physiological, personality, and social/cultural elements that sustain unhealthy behavior. Many psychological disorders, such as anorexia, illustrate this complexity as well. Females in certain cultures who tend to show certain personality characteristics may be more vulnerable to the problem and certainly risk dramatic physiological consequences from enduring anorexic behavior. Healthy aging will be influenced by a combination of genetics, effective physical regimens, a positive outlook, and social and cultural support. Human attachment also shows complex interaction since temperament from birth may influence the level of need regarding making human connections. Still, other factors such as cultural practices, access to resources, and personality factors can also contribute.

Theme D. Psychology Values Diversity, Promotes Equity, and Fosters Inclusion in Pursuit of a More Just Society

Psychologists tend to share a worldview that obligates us to strive to improve the human condition. We acknowledge that many injustices and inequities exist in the world, but we believe that learning and exercising psychology principles in service to improving lives can make a positive difference.

Facilitating fair and humane outcomes for humanity may seem to be a grandiose objective as part of an introductory psychology course, but we believe students should come away from the course with a greater understanding of the dynamics that generate bias, prejudice, and discrimination in all its varieties (racism, sexism, ageism, ableism, etc., and the intersection of these injustices). To those ends, psychologists believe that all should work to transcend our human frailties and diminish the negative effects and disparities generated by our differences.

Some psychologists have adopted the concept of "intersectionality" to help explain how individuals represent a composite of characteristics that influence how others respond to them. Not only do all individuals have identity elements that contribute to their own unique experience and self-perception, but also any aspect of that composite may stimulate responses from others that could be problematic and potentially unfair. For example, a given individual might be female, Muslim, lesbian, and hearing impaired. Every aspect of her intersectional identity may have been the basis for a lost opportunity or an episode of maltreatment. Articulating different aspects of identity provides a great opportunity to explore the impact of privilege, differential access, and social justice concerns.

Theme E. Our Perceptions and Biases Filter Our Experiences of the World Through an Imperfect Personal Lens

One of the most helpful objectives we can offer in introductory psychology is helping students understand and cope with their own inherent human imperfections. Human beings are, by default, flawed organisms. Our brains have evolved to process information in ways that make life easier to navigate, but sometimes those automatic reactions can misfire (Kahneman, 2011). We are good at coming to rapid conclusions that might short-circuit more complex and complete consideration of a problem. We fill in or embellish information in ways that reflect our own biases. We interpret events in ways that often allow us to save face or escape blame. Persuading students that as humans we have to be vigilant to guard against automatic responses can be instrumental in helping them live a more functional life.

We can illustrate various traps that influence our perceptions by exploring perceptual illusions in which case we often know the trick behind the illusion (e.g., the Muller–Lyer lines are equal), but we still fall for the distortion. We can examine how framing can influence judgment. In Loftus and Palmer's (1974) classic misinformation study, changing a single word in a description of a car crash influences participant perception of how fast the cars were moving. An assortment of cognitive errors (e.g., confirmation bias, hindsight bias, representative heuristic) can illustrate the shortcuts we resort to in making decisions. Our tendencies for self-protection produce distorted perceptions that contribute to self-serving and in-group biases.

Theme F. Applying Psychological Principles Can Change Our Lives, Organizations, and Communities in Positive Ways

Using psychology to foster positive changes can be an exciting prospect for students. Finding ways to implement the principles they have learned to live more satisfying lives can often be a deciding factor in whether students decide to pursue additional coursework in psychology. The level of change can be personal or more outward directed, looking at ways to improve systems that influence peers, families, communities, and even culture. Of course, psychology can also be used in negative ways, and students should be encouraged to apply change principles to produce positive rather than negative outcomes or not merely as an exercise in manipulation.

Students most directly benefit from the insight our discipline provides on how to be an effective student (i.e., memorization strategies, massed vs. distributed practice). Since all of us live stressful lives, enacting psychology principles to promote the most effective coping strategies can be immediately useful in producing more healthy management of life strains. Operant conditioning principles can help students develop personal improvement plans, such as increasing exercise or stopping smoking. Concepts and strategies discussed in social psychology can be deployed to promote conflict resolution. Finally, endorsing the pursuit of therapy to improve quality of life can be construed as an act of courage rather than weakness. This stance can be persuasive for students concerned about stigma related to getting professional help.

Beyond self-improvement, using psychology principles to improve community conditions can be illustrated in a variety of ways. Embarking on a service-learning project can demonstrate how to build community resilience under stress. Factoring in psychological impact may influence voting support for new public policy. For example, connecting the principles from different content areas, especially from the social psychology chapter, to better understand the Black Lives Matter movement, can provide a powerful real-world connection for students between the applied ideas of psychology based on empirical research and their daily lives.

Theme G. Ethical Principles Guide Psychology Research and Practice

Psychology's commitment to describe, explain, predict, and control behavior has sometimes produced some controversial research that has tarnished the reputation of the discipline as a whole. For example, the Stanford prison experiment (Haney et al., 1973) and the Milgram obedience research (1963) both represent practices that would be considered by today's standards as not just exploitative but also potentially harmful. The larger enterprise of scientific research has also historically engaged in controversial research, such as the Tuskegee experiments (Brandt, 1978), which represented appalling exploitation of the research participants.

Perhaps in part because research studies like these took place, psychology researchers and practitioners now carefully follow strict guidelines for the protection of those who participate in psychological research, whether human or nonhuman. Regulations exist to protect the rights of individuals, and researchers working under the auspices of formal organizations must submit their ideas for research to an institutional review board to justify that those rights will be recognized and protected. Violating the code of ethics can lead to loss of institutional funding at the federal level for researchers. Similarly, violations of the ethical codes pertaining to appropriate therapy carry penalties for those found guilty that may include suspension of practice.

Because deception has often played a part in social psychology research, this content area is particularly rich in opportunities to explore how researchers implemented or failed to implement participant protection. Discussing the use of animals in research also provides good background in ethical oversight that must happen in animal laboratories. Describing ethical guidelines that influence therapy may provide some reassurance to students who have been reluctant to seek help out of concerns for confidentiality.

CONCLUSION

Although we recognize these outcomes and objectives may be ambitious, we think they represent manageable strategies that can engender vibrant introductory psychology courses. We encourage instructors to think about how they could plan and collaborate with their colleagues to gain the infrastructure support, the bandwidth, and form the collaboration to reinvigorate their introductory psychology course. Are there teaching-centered support funds or grants available on campus, in the system, or in the state? Could an instructor persuade folks at the dean and provost level that such a course redesign might have beneficial effects on performance in postrequisite courses and other performance metrics elements, including retention in the major, retention at the college or university, and ultimately, graduation?

Launching a course redesign coupled with data collection strategy about the direct impact of the introductory psychology course could be an effective tactic in gaining campus support. In addition, all of the outcomes we have proposed in this chapter lend themselves to assessable strategies. The next chapter provides examples of how to measure these achievements.

REFERENCES

American Psychological Association. (2007). *APA guidelines for the undergraduate psychology major, Version 1.0.* https://teachpsych.org/Resources/Documents/otrp/resources/apapsymajorguidelines.pdf

American Psychological Association. (2011). *National standards for high school psychology curricula.* https://www.apa.org/education/k12/national-standards

American Psychological Association. (2013). *APA guidelines for the undergraduate psychology major: Version 2.0.* https://www.apa.org/ed/precollege/about/psymajor-guidelines.pdf

American Psychological Association. (2014). *Strengthening the common core of the introductory psychology course.* https://www.apa.org/ed/governance/bea/intro-psych-report.pdf

American Psychological Association. (2020). *The APA Introductory Psychology Initiative.* https://www.apa.org/ed/precollege/undergrad/introductory-psychology-initiative

Becker-Blease, K., Stevens, C., Witkow, M. R., & Almuaybid, A. (2019). Teaching modules boost scientific reasoning skills in small and large lecture introductory psychology classrooms. *Scholarship of Teaching and Learning in Psychology.* Advance online publication. https://doi.org/10.1037/stl0000173

Boatright-Horowitz, S. L., McSheffrey, S., Marraccini, M. E., & Harps-Logan, Y. (2019). The introductory psychology course from a more diverse human perspective. In J. A. Mena & K. Quina (Eds.), *Integrating multicultural and intersectionality into the psychology curriculum: Strategies for instructors* (pp. 211–223). American Psychological Association. https://doi.org/10.1037/0000137-017

Brandt, A. M. (1978). Racism and research: The case of the Tuskegee syphilis study. *The Hastings Center Report, 8*(6), 21–29.

College Board. (2019). *Program summary report.* https://secure-media.collegeboard.org/digitalServices/pdf/research/2019/Program-Summary-Report-2019.pdf

Diamond, R. M. (2008). *Designing and assessing courses and curricula: A practical guide* (3rd ed.). Jossey-Bass.

Dunn, D. S., Brewer, C. L., Cautin, R. L., Gurung, R. A., Keith, K. D., McGregor, L. N., & Voight, M. (2010). The undergraduate psychology curriculum: Call for a core. In D. F. Halpern (Ed.), *Undergraduate education in psychology: A blueprint for the future of the discipline* (pp. 47–61). American Psychological Association. https://doi.org/10.1037/12063-003

Dunn, D. S., & Hard, B. M. (Eds.). (2018). *Thematic approaches for teaching introductory psychology.* Cengage.

Festinger, L., & Carlsmith, J. M. (1959). Cognitive consequences of forced compliance. *Journal of Abnormal and Social Psychology, 58*(2), 203–210. https://doi.org/10.1037/h0041593

Greene, E. B. (1931). The retention of information learned in college courses. *The Journal of Educational Research, 24*(4), 262–273. https://doi.org/10.1080/00220671.1931.10880208

Gurung, R. A. R., Hackathorn, J., Enns, C., Frantz, S., Cacioppo, J. T., Loop, T., & Freeman, J. E. (2016). Strengthening introductory psychology: A new model for teaching the introductory course. *American Psychologist, 71*(2), 112–124. https://doi.org/10.1037/a0040012

Haney, C., Banks, W. C., & Zimbardo, P. G. (1973). A study of prisoners and guards in a simulated prison. *Naval Research Reviews, 30*, 4–17.

Hard, B. M. (2017, July). *What's the big idea? Teaching intro using integrative themes* [Conference session]. Sixth Annual Psychology One Conference, Palo Alto, CA, United States.

Hard, B. M., Lovett, J. M., & Brady, S. T. (2019). What do students remember about introductory psychology, years later? *Scholarship of Teaching and Learning in Psychology, 5*(1), 61–74. https://doi.org/10.1037/stl0000136

Homa, N., Hackathorn, J., Brown, C. M., Garaczynski, E. D., Solomon, R. T., Sanborn, U. A., & Gurung, R. A. R. (2013). An analysis of learning objectives and content coverage in introductory psychology syllabi. *Teaching of Psychology, 40*(3), 169–174. https://doi.org/10.1177/0098628313487456

Hund, A. M., & Bueno, D. (2015). Learning in out-of-class experiences: The importance of professional skills. *Psychology Learning & Teaching, 14*(1), 62–69. https://doi.org/10.1177/1475725714565232

International Baccalaureate Organization. (2019). *The IB Diploma Programme Final Statistical Bulletin.* https://ibo.org/contentassets/bc850970f4e54b87828f83c7976a4db6/dp-statistical-bulletin-may-2019.pdf

Jhangiani, R., & Hardin, E. E. (2015). Skill development in introductory psychology. *Scholarship of Teaching and Learning in Psychology, 1*(4), 362–376. https://doi.org/10.1037/stl0000049

Kahneman, D. (2011). *Thinking, fast and slow.* Farrar, Straus and Giroux.

Landrum, R. E., & Gurung, R. A. R. (2013). The memorability of introductory psychology revisited. *Teaching of Psychology, 40*(3), 222–227. https://doi.org/10.1177/0098628313487417

Loftus, E. F., & Palmer, J. C. (1974). Reconstruction of automobile destruction: An example of the interaction between language and memory. *Journal of Verbal Learning and Verbal Behavior, 13*(5), 585–589. https://doi.org/10.1016/S0022-5371(74)80011-3

Marzano, R. J. (2009). *Designing and teaching learning goals and objectives: Classroom strategies that work.* Marzano Research Laboratory/Solution Tree.

Milgram, S. (1963). Behavioral study of obedience. *The Journal of Abnormal and Social Psychology, 67*, 371–378. https://www.demenzemedicinagenerale.net/pdf/MilgramOriginalWork.pdf

Miller, M. J., & Carducci, B. J. (2015). Student perceptions of the knowledge, skills, and abilities desired by potential employers of psychology majors. *Scholarship of Teaching and Learning in Psychology, 1*(1), 38–47. https://doi.org/10.1037/stl0000015

Myers, D. G., & DeWall, C. N. (2017). *Psychology in everyday life* (4th ed.). Worth Publishers.

Norcross, J. C., Hailstorks, R., Aiken, L. S., Pfund, R. A., Stamm, K. E., & Christidis, P. (2016). Undergraduate study in psychology: Curriculum and assessment. *American Psychologist, 71*(2), 89–101. https://doi.org/10.1037/a0040095

Pfund, R. A., Norcross, J. C., Hailstorks, R., Stamm, K. E., & Christidis, P. (2018). Introduction to psychology: Course purposes, learning outcomes, and assessment practices. *Teaching of Psychology, 45*(3), 213–219. https://doi.org/10.1177/0098628318779257

Rickard, H. C., Rogers, R., Ellis, N. R., & Beidleman, W. B. (1988). Some retention, but not enough. *Teaching of Psychology, 15*(3), 151–152. https://doi.org/10.1207/s15328023top1503_14

Smith, R. A., & Fineburg, A. C. (2006). Standards and outcomes: Encouraging best practices in teaching introductory psychology. In D. S. Dunn & S. L. Chew (Eds.), *Best practices for teaching introduction to psychology* (pp. 179–194). Erlbaum.

Steuer, F., & Ham, K. W., II. (2008). Psychology textbooks: Examining their accuracy. *Teaching of Psychology, 35*(3), 160–168. https://doi.org/10.1080/00986280802189197

Stevens, C., Witkow, M. R., & Smelt, B. (2016). Strengthening scientific reasoning skills in introductory psychology: Evidence from community college and liberal arts classrooms. *Scholarship of Teaching and Learning in Psychology, 2*(4), 245–260. https://doi.org/10.1037/stl0000070

Stoloff, M. L. (2010). Addressing the multiple demands of teaching introductory psychology. In D. S. Dunn, M. A. McCarthy, B. Beins, & G. W. Hill IV (Eds.), *Best practices for teaching beginnings and endings in the psychology major: Research, cases, and recommendations* (pp. 15–29). Oxford University Press.

Strohmetz, D. B., Dolinsky, B., Jhangiani, R. S., Posey, D. C., Hardin, E. E., Shyu, V., & Klein, E. (2015). The skillful major: Psychology curricula in the 21st century. *Scholarship of Teaching and Learning in Psychology, 1*(3), 200–207. https://doi.org/10.1037/stl0000037

Suskie, L. (2009). *Assessing student learning: A common sense guide* (2nd ed.). Jossey-Bass.

U.S. Department of Education, Institute of Education Sciences, National Center for Education Statistics. (2011). *America's high school graduates: Results from the 2009 NAEP High School Transcript Study.* https://nces.ed.gov/pubsearch/pubsinfo.asp?pubid=2011462

Watson, D. L., Hagihari, D. K., & Tenney, A. L. (1999). Skill-building exercising and generalizing psychological concepts to daily life. *Teaching of Psychology, 26*(3), 193–195. https://doi.org/10.1207/S15328023TOP260306

Weiten, W. (2017). *Psychology: Themes and variations 10E.* Cengage Learning.

Weiten, W., & Houska, J. A. (2015). Introductory psychology: Unique challenges and opportunities. In D. S. Dunn (Ed.), *The Oxford handbook of undergraduate psychology education* (pp. 289–321). Oxford University Press.

Willingham, D. T., Hughes, E. M., & Dobolyi, D. G. (2015). The scientific status of learning styles theories. *Teaching of Psychology, 42*(3), 266–271. https://doi.org/10.1177/0098628315589505

4

ASSESSING STUDENT LEARNING OUTCOMES IN INTRODUCTORY PSYCHOLOGY

JANE S. HALONEN, JENNIFER L. W. THOMPSON, KRISTIN H. WHITLOCK, R. ERIC LANDRUM, AND SUE FRANTZ

KEY RECOMMENDATIONS

1. Incorporate assessment practices directly aligned to the student learning outcomes.

2. Select assessment strategies considering both the goal of the assessment and how the resulting data will be used.

How will the introductory psychology instructor know if their instructional efforts have been fruitful? Assessments meaningfully linked to carefully crafted student learning outcomes (SLOs) provide more robust evidence that students are learning what we want them to learn in the hope that our efforts as psychology educators can produce enduring effects even in the brief context of the introductory psychology course. We believe the introductory

https://doi.org/10.1037/0000260-005
Transforming Introductory Psychology: Expert Advice on Teacher Training, Course Design, and Student Success, R. A. R. Gurung and G. Neufeld (Editors)

psychology course has demonstrated value, as evidenced by how many other disciplines require introductory psychology as part of their major or minor course of study, but we could clearly do a better job of articulating what student learning should transpire from an introductory psychology course. Assessment done well is meticulous, informative, and instructive; it reflects psychology's fundamental goal of making sense of behavior using empirical investigation. In that vein, efforts from the Introductory Psychology Initiative (IPI; American Psychological Association, 2020) expressed through this chapter should help you address your assessment needs more easily and effectively should you choose to do so.

The term *assessment* stirs confusion and some controversy regarding its meaning. Some insist that the primary function of assessment is to assist students to learn what the course has to offer. They cite the Latin root *assere* (to sit beside) as a justification for why changes in student learning should be the priority in implementing assessment activities. The emphasis in this point of view is assessment *for* learning (Kirschner & Hendrick, 2020). Others advocate that the primary reason for assessment is to address accountability initiatives, constituting the assessment *of* learning. That is, faculty gather assessment data because they need to submit evidence (e.g., learning assurance) to an agent beyond the classroom (e.g., the department, the college, a program reviewer, or principal) that learning has taken place. In this function, data from student performance assists with determining program quality. A third perspective is that teachers conduct assessment for their own benefit to learn what worked and what did not work in their teaching strategies. As such, assessment evinces an intentional cycle of continuous improvement. Of course, in an ideal world, assessment could serve all purposes described here; robust and mature assessment plans are likely to be multipurpose (Stanny & Halonen, 2011). When designed carefully and executed thoughtfully, we believe that assessment data can legitimately serve all of those goals. In fact, many of our colleagues have written about the specific approaches for accomplishing rich assessment plans in psychology in the edited volume *Assessing Teaching and Learning in Psychology: Current and Future Perspectives* (Dunn et al., 2013).

Assessing what introductory psychology students learn in their first exposure to psychology is an important feature of course design. Still, to date, the community of psychology educators has not developed consensus on what good assessment practices in introductory psychology should entail. Ultimately all psychology educators should know what impact their courses have had on students. Getting assessment "right" matters—not only to provide students with meaningful feedback about what they know and can do but also to use the time and talents of faculty wisely in such a demanding endeavor.

THE INFLUENCE OF THE ASSESSMENT MOVEMENT

Fueled by many critics to question whether old measurement strategies could provide reasonable evidence of student learning, accountability efforts began to ramp up for both college and high school programs starting in the 1980s (Kuh et al., 2015). Traditional testing methods, such as exams populated by multiple-choice items, measure psychology content, but these strategies tend to tap low-level recall and recognition skills. Consequently, this approach provides a minimalist view of what a student knows as a result of the course but may shed little light on what a student can do at the conclusion of a course. For the past 4 decades, educators have been trying to determine how to improve the measurement of both content mastery and skills development.

Fortunately, some excellent generic advice has been available to educators, such as the classic *Classroom Assessment Techniques: A Handbook for College Teachers* (2nd ed.) by Angelo and Cross (1993). This discipline-agnostic volume is filled with good ideas about assessment that are mostly low-technology and include a good number of skill-based assessment approaches. To support skill development at the college level, the American Association of Colleges and Universities (2005) instituted the *Liberal Education and America's Promise* initiative, known as LEAP (https://www.aacu.org/leap). The skills-focused rubrics produced in LEAP have provided assistance to many undergraduate programs, although the skills addressed are not discipline-specific.

Formal assessment demands for accountability in psychology at the college level have increased over time. Most college programs face at least annual requirements to produce some kind of documentation that students are fulfilling the department's designated learning objectives. It may be that the programs are asked to complete periodic program reviews where assessment evidence must be prepared for internal and external consumption. These mandates have intensified developing some consensus on what students should know and be able to do as a function of studying psychology. Many introductory psychology college teachers are now obligated to provide documentation of student learning that goes beyond simply grade distribution.

The American Psychological Association (APA) has been active in providing assessment support for introductory psychology teachers in various contexts. At the college level, many departments in the United States have adopted the *APA Guidelines for Undergraduate Psychology: Version 2.0* (APA, 2013) to shape the accountability practices. The *Guidelines 2.0* specified what kinds of learning should take place at the end of 2- and 4-year programs. This document included a listing of assessment possibilities but did not include benchmarking information, offer evidence about the effectiveness of those approaches, or specify desirable outcomes at the introductory psychology course level.

Similar accountability demands have emerged in the high school setting as well. The *National Standards for High School Psychology Curricula* (APA, 2011) have undergone three revisions. Each iteration of the document has provided benchmark learning objectives for both developing a course and for the assessment of student learning. The *National Standards* include Content Standards, which are specific topics instructors may use as the basis to construct lessons (e.g., Encoding of Memory). Instruction on these topics should enable students to meet specific Performance Standards (e.g., 1.3 Discuss strategies for improving the encoding of memory). In addition, Performance Indicators are ways to assess student mastery of these Performance Standards (e.g., 1.3.a. Providing examples of uses of mnemonic devices, e.g., chunking, peg words). The *National Standards* offer a framework that provides teachers with clear direction about what to teach and suggestions for how to assess student learning.

In addition to the proposal of the pillar model for managing content choices, the APA (2014) Working Group on Strengthening the Common Core of the Introductory Psychology Course recommended that a universal assessment for introductory psychology should be developed. The Board of Educational Affairs (BEA) then established a second working group in response to this specific recommendation, giving it the charge of "developing a plan and identifying the necessary steps to create a universal assessment to measure introductory psychology students' mastery of content knowledge and skills" (APA, 2017, p. 1). This desire to create more assessment options for the introductory psychology course instructor is a good trend; however, we have mixed feelings about the need or mandate for a national assessment for introductory psychology. We address this complicated issue at the conclusion of this chapter.

Through the BEA, APA commissioned another group of educators facilitated by the Committee on Associate and Baccalaureate Education (CABE) to assemble strategies for assessment at an invitational conference that was called the Summit on National Assessment of Psychology (SNAP) in 2016. Summit attendees either reported or generated new examples of strategies that could assess outcomes specified in *Guidelines 2.0*. Despite a wealth of examples from SNAP that are now posted in Project Assessment (see pass.apa.org), relatively few assessment strategies at that time specifically addressed introductory psychology.

The number of introductory psychology strategies dramatically increased when educators from both the high school and college levels convened at the Summit on High School Psychology Education held in 2017. Their collective efforts formally developed a set of activities that could be added to the website specifically to address introductory psychology needs. In keeping with the design of the website, contributors identified their strategies (a) as "evidence based," meaning they designer had collected evidence to substantiate the claim that the desired learning had taken place, or (b) "evidence informed," meaning their designer had relied on empirical literature to generate new ideas about how the outcome could be measured but had not gathered definitive data to support a specific learning outcome. The website design also required a designation of whether the assessment measured formative (developing) or summative (ultimate) skills. (The website provided many of the examples, some of which we cite in a later section in this chapter.) Although this step represented progress in developing guidance for introductory psychology design, in the absence of widely accepted student learning outcomes for introductory psychology, the activities do not provide a systematic framework to support true assessment culture in the introductory psychology course. The development of student learning outcomes and objectives specific to introductory psychology should facilitate a unified and coherent strategy from which sound assessment practices can emerge.

Exhibits 4.1 through 4.14 provide exemplars for the outcomes and objectives set up in Chapter 3. We have collected these exemplars in the course of conversations and collaborations at SNAP, the High School Summit, and IPI-specific work. Many of the exemplars are listed as part of CABE's Project Assessment website (pass.apa.org) and we include their locations for direct access. In the exemplars offered, we provide a mix of both formative and summative assessment strategies. Some of the examples have generated assessment evidence (evidence based). Some are ripe for experimentation (evidence informed). We offer one assessment example for each of the learning outcomes and themes offered. All of these examples are not prescriptive but aspirational; they serve to model the kind of architecture that goes into good assessment design.

EXHIBIT 4.1. Exemplar of Objective 1.1

Objective 1.1	**Define and explain basic psychological concepts.**
Assessment title	The Restaurant for Zombies
Author & affiliation	Steve Jones Academy of Medicine Durham, NC
Link to more information	https://pass.apa.org/docs/restaurant-menu-for-zombies/
Description of assessment technique	This strategy is an alternative to multiple-choice testing involving a student's ability to apply content knowledge from the biological foundations chapter. Students are required to work in teams to develop seven dishes that would appeal to zombies. Students must generate the restaurant name, develop dishes and corresponding pictures of the dishes, and execute the menu professionally. Class time can be devoted to producing the work, or it can be done as an out-of-class project. In addition to solid performance data generated by applying the project rubric, the assessor indicated that students approach this learning task with an unusual degree of enthusiasm. They tend to be energetic in project time devoted in class, and later more traditional tests demonstrate effective retention of key concepts for what students typically regard as the hardest portion of the class.
Rubric available	Yes.
Additional details	A sample handout to provide to students as a Word file is available. This exercise has been identified as an evidence-informed practice.

EXHIBIT 4.2. Exemplar of Objective 1.2

Objective 1.2	**Interpret research findings related to psychological concepts.**
Assessment title	Group Influence Via Plastic Toys (Dinosaurs)
Author & affiliation	Virginia Welle Chippewa Falls Senior High School Chippewa Falls, WI
Link to more information	https://pass.apa.org/docs/group-influence-via-plastic-toys-e-g-dinosaurs/
Description of assessment technique	Students create dioramas illustrating social psychology concepts (e.g., social facilitation, groupthink, altruism) and explain their creations to the class. Teacher feedback allows for corrections of their interpretations.
Rubric available	No. The assessment is formative rather than summative.
Additional details	Although no feedback structure is offered, the web source includes photographs of students engaged in diorama creation.

EXHIBIT 4.3. Exemplar of Objective 1.3

Objective 1.3	**Apply psychological principles to personal growth and other aspects of everyday life.**
Assessment title	Applying Psychological Concepts to Everyday Experiences
Author & affiliation	Original Author: Kevin Clark Indiana University Kokomo, IN
	Adapted at the Summit on National Assessment of Psychology by Sue Frantz, Jane Halonen, Rebecca Hoss, Maureen McCarthy, Susan Nolan, Tom Pusateri, and Katherine Wickes
Link to more information	https://pass.apa.org/docs/applying-psychological-concepts-to-everyday-experiences/
Description of assessment technique	Clark published a summative assessment strategy for personalizing course concepts to help students learn them more effectively. In this design, he asked students to identify 10 examples from across a minimum of six chapters covered during the course that had the potential to have a transformative impact on their lives. The instructions specifically ask students to develop a three- to five-page essay in which 10 course ideas helped them understand something (about themselves, others, or society at large), helped them solve a problem or make better decisions, motivated them to change their lives, or otherwise had some kind of significant impact on understanding, thinking, motivation, or behavior.
Rubric available	Yes. Clark's work was adapted by the SNAP Goal 3 Committee to include a rubric that would help discriminate the quality of work submitted by students. The rubric offered three categories of feedback not linked specifically to point capture.
Additional details	Clark, K. M. (2010). Applied and transformed understanding in introductory psychology: Analysis of a final essay assignment. *Journal of the Scholarship of Teaching and Learning, 10*(3), 41–57.

Note. SNAP = Summit on National Assessment of Psychology.

EXHIBIT 4.4. Exemplar of Objective 2.1

Objective 2.1	**Describe the advantages and limitations of research strategies.**
Assessment title	Distinguishing Correlational vs. Experimental Research
Author & affiliation	Maria Vita Penn Manor High School Millersville, PA
Link to more information	https://pass.apa.org/?s=correlational
Description of assessment technique	A comprehensive strategy designed by Maria Vita allows students to demonstrate their grasp of correlational research and how it differs from experimental research. Five scenarios depict examples of research that could be conducted. For each scenario, students must designate whether the research design is correlational or experimental. If it is correlational, they must further speculate what a scatter plot might look like that would illustrate likely outcomes. If experimental, students must generate a likely histogram or bar graph to demonstrate those relationships. Part of the instructions involve helping students associate the proper terminology that tends to be used with either research strategy. The answer key models proper language to be used with the corresponding examples.
Rubric available	No. Answer key is available.
Additional details	There are extensive notes available that support and augment teaching this concept; this is an impressive resource.

EXHIBIT 4.5. Exemplar of Objective 2.2

Objective 2.2	**Evaluate, design, or conduct psychological research.**
Assessment title	Analyzing Potential Sociocultural Challenges in Scientific Inquiry
Author & affiliation	Jaclyn Ronquillo-Adachi Cerritos College Norwalk, CA
Link to more information	https://pass.apa.org/docs/analyzing-potential-sociocultural-challenges-in-scientific-inquiry/
Description of assessment technique	Students read an empirical study by Baumeister et al. (2005) from *Personality and Social Psychology*. The article discusses social exclusion's effects on self-regulation. Students analyze the sociocultural factors that influence the results and redesign the study to address those considerations.
Rubric available	Yes.
Additional details	This assessment may have particular appeal in helping students understand how sociocultural factors influence research questions.

EXHIBIT 4.6. Exemplar of Objective 2.3

Objective 2.3	**Draw logical and objective conclusions about behavior and mental processes from empirical evidence.**
Assessment title	Email A Friend
Author & affiliation	American Psychological Association, Working Group on Introductory Psychology Assessment Washington, DC
Link to more information	https://pass.apa.org/docs/email-to-a-friend/
Description of assessment technique	This exemplar offers an opportunity to apply psychological principles to address the challenges that face new psychology students. In an email format, students assume that one of their friends is struggling with doing well on her psychology exams. When questioned, she reveals the following:
	She sleeps, on average, 4 hours per night.
	She does all of her studying in one big cram session the evening before the exam.
	Her primary study technique is just rereading her notes and the chapters.
	She checks her phone about every 2 minutes for text messages or social media updates.
	As such, the response requires application of knowledge that comes from learning, sleep, and memory chapters. Although the email itself can be judged in terms of writing quality, conventional expression, and attention and civil response to the audience, the primary focus of the email addresses these indicators.
Rubric available	Yes.
Additional details	American Psychological Association, Working Group on Introductory Psychology Assessment. (2017). *Assessment of outcomes of the introductory course in psychology.* https://www.apa.org/ed/precollege/assessment-outcomes.pdf

EXHIBIT 4.7. Exemplar of Objective 2.4

Objective 2.4	**Examine how psychological science can be used to counter unsubstantiated statements, opinions, or beliefs.**
Assessment title	The Misconceptions Test
Author & affiliation	Jane Halonen University of West Florida Pensacola, FL
Link to more information	https://pass.apa.org/docs/the-misconceptions-test/
Description of assessment technique	Multiple instruments have been developed to identify how vulnerable students might be to the misconceptions that are ubiquitous regarding human behavior, but only recently have such inventories been adapted for assessment purposes, such as this one. This approach requires testing students' beliefs about such things as the validity of learning styles, the rumored 10% use of the brain, and the interchangeability of multiple personality disorder and schizophrenia on the first day of class. Conducting a posttest produces a significant change in students' vulnerability to believing things that do not stand up to empirical scrutiny.
Rubric available	Yes. An answer key is available.
Additional details	This test was derived from earlier work from the following: Lilienfeld, S. O., Lynn, S. B., Ruscio, J., & Beyerstein, B. L. (2010). *Fifty great myths of popular psychology: Shattering widespread misconceptions about human behavior.* Wiley-Blackwell. Taylor, A. K., & Kowalski, P. (2014). Students' misconceptions in psychology: How you ask matters . . . sometimes. *Journal of the Scholarship of Teaching and Learning, 12*(3), 62–77.

EXHIBIT 4.8. Exemplar of Theme A

Theme A	**Psychological science relies on empirical evidence and adapts as new data develop.**
Assessment title	Evaluating Evidence in Support of Research Questions
Author & affiliation	Jon Mueller North Central College Naperville, IL
Link to more information	https://pass.apa.org/docs/evaluating-evidence-in-support-of-research-questions-2/
Description of assessment technique	In this assignment, students evaluate seven types of evidence offered to support a causal claim. The categories of evidence include personal anecdotes to scientific research. Students judge the degree to which each type of evidence supports the causal claim.
Rubric available	Yes.
Additional details	The research examples offered are both contemporary and compelling to engage students in solving the challenge.

EXHIBIT 4.9. Exemplar of Theme B

Theme B	Psychology explains general principles that govern behavior while recognizing individual differences.
Assessment title	The Good Life
Author & affiliation	Jane S. Halonen University of West Florida Pensacola, FL
Link to more information	https://pass.apa.org/docs/the-good-life/
Description of assessment technique	In this strategy students initially develop a list of 10 elements that constitute for them what the "good life" is. Then students are invited to compare their list with either one that they can build from doing research on a very different culture or they can interview an actual person asking them to provide their good life requirements. The comparisons help students understand what good life elements might be culturally prescribed versus those that might differ from cultural expectations.
Rubric available	Yes.
Additional details	This assignment can be especially helpful for students who are preparing to study abroad. They can become familiar with the cultural norms of the place they will be visiting. Students are often surprised by both the commonalities and the differences that emerge in comparing the two cultures.

EXHIBIT 4.10. Exemplar of Theme C

Theme C	Psychological, biological, social, and cultural factors influence behavior and mental processes.
Assessment title	Understanding the Other
Author & affiliation	Ninh Nguyen Littleford Ball State University Muncie, IN Susan A. Nolan Seton Hall University South Orange, NJ
Link to more information	https://pass.apa.org/docs/understanding-the-other/
Description of assessment technique	This exercise highlights the role of social and cultural factors in defining reality. Students read an article published in *Psychology Teacher Network* written by the authors. Then they are asked to imagine some cultural conditions that are not consistent with their personal experiences after being given some examples (e.g., What if all U.S. presidents had been female? What if everyone had to get an IQ tattoo?). The students then reflect on what kinds of consequences might transpire.
Rubric available	Yes.
Additional details	This imaginative strategy offers subtle ways of addressing the complex factors that influence mental processes and behavior.

EXHIBIT 4.11. Exemplar of Theme D

Theme D	Psychology values diversity, promotes equity, and fosters inclusion in pursuit of a more just society.
Assessment title	Teaching Antiracism in a Large Introductory Psychology Class Can Make a Difference
Author & affiliation	Su Boatright-Horowitz University of Rhode Island Providence, RI
Link to more information	https://doi.org/10.1177/0021934704266508
Description of assessment technique	For her large enrollment (500+) introductory psychology course, Su Boatright-Horowitz developed five questions measuring attitudes about racism using an 11-point Likert-type agreement scale, and she administered this measure as a pretest, an immediate posttest and a delayed posttest. During the semester, she delivered a series of instructional modules about multiculturalism on campus and racism in the country, students watched films and participated in discussion groups. Teaching assistants presented information about White supremacists and related issues. This technique allows for changes to be tracked over time (not only within groups but also between groups when careful data planning is executed), and the type and nature of change can be studied for different subpopulations of students.
Rubric available	No (survey responses early in semester, late in semester).
Additional details	Boatright-Horowitz, S. L. (2005). Teaching antiracism in a large introductory psychology class: A course module and its evaluation. *Journal of Black Studies, 36*(1), 34–51. https://doi.org/10.1177/0021934704266508

EXHIBIT 4.12. Exemplar of Theme E

Theme E	Our perceptions and biases filter our experiences of the world through an imperfect personal lens.
Assessment title	Norm Violations and Attribution
Author & affiliation	Jane S. Halonen University of West Florida Pensacola, FL
Link to more information	https://pass.apa.org/docs/norm-violation-and-attribution
Description of assessment technique	In this assignment, students will violate a fairly benign social norm. (The instructions should emphasize that students should not take any legal or physical risks in the norm violation.) Their report of the experience should first detail what actions they chose, along with the rationale of why their intended actions would work as a norm violation. Next they describe what actually transpired. The final step is to apply attribution theory to perceptions of the motivations of their actions. Students must accurately reflect the difference between internal and external attributions and speculate about the effects of self-protective reflections.
Rubric available	Yes. Contact jhalonen@uwf.edu.
Additional details	Fundamental attribution theory is often very difficult to get across to beginning students. This application helps them distinguish actor versus observer roles.

EXHIBIT 4.13. Exemplar of Theme F

Theme F	Applying psychological principles can change our lives, organizations, and communities in positive ways.
Assessment title	Applying Psychological Principles to Improve Behavioral Health
Author & affiliation	American Psychological Association, Working Group on Introductory Psychology Assessment Washington, DC
Link to more information	https://pass.apa.org/docs/applying-psychological-principles-to-improve-behavioral-health/
Description of assessment technique	In this assignment, students are cast in the role of behavioral assistants working in health care where their focus is helping physicians recommend to patients how to stop smoking. They apply various course concepts (e.g., operant conditioning, framing, cognitive dissonance) to forge an effective strategy that can improve the smoker's life. The focus of the intervention can be varied to address any health care challenge (e.g., obesity, binge drinking, insufficient sleep).
Rubric available	Yes.
Additional details	American Psychological Association, Working Group on Introductory Psychology Assessment. (2017). *Assessment of outcomes of the introductory course in psychology*. https://www.apa.org/ed/precollege/assessment-outcomes.pdf

EXHIBIT 4.14. Exemplar of Theme G

Theme G	Ethical principles guide psychology research and practice.
Assessment title	Assessing Applications of Ethics in Psychological Research
Author & affiliation	Katherine Wickes Blinn College Brenham, TX
Link to more information	https://pass.apa.org/docs/assessing-applications-of-ethics-in-psychological-research/
Description of assessment technique	In preparation for this assignment, students read or watch videos regarding seminal research studies in psychology. Examples include the Kinsey studies, disobedience to authority, or the Stanford Prison Study. Students describe what unfolded in those studies, address the connection of the work to their course textbook. Then attention turns to ethics. They must determine whether the results of the research study are reliable or valid based on any potential compromise from ethical concerns.
Rubric available	Yes.
Additional details	The website reports data gathered using this strategy from a variety of course contexts.

One assessment approach that can determine whether the themes addressed in psychology have penetrated is to build in an opportunity for students to generate their own examples for the themes that we hope will stay with students long after the content has faded. Hard (2017) developed a summative strategy to conclude introductory psychology that allows students to personalize those themes. She allows students to reflect on the integrative nature of the themes. She either provides a specific integrating theme ("a big idea") and asks students to identify multiple examples from different content areas that reflect the themes or she lets students select from among the course's big ideas before generating their list of examples. Her account suggests that both she and her students find this approach provides a more constructive, meaningful conclusion to the introductory psychology experience.

ADOPTING OUTCOME-BASED DESIGN

Educators differ in the sophistication with which they approach outcome and assessment questions. However, if you are interested in framing your introductory psychology course around SLOs but have no idea where to start, this chapter should provide some inspiration. Alternatively, if you have wanted to break out of a singular commitment to multiple-choice testing, we have many assessment alternatives for you to consider. Even those with fairly sophisticated teaching and assessing strategies are likely to find some ideas that will rejuvenate practices that may have become less exciting not just to the students on the receiving end but to the person engineering the learning experiences.

As discussed in Chapter 2, one beginning framework to think about this process is backward course design (Fink, 2013; Wiggins & McTighe, 2005). In this type of course design, the first step is to establish your intentions for learning by identifying SLOs; this should be the centerpiece or cornerstone for any course (Step 1). All other decisions flow from what you want your students to know or be able to do by the conclusion of your course. Step 2 involves adopting strategies that measure whether you are successful in your intentions. The moniker "backward" is added to this label because so many instructors, when actually designing a course, either do not start with SLOs or do not include SLOs at all. In fact, many instructors may initiate course design by answering an email from their bookstore 4 months before that course is to even start. In backward course design, decisions about source material and a textbook (or not) should occur well after SLOs are determined and assessment practices are settled.

Changing the organizational structure of your course to adopt or adapt to new SLOs and assessment strategies could be quite a dramatic task. For example, your local assessment requirements may mandate that you act in concert with other introductory psychology teachers to provide some uniformity in proposed evidence across multiple sections per quarter. In fact, in some educational settings, the SLOs may be predetermined with little input from the teachers assigned to teach the class, for example. Effective collaboration on assessment questions, especially when expertise and enthusiasm vary among the course designers, can be both complex and time-consuming. Moreover, moving teachers to work through negative attitudes and adopt an authentic assessment culture can be somewhat daunting. Many assessment scholars (e.g., Dunn et al., 2020) have offered suggestions on ways to assist faculty in adopting and then thrive in that authentic assessment culture that promotes continuous improvement in teaching. We continue that tradition in this chapter.

Bernstein et al. (2010) captured how educator concerns might evolve from novice to expert in proposing his scientist–educator model (a training model analogous to the scientist, scientist–practitioner, and practitioner models). Here, we take the perspective of the scientist–educator and express different levels of expertise that reflect what could be applied to outcome and assessment design concerns:

- I don't know if what I am doing works, or if there is some other explanation.
- I want to know if what I am specifically doing is what is working, but I'm not sure how to address the problem.
- I know what I want my students to do, but I'm uncertain how to measure it.
- I have some ideas about outcomes and how to measure student performance, but I wonder if there are better, more efficient strategies?
- What can I do to transform student learning in profound ways and document those changes?

According to Dormant (2011), one of the most common (and perhaps most popular) of models that predict behavior change is the transtheoretical model of stages of changes by Prochaska and colleagues (Prochaska & DiClemente, 1983; Prochaska et al., 1994). The Prochaska and DiClemente (1983) transtheoretical model of stages of change includes five stages of change:

- *Precontemplation*: a person does not intend to act in the future either because the person does not know there is a problem or that the status quo is producing negative outcomes

- *Contemplation*: a person considers making a change in the future, but it is unclear if behavior change will occur

- *Preparation*: a person makes small steps toward real change and expresses beliefs that change will lead to positive outcomes

- *Action*: change transpires, and the person intends to keep the change going

- *Maintenance*: new behavior is established, and work may need to be done to prevent relapse

Dormant (2011) adopted the transtheoretical model in a faculty development context, producing the following descriptions of action that also unfold in predictable stages:

- *Awareness*: the person is passive about the potential change, may have little to no information about the change, and may not have much of an opinion about the change

- *Curiosity*: the person is now seeking information about the potential change, asking questions about ramifications and impact, especially personal impact

- *Mental tryout*: the person is in a precommitment phase, now imagining how they would make the change, thinking about how it would affect their job tasks

- *Hands-on tryout*: the commitment to change has been made by the person; they want to learn all the implementation details, express opinions and concerns about how the change may have an organizational impact

- *Adoption*: the person has now actively made and implemented the change; they can make suggestions for improvement; they are far enough into the process that they can now seek expert opinions about the processes

We have adapted Dormant's (2011) terminology to predict how educators might respond to the prospect of adopting APA IPI strategies:

- *Awareness*: "I don't really know about IPI or national efforts; I know there are other kinds of assessments beyond multiple choice, but I like to stick with what is traditional."

- *Curiosity*: "I've heard that IPI has proposed some new ideas about intro. How were the SLOs developed? What kind of support exists for developing new strategies?"

- *Mental tryout*: "Some of the new SLOs are innovative and would fit well with the mission of my institution. Our assessment approach could stand some freshening up, and this might help us with our upcoming program review."

- *Hands-on tryout*: "We are adopting most of the SLOs but may have challenges getting compliance across all of our intro sections. It may complicate our use of the learning management system and might require extra administrative time and support."

- *Adoption*: "The new SLOs have enhanced instructor enjoyment in teaching the course. Our course materials had become stale, and this approach allowed us to reconceptualize and repackage in new ways. The new assessments are challenging but provide real-world indicators of what students can do with the psychological knowledge they are acquiring."

We offer these brief fictional descriptors to help you imagine where you and teaching colleagues might be along these stair-step stages regarding SLOs and assessment aspirations and perhaps help you envision what might be the next suitable step to take in your assessment work. Our goal is not to get every reader to become an adopter of any specific outcome or assessment technique recommended in this chapter, nor is it necessary to get you to the final "adoption" stage. However, we think a reasonable goal is to "level up" from where you are to promote programmatic assessment maturity and be closer to the development of a meaningful assessment culture. If you were merely aware, we hope you will become curious. If you have been curious, we hope you will begin to imagine how some of the teaching and assessment strategies described in the previous section could assist you in achieving your goals. Perhaps you are ready to jump in with a hands-on tryout. If the description in the hands-on tryout section describes you, perhaps the work of the IPI will convince you that adoption is the appropriate next step.

CONDITIONS TO CONSIDER WHEN SELECTING AN ASSESSMENT APPROACH

After carefully consuming the contents of this book (particularly this chapter), or perhaps after noticing that so many introductory psychology instructors and programs use an assessment approach dissimilar from your own, you, your departmental committee, or perhaps your department as a whole has decided to update and upgrade your assessment approach. What are the factors or questions to consider in implementing an assessment plan for introductory psychology? We believe that there is no simplistic flowchart with yes–no responses that will funnel you to an ideal singular outcome; assessment is too complex for that solution, and there are too many stakeholders and constituencies influencing the path. In this section, we attempt to present some of the framing questions educators should ask about introductory psychology assessment; however, even in the space provided, this is not an exhaustive list of the conditions or determinants to consider when selecting your introductory psychology assessment.

What Is the Purpose of the Assessment?

Will you be administering an assessment to help students develop their skills? *Formative* assessment tends to be "low stakes," but increasingly educators are voicing preferences for assessments that provide a direct learning benefit to students. In contrast, *summative* assessment tends to be "high stakes," establishing whether students achieved a specific outcome may influence grades. The data from summative assessments can also factor into other purposes, such as teacher improvement or the evaluation of the quality of the teacher or program.

How and by Whom Will the Assessment Results Be Used?

Knowing who will see the resulting assessment data and understanding how those data may be used by others should influence your choice of an assessment approach in introductory psychology. Your constituencies and key stakeholders—and you need to know who those folks are—may use the assessment data you provide in the way you intended for it to be used, or not. Once any researcher releases data into the world, they lose control over the messaging of that data and how it may be used; thus, the origin story matters. For example, if you intend to interpret poor student performance to make the argument for more instructors to reduce class size, an administrator or legislator with a different agenda could use those poor performance data to make the case that introductory psychology is already ineffective, so why invest more resources in a sinking ship? Understand your local assessment climate and find out how key decision makers currently use and understand data.

What Is the Enrollment of Your Course?

With a small section of 30 students in your introductory course, you are more likely to consider a wider range of options for assessment because the workload is relatively small; when there are 500 students who enroll in your course, your thinking about assessment options will likely change. If you opted to require a 10-page APA Style paper at the end of the semester because you wanted to assess students' writing abilities as well as mastery of content in a particular area, it is much less daunting to consider evaluating 30 papers for assessment purposes at the end of the semester compared with 500 papers. Particularly if you do not have teaching assistants to handle the workload, enrollment will be a key factor in your choice of assessment.

When Should the Assessment Be Conducted?

Of course, the timing of an assessment is somewhat dependent on whether the purpose is formative or summative. Regardless of when an assessment is administered, you must be careful to ensure that all of the topics on the assessment instrument have been presented in the course. A summative assessment for introductory psychology can be administered as a cumulative final exam. If a separate assessment instrument is administered, steps must be taken to ensure students take the assessment seriously. Testing fatigue must also be considered.

What Is the Assessment's Footprint?

If you are conducting an assessment on your own course and on your own deadline, this task is much easier to accomplish than if you have to coordinate with multiple instructors and, in some cases, perhaps across multiple campuses or multiple locations where introductory psychology is coordinated across sections taught at high schools, satellite branch campuses, and so on. Ease of administration of the assessment instrument may be favored if data must be harvested across multiple locations.

What Is the Source of the Assessment Instrument?

Who generated the assessment instrument or the assessment process? Is it from the literature, an introductory psychology textbook publisher, or something homegrown in the department? Is it content focused, or does it assess a skill that introductory psychology students are expected to acquire by the conclusion of the course?

Is There a Cost Involved to Administer the Assessment?

Using nationally normed tests typically entails expense. If a program hasn't allocated funds to cover the cost of assessments, those may be passed on to students in the form of special fees. Even if there is no posted or published cost to administer the assessment, there are time, resource, and expertise costs in administration, scoring, and interpretation of assessments.

Is Your Course Offered Face-to-Face, Online Remote (Synchronous), or Online Asynchronous?

The instructional modality of your course may influence your selection of an assessment technique. The face-to-face mode generally gives us the greater number of options, but online technologies may allow us to leverage opportunities we typically do not consider. In a larger introductory psychology class, you might not be able to afford the time in class to have each student give a 10-minute speech to demonstrate oral communication skills as part of an assessment, but in the online course, you might have those students prepare a 10-minute podcast and upload the file to the Learning Management System (in fact, the same podcast assignment could be used in the face-to-face class as well). Instructors often think that assessment is easier face-to-face because of familiarity with the modality, but many of the assessments used in face-to-face courses can be administered in an online fashion at this time.

Who Is Administering the Assessment to Students?

Depending on institutional context, it may matter who is administering the assessment to introductory psychology students. Sometimes it matters if an outside source—that is, someone other than the instructor, is the person administering the assessment; it will be seen as more serious or more "institutional."

Is It Being Used for Institutional Evaluation Purposes or Research Purposes?

From the departmental and instructor perspective, there must be clarity about whether the collection of assessment data in this context is institutional research or whether the research represents teaching and learning scholarship that will be presented to a broader audience. If these data are considered institutional research, meaning that there is no planned presentation of these data beyond campus officials (e.g., local administrators or a Board of Regents or State Board), then no additional approvals are likely needed. However, if this becomes a research project where it is likely that the data will be aggregated and presented at a regional or national conference or convention or submitted for publication, the assessment data become research data, and the entire assessment process will require institutional review board (IRB) approval. Check with your local IRB and Institutional Research Office to be certain about your local rules.

How Are Students Motivated to Perform Their Best on the Assessment?

The motivation of those individuals completing assessment instruments is of great importance to those who study assessment outcomes and data; a full presentation of the complexity of this issue is not possible here. Needless to say, the more serious and sincere introductory psychology students are in doing their best on the assessment presented, the more valid and robust the outcomes (i.e., the scores) will be. If the assessment outcomes are fair representations of what introductory psychology students know and can do, then the instructional and administrative decisions made based on those data have a better chance of being sound decisions and future-enhancing. If students "blow off" the assessment and scores are not valid, then decisions will be made on a faulty foundation.

What Is the Time Turnaround Needed for the Assessment Outcomes?

Depending on the audience for your assessment data and how quickly the data are needed, these parameters could influence your choice in an assessment approach. If the data are needed quickly, you are more likely to rely on a content-based approach that has closed-ended responses, such as multiple-choice items in an LMS or scantron sheet—items that have a singular correct answer that can be machine-scored. If there is time, then more labor-intensive scoring systems can be used for different assessment techniques that may focus on either content or skills. A problem-solving task that involves the application of critical thinking skills using the content acquired in introductory psychology would likely not be an assessment outcome that could be quickly scored unless the size of the class was particularly small.

Are You More Interested in Content Knowledge or Skill Acquisition?

For the bulk of the existence of the introductory psychology course, a traditional approach to assessment has often been in the testing of vocabulary in one form or another. A student new to the discipline cannot begin to understand the science of human behavior until they understand its terminology. Thus, testing for the content of introductory psychology through publisher-supplied test-item files or test banks with multiple-choice questions, fill-in-the-blank questions, true–false items, and essay question suggestions have been commonplace for decades. This approach tends to primarily focus on content knowledge acquisition, but some instructors, and often depending on class size, also incorporate writing prompts in the form of short essays and term papers in the introductory course. By adding this step, they integrate the practice of skill acquisition in practicing writing (and often writing practice in specific APA format) with the students' demonstration of their understanding of content knowledge by writing about introductory concepts being studied.

Is There an Institutional Theme or Affiliation That May Be Informing Assessment?

There are instances where an institutional theme or affiliation may influence the lens through which assessment is viewed. For instance, some institutions have a dedicated focus to civic engagement, are Hispanic serving institutions, or may have a specific religious affiliation. Depending on the affiliation or specialty of the institution, this relationship may affect the assessment choices made in introductory psychology, as well as the interpretation about what is done with those assessment data and how the data inform future plans. If there is an institutional mission, then assessment data may not only be informing the department about how students are performing regarding curriculum goals, but those data might also be used to help inform if a university's mission is being met.

Please remember that this is not a comprehensive or exhaustive list of conditions that one might consider when selecting an assessment approach at your local institution; your individual results may vary. Caution: Your assessment results in the rear-view mirror may be larger than they appear in real life. Proceed with care.

STARTING FROM SCRATCH

Rather than adopting an existing assessment, instructors can certainly build their own strategies for determining what students know and can do as a result of their study in introductory psychology. This portion of the chapter provides a demonstration of the backward design process (see Fink, 2013) that can generate an effective and efficient assessment process. For our purposes, we will begin by choosing an outcome related to the Key Themes SLO and then complete the typical steps of assessment design through "closing the loop." In this case, closing the loop can transpire in making a conclusion that influences a summative judgment about individual student achievement, in providing evidence of high-quality educational process to an external judge, or in offering some direction for improvement in teaching tactics. The steps are as follows:

1. Identify the desired outcome.
2. Designate an appropriate context in which students can demonstrate the outcome.
3. Deliver instruction that highlights and provides practice with the skills and themes.
4. Design an assignment that reflects the context and the targeted outcome.
5. Specify expectations for student performance.
6. Use the data to promote continuous improvement.

We now review each step in detail.

Step 1: Identify the Desired Outcome

The first step in the process is targeting the specific outcome for which we wish to generate evidence. In this example, we focus on generating an assessment connected to Outcome 3 Theme C: Psychological, biological, social, and cultural factors influence behavior and mental processes. The underlying value of this outcome is helping students move away from a black-and-white or dualistic worldview (see Perry, 1960) to the perspective that most behaviors derive from complex factors. An additional advantage in focusing on this outcome is that practice with the bio–psycho–social–cultural approach can help teach students how to be more variable minded (cf. Halonen & Gray, 2016), meaning that students can learn to become more inquisitive about identifying all potential contributing factors rather than settling for the first compelling causal explanation.

Step 2: Designate an Appropriate Context in Which Students Can Demonstrate the Outcome

Because this theme is pervasive throughout the content of introductory psychology, finding the proper context for teaching and assessing the use of the bio–psycho–social–cultural framework is relatively easy. Developmental psychology phenomena (e.g., parenting practices, attachment behavior, rituals surrounding death and dying) can serve as an excellent vehicle for multilayered analysis. Similarly, behaviors in health psychology (e.g., smoking, drug and alcohol abuse, eating disorders) lend themselves to the use of multiple perspectives. Behavior disorders, gender development, intelligence testing, and even social phenomena can be analyzed for the range of factors that contribute to the behavior in question.

Current events also tend to be rich in behaviors that could be scrutinized from the standpoint of the bio–psycho–social–cultural model. For example, when the country effectively shut down from the threat of COVID-19 in 2020, the contributing factors were broad and the ramifications of the shutdown were also far-reaching. The #MeToo movement can be understood in a more comprehensive fashion when we entertain how all those different elements of the model contribute. As well, the social justice movement clearly has social and cultural influences, but digging more deeply into the biological and psychological variables will engender a more defensible explanation about the rich causes and ideally help us predict how the phenomenon may influence bio–psycho–social–cultural variables in return. For example, did the heat of the summer months account for some of the aggression reported in connection with the protests? Did media coverage inspire more participation in the movement through modeling?

Another context that would work for promoting the model is examining a proposed public policy. For example, in 1998 a southern governor decided to allocate more than $100,000 of the state budget to providing an audiotape of Mozart music in the belief that early exposure would accelerate intellectual development (Goode, 1999). Although a meta-analysis of research on the phenomenon demonstrated that the original report couldn't be replicated (Pietschnig et al., 2010), the decision to expend such a significant portion of state funding based on such limited evidence represents a great opportunity to explore variables of different types to push children to reach their potential. The model could also be invoked to predict what kinds of consequences might arise biologically, psychologically, socially, and culturally from the actions that followed the distribution of the Mozart CDs. Although the Mozart debacle is an egregious example of bad public policy, any current proposal that affects behavior could be used as a context for practice with the model. How do the major areas in the model frame how we understand a given phenomenon?

Step 3: Deliver Instruction That Highlights and Provides Practice With the Skills and Themes

In most psychology textbooks, authors tend to highlight the interaction of levels of analysis as part of the framework that will unfold in the text, whether it be a "big idea" or a "theme." Therefore, when authors provide such organizing frameworks to orient students to the values that will unfold in their texts, instructors need to review those themes in an explicit way to set the stage for the discussion that will be infused throughout the course. In addition, instructors should be vigilant when looking at complex phenomena throughout the course to seize the moment to produce reminders about the value of the bio–psycho–social–cultural model in producing a more well-rounded understanding of the phenomenon. However, before a formal assessment of whether students grasp the significance of different levels of analysis, providing a fresh example that relates to the forthcoming assignment will more likely produce the greatest intellectual performances from students on the assignment.

Step 4: Design an Assignment That Reflects the Context and the Targeted Outcome

Assignment options can vary. Although multiple choice questions might be derived for some themes or outcomes, a more likely course of action for assessing what students have learned regarding thematic insights is likely to be an essay question. For example, an essay question could simply ask students to speculate how the bio–psycho–social–cultural model explains the origins of shoplifting. For example:

- *Biological*: Could there be an arousal deficiency that encourages inappropriate risk-taking?
- *Psychological*: How might a shoplifting episode illustrate moral development?
- *Social*: To what extent can peers influence law-breaking behavior?
- *Cultural*: How might socioeconomic factors play a role in a shoplifting decision?

To encourage integrative insights, the question could also prompt students to discuss the value of applying the model. An adventurous adaptation of this approach might be to allow students to pick a behavioral phenomenon and then exercise the model in explaining how the levels of analysis contribute to an integrated understanding of the behavior about which they expressed intrinsic interest.

Another format shifts the assignment to a group project akin to Aronson's jigsaw design (Aronson et al., 1978). A group of students could be assigned a public policy issue, such as proposals to change the legal drinking age. Each member of the group could be asked to develop one dimension of the model. What insight might develop on the problem if we view it from the standpoint of biology? Of culture? Then students could bring their individual observations back to the table to craft a public service announcement in which they take and defend an integrated stand in relation to the targeted issue.

Step 5: Specify Expectations for Student Performance

In this stage, we offer two types of rubric designs for making determinations of the level of student achievement in a new assessment strategy. We begin with a more holistic approach that tends to be especially useful when instructors collect data that will eventually be submitted to an external evaluator (e.g., a principal, an accrediting agency). Achievement levels are designated as "exceeds," "meets," or "does not meet" as quality standards in an assignment. The collective weight of those achievements can also be used to determine a grade. Once the evaluative scale has been established, the instructor should identify the component behaviors, which will serve as performance criteria.

For example, if we decided to ask students to deliberate the rich variables that influence shoplifting, the rubric for this essay question could be configured in a manner shown in Exhibit 4.15.

EXHIBIT 4.15. A Holistic Rubric for an Essay Question on Shoplifting According to the Bio-Psycho-Social-Cultural Model

Criterion	Exceeds expectation	Meets expectation	Does not meet expectation
Follows instructions			
Accurately describes target behavior			
Provides evidence derived from all model dimensions			
Identifies value of explicit use of a model			

An analytic rubric may translate more easily to grading. In the example of the development of a public service announcement, suppose we have designated the assignment as an effort that will contribute 50 points toward the students' grades. A possible rubric that would help students clarify what kind of performance would be satisfying is presented in Exhibit 4.16.

EXHIBIT 4.16. An Analytic Rubric Evaluating the Bio-Psycho-Social-Cultural Model in a Group Assignment Developing a Public Service Announcement

Criterion	10 points: superb execution	8 points: proficient execution	6 points: problematic execution	4 points: incomplete execution	0 points: missing execution
Follows instructions					
Identifies and describes behavior					
Presents aesthetically pleasing material					
Represents all four dimensions of model in execution					
Proper conventions and professionalism					

Gather the Data From Student Performance

The use of rubrics tends to facilitate greater clarity for students in grasping what instructors want in a given assignment, but there are also advantages for instructors. A well-designed rubric tends to speed up grading. With a rubric applied blindly to student submissions, the grading process can also more fairly address equity concerns.

The results can be factors in determining grades. Alternatively, compiling the data can provide insight into the overall process. Disappointing patterns can reflect that improvements might be necessary either in the instruction delivery or in the assessment design. Similarly, the aggregated data may be harvested and reported according to program specifications. Pertaining to the latter situation, a holistic approach may be the most satisfactory (e.g., what percentage of students at least met expectations in relation to the targeted outcome?).

Step 6: Use the Data to Promote Continuous Improvement

Feedback to students can reinforce what students have accomplished in their studies and highlight where their understanding or skill development still may be deficient. To maximize impact on student development, instructors should require some process that engages students to read and benefit from the feedback. For example, following up with a discussion prompt (e.g., "What lessons can you extract from the feedback that might influence how you prepare for similar challenges in the future?") will help students incorporate changes that can enhance their future success.

Assessment strategies tend to be works in continuous progress. On the basis of the direct results of the assessment, instructors may redesign instruction or modify how the outcome is assessed. Most assessment-oriented faculty recognize that a well-designed rubric may be able to collect important information on more than one target outcome from one project. They also accept that a teaching or assessing strategy rarely is going to be perfect upon its first use; therefore, most faculty have the expectation that the process will need continual fine-tuning. Instructors can also gather feedback post hoc from students on how well the strategy worked. By asking students which elements of the process could be improved, the faculty member can harvest helpful suggestions that might make a difference on the next implementation.

Despite the fact that homegrown assessments offer the greatest degree of autonomy in instructional design, we recognize that many faculty would simply prefer to implement assessment strategies that are more plug and play. This expressed preference naturally raises the question about the value of developing a national assessment strategy that could be implemented across courses. Therefore, we conclude our discussion by taking on this question: Should there be a national measure for achieving skills and learning content in introductory psychology?

THE NATIONAL ASSESSMENT QUESTION

When confronted with demands for accountability data, many departments ponder why no standard test has been developed to assist with assessment concerns related to introductory psychology. There are proxies available, such as the Psychology Area Concentration Achievement Test (PACAT), the GRE Subject Test in Psychology, the ETS Major Field Test in Psychology, but these instruments are for assessing content knowledge of the psychology major at the time of the conclusion of the undergraduate degree program. Some measures of psychological knowledge at the beginning level are publicly available, such as the recently developed introductory psychology Knowledge Inventory (Solomon et al., 2019) and the Psychology Knowledge Questionnaire (Thompson & Zamboanga, 2004). These instruments offer a variety of reliable and valid means of measuring content, but their focus is primarily on the discipline's content.

A nationally normed inventory for introductory psychology has not yet been universally accepted, and more reasons exist as to why such a strategy might not be in the best interest of the psychological community. Developing a standardized test is an extremely challenging proposition. Developing a reliable and valid measure is both time-consuming and labor-intensive. If such a test were to be developed, security measures would likely be problematic. We increasingly hear reports of compromised test banks that actively discourage faculty from using test questions engineered by publishers. The same security threat would exist for a standardized exam for introductory psychology if the exam were unchanging.

If an exam were to change every year, the exam would need the kind of testing development and financial support that is apparent in the Advanced Placement Psychology exam. This necessity represents no small undertaking. It is unclear that there would be sufficient profit in this question to promote such an investment. Beyond mechanical issues, nationally normed tests always struggle with the challenge of demographic influences in the tested population. These issues become even more complicated when one recognizes that introductory psychology is taught at the university, college, community college, and high school levels. In addition, colleges that are highly selective may have inherent advantages in accountability through selection bias that may undermine the use of a "standardized" test with disadvantaged, underrepresented populations.

A final rationale for not supporting the development and use of such an instrument is that it would most likely reinforce low-level content-related skills of recognizing and recalling rather than focusing on the acquisition of skills. The very thrust of the importance of the assessment movement would be lost if psychology programs could simply dispatch their responsibilities through a simple-to-administer multiple-choice test. In the absence of such definitive instruments, teachers should be encouraged to explore skill development and assessment where feasible. In fact, in the best traditions of psychometrics, multiple measures would ideally be used that converge on the key aspects of knowledge and skills to be learned and performed.

CONCLUSION

The introductory psychology course is the tie that binds throughout all levels and specialties of psychological science where the vast majority of our students and our citizens first systematically learn about the principles, theories, and laws that comprise psychology. The practice, public interest, education, and science of psychology all have an essential stake in the introductory psychology course. Introductory psychology instructors understand all too well that this is the course—the one and only psychology course— that many college students will complete in the United States. It is our chance to tell the story of psychology as a science, that is, the STEM—science, technology, engineering, and math—story of psychology. The amount of effort and expertise that we invest into the introductory psychology course and our students will never be too much, and the potential return on our investment is limitless.

REFERENCES

American Psychological Association. (2011). *National standards for high school psychology curricula.* https://www.apa.org/education/k12/psychology-curricula.pdf
American Psychological Association. (2013). *APA guidelines for the undergraduate psychology major: Version 2.0.* https://www.apa.org/ed/precollege/about/psymajor-guidelines.pdf
American Psychological Association. (2014). *Strengthening the common core of the introductory psychology course.* American Psychological Association, Board of Educational Affairs. http://www.apa.org/ed/governance/bea/intro-psych-report.pdf

American Psychological Association. (2020). *The APA Introductory Psychology Initiative.* https://www.apa.org/ed/precollege/undergrad/introductory-psychology-initiative

American Psychological Association, Working Group on Introductory Psychology Assessment. (2017). *Assessment of outcomes of the introductory course in psychology.* https://www.apa.org/ed/precollege/assessment-outcomes.pdf

Angelo, T. A., & Cross, K. P. (1993). *Classroom assessment techniques: A handbook for college teachers* (2nd ed.). Jossey-Bass.

Aronson, E., Blaney, N., Stephin, C., Sikes, J., & Snapp, M. (1978). *The jigsaw classroom.* Sage Publications.

Association of American Colleges & Universities. (2005). *Liberal education and America's promise.* https://www.aacu.org/leap

Baumeister, R. F., DeWall, C. N., Ciarocco, N. J., & Twenge, J. M. (2005). Social exclusion impairs self-regulation. *Journal of Personality and Social Psychology, 88*(4), 589–604. https://doi.org/10.1037/0022-3514.88.4.589

Bernstein, D. J., Addison, W., Altman, C., Hollister, D., Komarraju, M., & Shore, C. (2010). Toward a scientist–educator model of teaching psychology. In D. F. Halpern (Ed.), *Undergraduate education in psychology: A blueprint for the future of the discipline* (pp. 29–45). American Psychological Association. https://doi.org/10.1037/12063-002

Boatright-Horowitz, S. L. (2005). Teaching antiracism in a large introductory psychology class: A course module and its evaluation. *Journal of Black Studies, 36*(1), 34–51. https://doi.org/10.1177/0021934704266508

Dormant, D. (2011). *The chocolate model of change.* Lulu.

Dunn, D. S., Baker, S. C., Mehrotra, C. M., Landrum, R. E., & McCarthy, M. A. (Eds.). (2013). *Assessing teaching and learning in psychology: Current and future perspectives.* Wadsworth Cengage.

Dunn, D. S., Troisi, J. D., & Baker, S. C. (2020). Faculty receptivity to assessment: Changing the climate for evaluating teaching and learning in psychology. *Scholarship of Teaching and Learning in Psychology, 6*(3), 244–253.

Fink, D. (2013). *Creating significant learning experiences: An integrated approach to designing college courses* (Rev. ed.). Jossey-Bass.

Goode, E. (1999, August 3). Mozart for baby? Some say, maybe not. *The New York Times,* p. f.

Halonen, J. S., & Gray, C. (2016). *The critical thinking companion* (3rd ed.). Worth Publishers.

Hard, B. M. (2017, July). What's the big idea? Teaching intro using integrative themes. *The Hastings Center Report, 8*(6), 21–29. https://doi.org/10.2307/3561468

Kirschner, P. A., & Hendrick, C. (2020). *How learning happens: Seminal works in educational psychology and what they mean in practice.* Routledge. https://doi.org/10.4324/9780429061523

Kuh, G. D., Ikenberry, S. O., Jankowski, N. A., Cain, T. R., Ewell, P. T., Hutchings, P., & Kinzie, J. (2015). *Using evidence of student learning to improve higher education.* National Institute for Learning Outcomes Assessment and Jossey-Bass.

Perry, W. G., Jr. (1960). *Forms of intellectual and ethical development in the college years: A scheme.* Holt, Rinehart, & Winston.

Pietschnig, J., Voracek, M., & Formann, A. K. (2010). Mozart effect—Schmozart effect: A meta-analysis. *Intelligence, 38*(3), 314–323. https://doi.org/10.1016/j.intell.2010.03.001

Prochaska, J. O., & DiClemente, C. C. (1983). Stages and processes of self-change of smoking: Toward an integrative model of change. *Journal of Consulting and Clinical Psychology, 51*(3), 390–395. https://doi.org/10.1037/0022-006X.51.3.390

Prochaska, J. O., Velicer, W. F., Rossi, J. S., Goldstein, M. G., Marcus, B. H., Rakowski, W., Fiore, C., Harlow, L. L., Redding, C. A., Rosenbloom, D., & Rossi, S. R. (1994). Stages of change and decisional balance for 12 problem behaviors. *Health Psychology, 13*(1), 39–46. https://doi.org/10.1037/0278-6133.13.1.39

Solomon, E. D., Bugg, J. M., Rowell, S. F., McDaniel, M. A., Frey, R. F., & Mattson, P. S. (2019). Development and validation of an introductory psychology knowledge inventory. *Scholarship of Teaching and Learning in Psychology.* Advance online publication. https://doi.org/10.1037/stl0000172

Stanny, C. J., & Halonen, J. S. (2011). Accreditation, accountability, and assessment: Faculty development's role in addressing multiple agendas. In L. Stefani (Ed.), *Evaluating the effectiveness of academic development practice: A professional guide* (pp. 169–182). Routledge.

Thompson, R. A., & Zamboanga, B. L. (2004). Academic aptitude and prior knowledge as predictors of student achievement in introduction to psychology. *Journal of Educational Psychology, 96*(4), 778–784. https://doi.org/10.1037/0022-0663.96.4.778

Wiggins, G., & McTighe, J. (2005). *Understanding by design* (2nd ed.). Association for Supervision and Curriculum Development.

5

NAVIGATING THE NUANCES OF TEACHING INTRODUCTORY PSYCHOLOGY

A Roadmap for Implementing Evidence-Based Instructional Methods

DANAE L. HUDSON, AARON S. RICHMOND,
BRIDGETTE MARTIN HARD, DANA S. DUNN,
AND ROBIN MUSSELMAN

KEY RECOMMENDATIONS

1. Choose evidence-based instructional methods that accomplish the course goals, while taking into account institutional, student, and instructor variables that could influence the outcomes.

2. Expect the unexpected. Think through alternate forms of instructional delivery and strategies to support students should a local, national, or global situation interfere with teaching and learning.

3. Recognize or anticipate idiosyncratic introductory psychology teaching challenges and develop the course to specifically address these challenges.

4. Use the decision tree provided at the end of this chapter to guide the choice of instructional methods for introductory psychology.

https://doi.org/10.1037/0000260-006
Transforming Introductory Psychology: Expert Advice on Teacher Training, Course Design, and Student Success, R. A. R. Gurung and G. Neufeld (Editors)

So far, we have provided a rationale for why introductory psychology is such a valuable course in higher education (see Chapter 1), offered an evidence-informed framework for designing the course (Chapter 2), introduced the Introductory Psychology Initiative's (IPI; American Psychological Association [APA], 2020) student learning outcomes (SLOs), and provided suggestions for how an instructor can assess whether these learning outcomes have been achieved (Chapters 3 and 4). We have not yet discussed how to teach the content and skills associated with an introductory psychology course. Imagine this process as a map: We have already identified the starting point (i.e., SLOs) and the destination (i.e., assessment of those SLOs). This chapter provides recommendations for how to navigate from the course's starting point to its destination. As with any map, there are several routes from point A to point B. When choosing the best route, various factors must be considered. This chapter does not provide a set of turn-by-turn directions for teaching introductory psychology. Rather, we present evidence-based instructional methods and discuss the instructional considerations needed to effectively implement these methods in a course. The chapter concludes with an example of how to integrate and use this information when designing an introductory psychology course. Therefore, the purpose of this chapter is to provide an empirically supported structure for teaching introductory psychology that contains all the building blocks necessary to create a course that uses evidence-based instructional methods and fits each instructor's specific institution, student body, and own personality.

A REVIEW OF EVIDENCE-BASED INTRODUCTORY PSYCHOLOGY INSTRUCTIONAL METHODS

There are many ways to teach introductory psychology well and many ways to teach introductory psychology poorly. Additionally, there is not one particular instructional method that solves all of the challenges of teaching introductory psychology and ensures success (Richmond et al., 2015, 2021). Thus, introductory psychology instructors need to employ a variety of techniques flexibly and adaptably. In a national study, Boysen and colleagues (2015) found that the best teachers use more than one instructional method, along with effective teaching skills and behaviors. As Richmond et al. (2015) suggested, model teachers tend to adapt their instructional methods to the specific conditions of the course. For example, in a small honors section of introductory psychology, the instructor may use collaborative learning and the Socratic instructional method more than direct instruction.

Although we know that many instructors vary their instructional methods, it is not yet clear how much they use various instructional methods within an introductory psychology course.

WHAT DO THE DATA TELL US ABOUT WHICH INSTRUCTIONAL METHODS TO USE?

In a recent national study, the IPI Census found that introductory psychology instructors use a wide variety of instructional methods (Richmond et al., 2021), but the most commonly used method was direct instruction, which involves lecturing or otherwise conveying course content directly to students. The use of direct instruction positively correlated with class size, such that the larger classes tended to rely more on direct instruction than did the smaller classes. Direct instruction was followed by active learning, cooperative learning, experiential learning, and the Socratic method as the next most popular instructional methods. The least used instructional methods were team-based, just-in-time teaching, and inquiry-based instruction. Moreover, Richmond and colleagues found that the use of one instructional method (e.g., experiential learning) did not preclude the use of another instructional method (e.g., direct instruction). In the end, this study demonstrated that instructors of psychology use a wide variety of instructional methods. Instructors of introductory psychology should adapt their instructional methods based on their SLOs, competency in using the specific instructional methods, and the constraints of the course.

Experienced and effective instructors of introductory psychology are not looking for the "right" instructional method. They recognize that the solution is multiplistic and often needs to adapt based on the needs and format of the class. Therefore, we put together a list of some of the more common and effective instructional methods used. Exhibit 5.1 illustrates a collection of instructional methods and strategies that are shown to be effective in teaching introductory psychology. In the exhibit, we first define the instructional method (i.e., including the underlying instructional theory and design). We then offer examples of instructional strategies for that method (i.e., how that instructional method may be implemented). Finally, we provide a set of resources containing specific evidence-based or informed examples of the instructional method. In addition to the resources described in Exhibit 5.1, we also recommend several resources that the Society for the Teaching of Psychology (APA Division 2) has developed for teaching introductory psychology. For example,

EXHIBIT 5.1. Types of Instructional Methods for Introductory Psychology: Definitions, Strategies, and Examples

Active learning

Definition: Students engage in either small or large group activities that connect material-to-be-learned to prior knowledge through engagement.

Instructional Strategies: Background knowledge probe, 1-minute-paper, elaborative interrogation, learning logs, three-step interview, muddiest point, etc.

Examples: Social conformity (Bleske-Rechek, 2001), in-class writing (Butler et al., 2001), developmental theories (Richmond & Hagan, 2011), multiculturalism (Warren, 2006)

Collaborative or cooperative learning

Definition: Students work together, typically in groups of two or more, with a shared goal such as to complete a task, solve a problem, or learn a new concept.

Instructional Strategies: Research teams, think–pair–share, number heads, group roundtables, jigsaw, etc.

Examples: Motivation and learning (Brothen, 1991), social psychology (Giordano & Hammer, 1999), science laboratory (Newcomb & Bagwell, 1997), neuroscience (Sheldon, 2000)

Problem-based learning

Definition: Students can either work individually or in groups to solve a particular problem. Typically, the problem is open-ended, and students progress through a series of modeled steps to solve the problem.

Instructional Strategies: Articulate what the learning outcomes are, establish rules to solve the problem, identify germane information, execute solutions, then discuss findings.

Examples: Pseudoscience (Lawson & Brown, 2018), sensation and perception (Kreiner, 2009), laboratory experience (Peterson & Sesma, 2017), behaviorism (Shields & Gredler, 2003)

Interteaching

Definition: A self-directed learning method that requires students to engage in course material before class and uses reinforcements to drive student motivation where the instructor serves as a guide or facilitator.

Instructional Strategies: Before class, students fill out a "prep-guide" on assigned read-ing and receive some reward (points). During class, the instructor roams from groups or pairs of students who are working on a guided discussion based on the prep guide and helps with any misconceptions or confusion. At the end, students complete a feedback form about the session.

Examples: Biopsychology (Saville et al., 2005, 2014)

Just-in-time teaching

Definition: Students complete preassessments before class, then the instructor uses their performance to modify the lesson to clarify any misconceptions.

Instructional Strategies: Active learning questions, prompting questions, warm-ups, puzzles, or "goodfors" (i.e., essays that connect material to the real world)

Examples: Statistics (Benedict & Anderton, 2004), general implementation (Hudson et al., 2014)

EXHIBIT 5.1. Types of Instructional Methods for Introductory Psychology: Definitions, Strategies, and Examples (*Continued*)

Experiential learning

Definition: Students acquire knowledge and skills from directly experiencing the content to be learned.

Instructional Strategies: Service learning projects, lab experiments, in-class activities, blogging, simulations, research projects, interviews

Examples: Clinical and counseling and cultural psychology (Kretchmar, 2001), learning and educational psychology (Muir & van der Linden, 2009), cognitive processes and metacognition (Richmond et al., 2017)

Inquiry-based learning

Definition: Students are required to create a question, collect evidence, analyze evidence, connect evidence to the knowledge they are trying to learn, and justify their explanation.

Instructional Strategies: Scientific process, elaborative interrogation (i.e., why questioning), self-explanation, self-generated examples, class discussion, case studies, fieldwork, etc.

Examples: Moral development theory (Richmond et al., 2015), research methods (Thieman et al., 2009)

Socratic teaching

Definition: Students and instructors have an open dialogue about course content. The role of the instructor is to ask probing questions to students in an effort to challenge their beliefs.

Instructional Strategies: Seminars, Socratic circles, 1-minute papers and discussion, what's the principle, self-explanation, expansive questions, muddiest point, invented dialogues

Examples: General implementation (Gose, 2009), history of psychology (Sternberg, 1998)

Direct instruction

Definition: An instructor-led set of instructions "directs" the student to learn specific material.

Instructional Strategies: Lecture, demonstrations, scaffolding, lecture notes

Examples: Critical thinking and argument analysis (Bensley et al., 2010), general implementation (Zayac et al., 2016)

Note. Data from Slavich and Zimbardo (2012) and Richmond et al. (2016).

Introductory Psychology Teaching Primer: A Guide for New Teachers of Psych 101 (Afful et al., 2013; Leder-Elder et al., 2015) and *Teaching Introductory Psychology: Tips from ToP* (Griggs & Jackson, 2011) are excellent resources for instructional methods and evidence-based practices.

It appears that direct instruction is popular among introductory psychology teachers (Richmond et al., 2021) but that many other instructional methods are also used (e.g., active learning, Socratic, problem-based) to teach a variety of psychological concepts. In the end, although instructional methods are important, equally important is how instructors choose and adapt each type of instruction to suit their students' needs, the learning outcomes, and other peripheral factors that can influence the course experience.

INSTRUCTIONAL CONSIDERATIONS: TAILORING INSTRUCTIONAL METHODS TO FIT THE ENVIRONMENT

Many helpful resources exist that guide instructors through the typical steps of preparing to teach a class (Gurung et al., 2016; Hudson, 2021). Many of these activities have already been discussed in previous chapters of this book (i.e., designing course learning objectives, choosing course content, and assessment strategies). In addition to these important decisions, numerous other interacting factors must be thoughtfully considered. Our tendency is to view these various considerations as constraints (e.g., "I have to teach in this small, old classroom, so I'm not going to be able to engage with my students in a meaningful way"). There are certainly constraints in teaching, but constraints can evolve into opportunities to generate creative solutions to age-old problems. We encourage instructors to see their educational environment in terms of affordances rather than constraints. Affordances describe what your environment offers rather than what it withholds (Gibson, 2015). Teachers must consider many factors, which we have categorized into institutional, student, and instructor domains. Although this categorization provides a useful framework for discussion, we recognize that many of the factors instructors need to consider can span multiple categories.

Institutional Factors That Influence Teaching

Psychology teachers rarely have 100% control over all aspects of their class. Many decisions about a course are made on an institutional level with little to no input from the instructor. As a result, instructors are left to develop a pedagogically sound course that fits the criteria defined by their institution. According to the results from the IPI census (Richmond et al., 2021), the vast majority of institutions (87.4%) offered introductory psychology in a single semester (or quarter). Therefore, in most cases, all content from introductory psychology is provided by the same instructor and in the same location.

Physical Space

The physical space in which the course is delivered is an example of an important institutional factor over which an instructor often has little control. Classrooms vary in size, seating arrangement, desk space, and general decor. Although evidence of the impact of such features on learning is limited, students' perceptions and behaviors are influenced by their physical environment (Hyun et al., 2017; Nicol et al., 2018; Walker & Baepler, 2017). In a study comparing students who attended class in a large auditorium to students who had class in a traditional classroom, students were less likely to attend class when it was held in the auditorium, and they indicated more difficulty hearing their peers than did students in traditional classrooms (Young et al., 2017). Active learning classrooms (ALCs) are technology-enabled, student-centered spaces that facilitate active learning pedagogies (Brooks, 2019). Students rate comfort, engagement, and perceptions of learning more favorably in ALC classrooms (Chiu & Cheng, 2017; Mui et al., 2019). Of course, active learning can take place in any classroom environment, and some classrooms have moveable seats that can be adjusted to facilitate student interaction. If possible, view the learning space before course development. If students will need laptops, phones, or tablets to participate in class, instructors should consider whether Wi-Fi is available and if it offers enough bandwidth to accommodate the number of students in the class. Typically, greater numbers of students are more taxing on the various technologies employed in the class.

Class Size

Class size is a frequent discussion within departments and also tends to be a variable over which instructors have limited input. The IPI Census confirmed a wide range in how many students are typically enrolled in a section of introductory psychology (Richmond et al., 2021). The mean number of students per section was 67.85; however, the standard deviation was 109.06. The median number of students in a class was 35, but the range was 997. Data from the IPI Census indicated that on average, doctoral institutions had the largest classes, followed by master's institutions, baccalaureate, 2-year colleges, and high schools, respectively (Richmond et al., 2021). If instructors can exert choice over class size, they should choose a class size that fits with their preferred modality, instructional methods, and teaching style.

Course Delivery

Introductory psychology is taught in a variety of modalities (Garratt-Reed et al., 2016). The traditional face-to-face format means students interact directly with the instructor by attending a lecture and/or discussion class totaling approximately 2 to 3 hours each week. According to the IPI Census, the vast majority of instructors (83.6%) indicated that they taught introductory psychology in a face-to-face format (although many may also teach in other modalities). Alternatively, students can enroll in online versions of the course where they complete readings and assignments off campus (typically through a learning management system) and then communicate with their instructor and peers online. Hybrid, or blended, courses have both an online and face-to-face component. A common variation is the flipped class, which provides instructional content outside the classroom, usually in an online format, while homework, an activity traditionally assigned to be completed outside the classroom is brought into the classroom in a live, interactive manner. All modalities can be an effective way to teach if the course has been thoughtfully planned and paired with appropriate instructional methods. However, there is strong evidence suggesting that blended or hybrid classes can significantly improve learning outcomes and increase retention compared with traditional, lecture-based courses (Alammary, 2019; Hudson et al., 2014, 2015; Vo et al., 2017).

Length of the Course
The majority (87.3%) of respondents to the IPI Census indicated that they taught introductory psychology in a semester-long (e.g., 14–16 weeks) format, whereas 6.4% of instructors reported teaching the course on a quarter system (e.g., 10–11 weeks). A national study involving psychology departments (Norcross et al., 2016) and class-level research (Deichert et al., 2016) suggested that there was little difference in structure and outcomes between courses of varying lengths. However, instructors should consider the amount of time available to teach the course when planning the pacing and nature of assignments.

Institutional Resources
Before embarking on a road trip, there are many factors to consider. The budget for the trip will determine whether hotel rooms or campsites are to be reserved. The types of activities planned will also depend on the opportunities and resources available. The trip can be exciting regardless of the circumstances, but it is important to know what resources are available before departing. Similarly, institutions vary considerably in the amount of resources they provide to introductory psychology instructors. Some programs have paid graduate assistants available to help with course management, which affords the instructor opportunities to include various forms

of assessment and projects that involve writing (e.g., Hard et al., 2019). Other programs with smaller budgets use undergraduate learning assistants to assist with large classes (Whisenhunt et al., 2019). In addition to course staff, support can be provided in the form of administrative help, a budget to purchase supplies for classroom activities and demonstrations, access to instructional designers, and travel funds for professional development. Before course development, be sure to clarify the type and amount of institutional support available. If the support appears inadequate, instructors should use empirical evidence and data from their own classes, if possible, to justify requesting additional resources to effectively teach the course.

Student Characteristics to Consider

Introductory psychology is considered a "gateway course" because it is usually the first class that a student takes within the psychology discipline. Additionally, the course is typically part of the larger general education curriculum and therefore attracts a wide range of students from various majors (see Chapter 1). The characteristics of the students enrolled in the course influence how the course will be taught, what level of materials will be used, the pace of the course, the nature of the assignments, quizzes and exams, and other forms of assessment. As a first step in understanding the students in introductory psychology, an instructor should know if their institution is highly selective in terms of admission requirements or if there are few or no barriers to being admitted (i.e., open enrollment).

Diversity of Students Within the Context of the Institution

In addition, the instructor should be familiar with the extent of diversity at the institution. Is the institution a minority-serving institution, which describes a group of federally designated colleges and universities that are categorized based on enrollment criteria (Espinosa et al., 2017)? If so, what is the nature of, and historical context, of the institution? Is the institution a Predominantly Black Institution, Historically Black College or University, Hispanic-Serving Institution, Tribal College or University, Alaska Native– and Native Hawaiian–Serving Institution, Asian American and Native American Pacific Islander–Serving Institution, or Native American–Serving, Nontribal Institution? Even if the institution is minority-serving, it is important to recognize that minoritized students are a heterogeneous group, and their college experiences vary widely (Stewart, 2013). In this post–George Floyd era of education, all instructors should take an active role in gathering information from university administrators, the department or program chair, teaching peers, and their own students so they can develop a welcoming and inclusive course design that will engage all students.

Diversity of Students' Background and Experiences

The population of students in U.S. higher education is more diverse than it has ever been. A recent report on race and ethnicity in higher education outlined how students of color in the undergraduate population increased from 29.6% in 1996 to 45.2% in 2016 (Espinosa et al., 2019). Diversity, of course, includes much more than race and ethnicity, and recognizing the intersectionality of race, gender, sexuality, socioeconomic status, and other environmental experiences is a complicated but necessary endeavor for each instructor (Nichols & Stahl, 2019). Some instructors have reported offering students a voluntary questionnaire at the beginning of the semester to share their background experiences, which may include whether students are veterans. The post-9/11 GI Bill was introduced in 2009 and offers educational benefits to veterans; since that time, approximately 100,000 degrees each year have been awarded to veterans (Cate et al., 2017). Veterans tend to be predominantly male, over age 25, and 46% report having children (Cate & Davis, 2016). Mental health issues continue to be a source of concern among veterans returning to college (Albright et al., 2017; Fortney et al., 2016) but have also been identified as a significant issue among traditional college students (Forbes et al., 2019). Student mental health centers have had difficulty keeping up with the demand, and financial constraints often prevent students from seeking psychological services from the community. These financial hardships lead many students to work an enormous number of hours each week in addition to taking college courses. Despite the number of students who work while attending college, there are a significant number of students who experience housing and food insecurity on a regular basis (Nikolaus et al., 2020; Silva et al., 2017). Instructors must recognize the difficult reality that each one of these aspects of diversity has been shown to be negatively associated with academic performance (Grossbard et al., 2014; Oyserman & Lewis, 2017; Sansone, 2019; Weaver et al., 2020). As discussed in Chapter 2, part of our job as instructors is to design a course that is inclusive, sensitive to the challenges students face, and provides a space and curriculum for all students to be successful.

Instructor Variables That Influence Teaching

Instructors vary in how much autonomy they have in choosing an instructional modality and subsequent course design. Many introductory psychology instructors appear to have some influence over textbook choice and the development of SLOs. According to the IPI Census, 52.4% of instructors had complete control over their textbook choice and 24.8% created their own SLOs. Interestingly, 63.2% of respondents reported that all sections of introductory psychology at their institution used a common set of SLOs. Previous research has suggested consistency across sections of introductory psychology can reduce course drift (i.e., students shifting between sections because of differing course requirements) and lead to a significant reduction in the number of students who withdraw from the course (Hudson et al., 2015). These data imply that introductory psychology is likely to be a course with shared governance among faculty and administrators, which is an important consideration if given the option of teaching the course.

Personality Characteristics
Some of the best practical advice that can be given to new teachers is to "know yourself." Do your specific personality characteristics mesh with a particular instructional modality? In a study comparing instructor personality characteristics in a face-to-face and online introductory course, the researchers found significantly higher scores on extraversion and agreeableness among instructors of face-to-face classes (Evans, 2017). These results suggested that the face-to-face modality provided an outlet of expression for instructors with these specific personality traits.

In addition to personality, choosing instructional methods (see Exhibit 5.1) should also take into account the instructor's teaching philosophy and level of comfort with different educational strategies. For example, many hybrid/ blended and online courses make use of digital technologies to address various course challenges (e.g., reading, engagement, critical thinking). Technology has its pros and cons and often requires the ability to adapt quickly and problem solve technological issues that inevitably arise (Eiland & Todd, 2019). Before adopting a new technology, instructors should determine whether the technology has the potential to solve an educational problem. Choosing a technology just because "everybody is using it" is not a good pedagogical strategy. Furthermore, instructors must realistically assess their own comfort level with technology. Instructors who are fearful or lack confidence with new technologies often struggle with implementation and student buy-in. There are still many fantastic, engaging, and successful instructors who use chalk as their primary teaching tool.

Tackling a new technology can be a daunting task but can be manageable if instructors have an open mind and take advantage of training opportunities, which can include informal offers to help from other more experienced faculty members. Teachers of psychology are a generous and helpful group of people. If local colleagues are not available to help, national colleagues such as those found through the Society for the Teaching of Psychology (APA Division 2) can be a tremendous source of support when tackling new technologies and other pedagogical challenges.

Experience and Knowledge of Content

In introductory psychology, a wide variety of experience teaching the course and with the basic content knowledge is required to teach the course effectively. As Richmond and colleagues (2021) reported, among the more than 800 teachers of introductory psychology in their sample, those who had less experience (i.e., graduate students and new teachers) typically had more training, but they faced more challenges in their teaching as opposed to instructors who had more experience. In addition, many teachers reported that they lacked expertise to teach such a wide range of topics (Richmond et al., 2021).

So, where does this leave us? The good news is that many of the inexperienced teachers are also receiving more training (Richmond et al., 2021). Regardless, it is imperative to support introductory psychology teachers with the proper pedagogical training for them to enter the classroom and be effective (see Chapter 7, this volume, on training models). Moreover, it is also important to stress to new introductory psychology teachers that it is ideal to teach and assess all of the student learning objectives; however, they do not need to teach every concept in the textbook. As Dunn and Halonen (2017) stated, going deeper into course content on a limited number of concepts is far more important and increases students' retention of knowledge and skills than just providing a shallow cover of a multitude of concepts. Finally, it appears that when considering hiring or assigning introductory psychology instructors, department chairs and program directors should consider both experience and the ability of the individual teacher to cover the needed content.

Challenges Specific to Introductory Psychology

All instructors encounter general teaching challenges. Introductory psychology instructors may experience additional challenges specific to this introductory course. These challenges may be inherent in the course itself or result from an interaction of the personality of the instructor and the course design. In the IPI Census, we provided participants with a list of

18 challenges specific to introductory psychology. The results from the census indicated the top five most challenging aspects of teaching:

1. time to thoughtfully grade or provide feedback on writing,
2. getting students to read assignments,
3. getting students to think critically,
4. assessing higher level learning, and
5. managing a wide range of student abilities, skills, and knowledge.

We imagine many instructors will agree with these difficulties or barriers to success in their own courses. Are these challenges viewed as constraints or affordances? The way in which instructors view these problems can have an impact on how they are addressed. Problems that are viewed as threats or unsolvable tend to lead to feeling overwhelmed, whereas problems that are viewed as a challenge can spark the energy and motivation needed to find a solution (Gaab et al., 2005).

Other Considerations: Expect the Unexpected

Sometimes unexpected circumstances require instructors to abruptly change modalities—sometimes temporarily, as in the cases of severe weather or instructor illness, other times more permanently. The COVID-19 pandemic during the spring 2020 semester resulted in a surge of remote learning, or what has been referred to as emergency remote teaching (Hodges et al., 2020). Remote learning is distinguished from online learning in that the course is developed as a face-to-face course but the instruction is delivered online, sometimes synchronously, meaning all students are online with the instructor in real time. There may be times, as was the case in spring 2020, when courses have to quickly pivot to remote learning despite their original design in another modality.

Although this experience was difficult and anxiety-provoking in many ways, it also taught us some valuable lessons, especially the value in considering how unanticipated interruptions (e.g., inclement weather, natural disasters, public health crises, international incidents) can affect our planned course. This academic season also highlighted the value of collaboration in teaching psychology, as instructors of psychology came together through social media to brainstorm action plans, share resources, and pose thoughtful questions about how to move forward.

The discussions that emerged from instructor experiences over the remaining spring semester ultimately prompted calls for new course designs that have built-in flexibility and are quickly amenable to change (e.g., resilient pedagogy, adaptable course design; Bruff, 2020; Eyler, 2020). These designs can inspire an entire course model, such as the HyFlex model, and/or specific instructional methods and strategies that are easily adaptable and have already been shown to have efficacy in face-to-face and online environments. Regardless of the modality in which the introductory psychology course will be delivered, instructors should seek appropriate training and continue to participate in professional development as technology and pedagogical empirical evidence evolves.

DECISION TREE FOR SELECTING INSTRUCTIONAL METHODS FOR INTRODUCTORY PSYCHOLOGY

So far, we have summarized a large set of instructional methods as well as considerations that instructors must evaluate to inform the practical teaching of their course. Chapter 4 demonstrated the use of backward design with a six-step process. Here, we offer a similar process, in the form of a decision tree, to guide instructors in choosing instructional methods to achieve desired results, given institutional, student, and instructor considerations. The decision tree uses a modified backward design procedure. As described in Chapters 2 and 3, backward design was created to help instructors anticipate both the learning and teaching of the goals and specific situational factors of the course to inform decision-making to best achieve the goals of the instructor (Wiggins & McTighe, 2005). There are three main stages to backward design. First, instructors need to identify the desired results. Second, they need to determine what evidence would demonstrate that students are achieving their learning objectives or goals. Third, instructors need to select instructional methods and strategies to achieve their student learning objectives and goals (Wiggins & McTighe, 2005). As described in the following paragraphs, our decision tree is a six-step process.

In Step 1, instructors need to identify and define *student learning outcomes* for their course. This is what Wiggins and McTighe (2005) would refer to as "desired results." In the context of introductory psychology, Step 1 outlines specific student learning objectives. Wiggins and McTighe suggested that instructors consider what they want their students to learn. Is it a skill, or is it a specific concept? What are the big ideas you want your students to retain? Once this step has been completed, instructors can then proceed to Step 2.

In Step 2, instructors need to plan for *specific instructional considerations*. As an intermediate step to backward design, we believe it is important to understand the situational context of your course (as previously discussed) and how those institutional, student, and instructor factors will affect how the class is designed. Moreover, it is these instructional considerations that will inform the decisions made in each of the following steps (e.g., assessment, which instructional method to use). Now that instructors have identified the SLO and the particular unique instructional considerations, they need to complete Step 3—how to assess students.

In Step 3, instructors must *determine the appropriate assessments* that will demonstrate that students are achieving the student learning outcome selected. In the Wiggins and McTighe (2005) model, this is Stage 2— *evidence and assessment.* In this step, instructors consider what evidence students may provide to demonstrate their understanding of core targeted content. For instance, do instructors use quizzes, exams, discussions, formative feedback, summative feedback, or a laboratory write-up? Well, the simple answer is—it depends. While choosing the assessment is an important task, instructors need to choose the assessment that fits both the individual characteristics of your students and the specific student learning objective. For example, if you have a class size of 475 students, choosing essay-style exams may not be feasible or practical. Whereas if you are assessing the APA IPI SLO *1.1. Define and explain basic psychological concepts,* you may want to use real-time response systems (e.g., iClickers, Cahoots) or immediate feedback assessment technique (IF-AT; Richmond, 2017) as short multiple-choice quiz questions. Or if you want to assess the APA IPI SLO *2.4. Evaluate how psychological science can be used to counter unsubstantiated statements, opinions, or beliefs* and you are at a small community college, you may want to use collaborative learning in conjunction with the Currency, Relevance, Authority, Accuracy, and Purpose (CRAAP Test) to evaluate articles (Sawyer & Obeid, 2017).

To help you select assessments that align with the APA Guidelines 2.0 learning goals, APA has created a great resource for various assessments called Project Assessment (PASS; APA, n.d.). It consists of a repository of more than 100 assessments for introductory and other psychology courses. PASS is searchable and is organized by APA (2013) *Guidelines 2.0* learning goals, topic, and type of assessment. Once the student learning objective, instructional considerations, and assessments have been determined, instructors must select an instructional method.

Step 4 in the decision tree process is to *choose the most effective instructional method* to achieve the student learning objective. As illustrated in Exhibit 5.1, many types of instructional methods are evidence based. When deciding which method to choose, it is, again, important to first consider the

SLO. For example, if the objective is centered on effective communication, cooperative learning instruction may be more effective than direct instruction for helping students fulfill that objective. However, instructors must also consider instructional considerations, such as physical space and format. For example, cooperative learning instruction in a large lecture hall may prove difficult to accomplish. Or using just-in-time teaching may be effective in a hybrid or blended class format where students are completing online work before coming to class. It is important to remember that the most effective college and university teachers are adept at selecting various instructional methods and adapting to the given situation (Richmond et al., 2016).

Now that Steps 1 through 4 are completed, Step 5 requires that the instructor chooses and implements the *most effective instructional techniques* that are consistent with the theory of the instructional method. As illustrated in Exhibit 5.1, it is important to match the technique with the method. For example, if an instructor chooses problem-based instruction as a method but then chooses only to provide lecture-based classes, then it is likely the students will not achieve the learning goal based on the assessments designed and implemented. Therefore, when using problem-based learning, instructors should follow the sequential steps by having students articulate the learning outcome, establish the rules to solve the problem, identify important information, execute the solution, and then have them discuss their findings. Again, effective teachers will use various instructional methods with corresponding techniques or strategies throughout their course. They will, however, use specific methods and techniques for specific learning outcomes (Richmond et al., 2016).

The final step, Step 6, is to *reflect and adapt*. Because teaching is an ever-evolving state, instructors of introductory psychology need to reflect on the decisions made: What worked and what did not? In this process and step, it is important to solicit feedback from students (Boysen et al., 2015). This feedback may come in the form of end-of-semester student ratings of instruction or, better yet, near the beginning and middle of the semester so that student feedback can lead to real-time needed adjustments to best serve your students.

To help introductory psychology instructors, we have developed a short case study and provided a worked-example using the decision tree described here as our framework. As illustrated in Exhibit 5.2, Naeda Ushond is faced with a few dilemmas in her introductory psychology course. In Exhibit 5.3, we have walked through the six-step decision tree to illustrate how instructors of introductory psychology may go about articulating and addressing challenges that arise in teaching.

EXHIBIT 5.2. Case Study: Naeda Ushond—The Dilemma of Teaching a Large Class of Introductory Psychology in a Blended Format

Naeda Ushond teaches at a large open-enrollment public university that has been designated as a Hispanic Serving Institution. Her typical introductory psychology course (she teaches two sections each term) has 200 students and is a general education course with 95% nonpsychology majors enrolled. The majority of her students are first-generation college students, more than 40% identify as Latinx, and more than two thirds of her class identify as minorities. Because of the class size and the limited space on campus, she is only able to meet once per week in a large lecture hall, with the remaining class time spent online. She has a few undergraduate teaching assistants that help her with student emails and some "objective" grading. Naeda is a passionate and effective instructor, but she struggles with how to assess student learning meaningfully in this large class while balancing the demands of her other classes as well. Although she is confident and effective in engaging her students when face-to-face, she is frustrated by the difficulty she experiences in trying to engage her students online. In fact, students often provide feedback on their end-of-the-semester student evaluations of instruction that she is approachable, reliable, and an effective communicator in class, but when they have to work online, it seems like she is a different teacher altogether. Recently, Naeda confided with her colleagues that she thinks she may be covering too many chapters but is conflicted because she believes that covering 16 chapters is the only way to meet the student learning objectives for the course. She knows something needs to change, but she is overwhelmed and isn't sure where to start.

EXHIBIT 5.3. Worked Example of Six-Step Decision Tree for Naeda Ushond—The Dilemma of Teaching a Large Class of Introductory Psychology in a Blended Format

Problem to solve: Not effectively engaging or assessing students in the online component of the course.

Step 1: Student Learning Objective

How to: Reflect on the problem and choose a student learning outcome (SLO) that specifically addresses the problem. *For example, students (and the instructor) are bored with basic online discussion boards focusing on content from the chapters. The content feels static and not meaningful.*

Solution: I want to choose an SLO that is relevant, interesting, and conducive to discussion outside of class. For example, *Apply psychological principles to everyday life.*[a] (Given the climate during the fall 2020 semester, I chose to focus on the topic of Implicit Bias and Police Work.)

Step 2: Instructional considerations

How to: Are there any physical or administrative constraints that could interfere with my SLO? Consider how my students in my class, at my institution, may respond to this SLO.

Solution: I have a large class of 200 students and would like to avoid having to grade multiple discussion-board posts. I have a number of minoritized students in my class. Also, there are likely students who, despite being presented with psychological data, will deny that implicit bias exists in the police departments. I need to thoughtfully develop guidelines for student interactions and provide training for my undergraduate teaching assistants to respond in a caring and culturally sensitive way. At my institution, all students have access to video conferencing through our learning management system.

(continues)

EXHIBIT 5.3. Worked Example of Six-Step Decision Tree for Naeda Ushond–The Dilemma of Teaching a Large Class of Introductory Psychology in a Blended Format (*Continued*)

Step 3: Assessment

How to: How will I know if my students have demonstrated the ability to apply psychological principles to everyday life?

Solution: Scaffolded, low-stakes group discussions and assignments related to assigned readings. Teaching assistants will monitor discussion boards, and quizzes will be auto-graded.

Final group project: Students will choose to develop one of the following (groups will have to sign up for a project or propose their own to ensure a range of options and manage end of semester grading):

1. Community educational digital brochure

2. Training module for local police

3. Class presentation (recorded and posted to LMS)

4. Written assignment: A family friend asks what you are studying in your classes, and you tell them about this assignment. They respond with, "Racism in the police department is a myth." Write a response to this person that incorporates psychological science.

Step 4: Instructional methods

How to: Is there one particular method that will help me to engage my students?

Solution: Cooperative learning or problem-based learning. Both of these methods rely on students engaging with one another and can be carried out in an online environment. The topic is relevant and one about which students are likely to have opinions.

Step 5: Instructional technique

How to: Once I have chosen a method(s), which technique(s) can I use with my students to teach, engage, and assess them?

Solution: Low-stakes multiple-choice quizzes will be used to ensure students are completing the readings. Discussion-board posts will be used to encourage critical thinking and provide students with a space to post updates on their projects. I will use video-sharing educational technology for a group member to introduce their final project and direct students where to find it on the LMS. Students will provide feedback (via video-sharing) for a minimum of two projects from each category. Students must initially comment on projects that have fewer than five comments already.

Step 6: Reflect and adapt

How to: Keep notes throughout the semester about what is working and what isn't. Incorporate new ideas into notes related to each chapter or assignment. Be sure to survey students (ideally throughout the semester) to obtain feedback regarding instructional methods and strategies. Make questions specific, and provide an open-ended question for students to give specific suggestions.

Solution: Use Trello to organize thoughts and feedback regarding the online portion of the class. Develop a Qualtrics survey to gather feedback from students at midterm and at the end of the course. Update syllabus at the end of the semester to ensure ideas are retained and incorporated the following semester.

Note. LMS = learning management system. [a]This SLO was selected from a list of recommended SLOs from the American Psychological Association's Introductory Psychology Initiative (APA, 2020).

CONCLUSION

Designing an effective and engaging introductory psychology course requires an awareness of general teaching principles, course models, and situation-specific factors that can affect course outcomes. In this chapter, we have provided suggestions, guidelines, and important aspects to consider when designing an introductory psychology course. First and foremost, instructors should identify and evaluate the various instructional methods and considerations that will provide the foundation on which their course will be built. They need to recognize that teaching involves a starting point with many possible routes to a destination, while acknowledging that the constitution of each of those routes may be different. How instructors navigate the route depends on the factors specific to each one. There typically isn't one "right path," and there are many scenarios where we can lose our way. Choosing a smart car to drive through rugged terrain isn't likely to lead to positive outcomes. Likewise, choosing instructional methods and strategies that don't take into account the situation-specific, institutional considerations will likely result in an unsatisfying educational experience for the instructor and their students.

Selecting appropriate instructional methods is critical. This chapter has reviewed many of the common and evidence-based instructional methods applicable to introductory psychology and acknowledged there is no one-size-fits-all approach to teaching. Every introductory psychology course will be slightly different and have its own character. Through a case study and worked example, we modeled how an instructor might approach the course design process. By following the six steps outlined in the decision tree, instructors can organize the process of planning and executing the course and inevitably improve their teaching skills at the same time. If instructors use the principles outlined in Chapter 2 as a framework for course design, adopt the SLOs and associated assessment strategies presented in Chapters 3 and 4, and integrate the evidence-based recommendations for choosing instructional methods in this chapter, the stage will be set for students to experience a coherent, engaging, and inclusive course that showcases all that introductory psychology has to offer.

REFERENCES

Afful, S. E., Good, J. J., Keeley, J., Leder, S., & Stiegler-Balfour, J. J. (2013). *Introductory Psychology teaching primer: A guide for new teachers of Psych 101*. Society for the Teaching of Psychology. http://teachpsych.org/ebooks/intro2013/index.php

Alammary, A. (2019). Blended learning models for introductory programming courses: A systematic review. *PLOS ONE, 14*(9), e0221765. https://doi.org/10.1371/journal.pone.0221765

Albright, D. L., Fletcher, K. L., Pelts, M. D., & Taliaferro, L. (2017). Use of college mental health services among student veterans. *Best Practices in Mental Health*, *13*(1), 66–80.

American Psychological Association. (n.d.). Project assessment (PASS). http://pass.apa.org/

American Psychological Association. (2013). *APA guidelines for the undergraduate psychology major: Version 2.0.* https://www.apa.org/ed/precollege/about/psymajor-guidelines.pdf

American Psychological Association. (2020). *The APA Introductory Psychology Initiative.* https://www.apa.org/ed/precollege/undergrad/introductory-psychology-initiative

Benedict, J. O., & Anderton, J. B. (2004). Applying Just-in-Time Teaching approach to teaching statistics. *Teaching of Psychology*, *31*(3), 197–199.

Bensley, D. A., Crowe, D. S., Bernhardt, P., Buckner, C., & Allman, A. L. (2010). Teaching and assessing critical thinking skills for argument analysis in psychology. *Teaching of Psychology*, *37*(2), 91–96. https://doi.org/10.1080/00986281003626656

Bleske-Rechek, A. L. (2001). Obedience, conformity, and social roles: Active learning in a large introductory psychology class. *Teaching of Psychology*, *28*(4), 260–262. https://doi.org/10.1207/S15328023TOP2804_05

Boysen, G. A., Richmond, A. S., & Gurung, R. A. R. (2015). Model teaching criteria for psychology: Initial documentation of teachers' self-reported competency. *Scholarship of Teaching and Learning in Psychology*, *1*(1), 48–59. https://doi.org/10.1037/stl0000023

Brooks, D. C. (2019). Active learning classrooms (ALCs). In S. Yu, H. Niemi, & J. Mason (Eds.), *Shaping future schools with digital technology: Perspectives on rethinking and reforming education* (pp. 41–56). Springer. https://doi.org/10.1007/978-981-13-9439-3_3

Brothen, T. (1991). Implementing a computer-assisted cooperative learning model for introductory psychology. *Teaching of Psychology*, *18*(3), 183–185. https://doi.org/10.1207/s15328023top1803_18

Bruff, D. [@derekbruff]. (2020, April 3). *"Pivotable" course design . . . planning an on-campus course that can be moved fully online on short notice* [Tweet]. Twitter. https://twitter.com/derekbruff/status/1246120740027543552

Butler, A., Phillmann, K. B., & Smart, L. (2001). Active learning within a lecture: Assessing the impact of short, in-class writing exercises. *Teaching of Psychology*, *28*(4), 257–259. https://doi.org/10.1207/S15328023TOP2804_04

Cate, C. A., & Davis, T. (2016). Student veteran demographics: Select results from Student Veterans of America. *SVA Spotlight*, *2*(1), 1–7.

Cate, C. A., Lyon, J. S., Schmeling, J., & Bogue, B. Y. (2017). *National veteran education success tracker: A report on the academic success of student veterans using the Post-9/11 GI Bill.* Student Veterans of America.

Chiu, P. H. P., & Cheng, S. H. (2017). Effects of active learning classrooms on student learning: A two-year empirical investigation on student perceptions and academic performance. *Higher Education Research & Development*, *36*(2), 269–279. https://doi.org/10.1080/07294360.2016.1196475

Deichert, N. T., Maxwell, S. J., & Klotz, J. (2016). Retention of information taught in introductory psychology courses across different accelerated course formats. *Teaching of Psychology*, *43*(1), 4–9. https://doi.org/10.1177/0098628315619725

Dunn, D. S., & Halonen, J. S. (2017). *The psychology major companion: Everything you need to know to get where you want to go.* Worth.

Eiland, L. S., & Todd, T. J. (2019). Considerations when incorporating technology into classroom and experiential teaching. *The Journal of Pediatric Pharmacology and Therapeutics, 24*(4), 270–275. https://doi.org/10.5863/1551-6776-24.4.270

Espinosa, L. L., Turk, J. M., & Taylor, M. (2017). *Pulling back the curtain: Enrollment and outcomes at minority serving institutions.* https://vtechworks.lib.vt.edu/bitstream/handle/10919/83978/PullingBackCurtain.pdf?sequence=1&isAllowed=y

Espinosa, L. L., Turk, J. M., Taylor, M., & Chessman, H. M. (2019). *Race and ethnicity in higher education: A status report.* https://vtechworks.lib.vt.edu/bitstream/handle/10919/89187/RaceEthnicityHighEducation.pdf?sequence=1&isAllowed=y

Evans, S. M. (2017). Personalities of introductory course instructors and course completion: A correlational study. *Journal of College Student Retention, 22*(1), 2–16. https://doi.org/10.1177/1521025117720389

Eyler, J. [@joshua_r_eyler]. (2020, June 8). *I have been poring over the possibilities for effective pedagogical models and course design approaches for the fall. There is only* [Tweet]. Twitter. https://twitter.com/joshua_r_eyler/status/1270049889678999552

Forbes, F. M., Whisenhunt, B. L., Citterio, C., Jordan, A. K., Robinson, D., & Deal, W. P. (2019). Making mental health a priority on college campuses: Implementing large scale screening and follow-up in a high enrollment gateway course. *Journal of American College Health*, 1–8. https://doi.org/10.1080/07448481.2019.1665051

Fortney, J. C., Curran, G. M., Hunt, J. B., Cheney, A. M., Lu, L., Valenstein, M., & Eisenberg, D. (2016). Prevalence of probable mental disorders and help-seeking behaviors among veteran and non-veteran community college students. *General Hospital Psychiatry, 38*, 99–104. https://doi.org/10.1016/j.genhosppsych.2015.09.007

Gaab, J., Rohleder, N., Nater, U. M., & Ehlert, U. (2005). Psychological determinants of the cortisol stress response: The role of anticipatory cognitive appraisal. *Psychoneuroendocrinology, 30*(6), 599–610. https://doi.org/10.1016/j.psyneuen.2005.02.001

Garratt-Reed, D., Roberts, L. D., & Heritage, B. (2016). Grades, student satisfaction and retention in online and face-to-face introductory psychology units: A test of equivalency theory. *Frontiers in Psychology, 7*, 673. Advance online publication. https://doi.org/10.3389/fpsyg.2016.00673

Gibson, J. J. (2015). *The ecological approach to visual perception.* Psychology Press.

Giordano, P. J., & Hammer, E. Y. (1999). In-class collaborative learning: Practical suggestions from the teaching trenches. *Teaching of Psychology, 26*(1), 42–44. https://doi.org/10.1207/s15328023top2601_9

Gose, M. (2009). When Socratic dialogue is flagging: Questions and strategies for engaging students. *College Teaching, 57*(1), 45–50. https://doi.org/10.3200/CTCH.57.1.45-50

Griggs, R. A., & Jackson, S. L. (2011). *Teaching introductory psychology: Tips from ToP.* Society for the Teaching of Psychology. http://teachpsych.org/ebooks/tips2011/index.php

Grossbard, J. R., Widome, R., Lust, K., Simpson, T. L., Lostutter, T. W., & Saxon, A. (2014). High-risk drinking and academic performance among college student veterans. *Journal of Alcohol and Drug Education, 58*(3), 28–47.

Gurung, R. A. R., Hackathorn, J., Enns, C., Frantz, S., Cacioppo, J. T., Loop, T., & Freeman, J. E. (2016). Strengthening introductory psychology: A new model for teaching the introductory course. *American Psychologist, 71*(2), 112–124. https://doi.org/10.1037/a0040012

Hard, B. M., Lovett, J. M., & Brady, S. T. (2019). What do students remember about introductory psychology, years later? *Scholarship of Teaching and Learning in Psychology, 5*(1), 61–74. https://doi.org/10.1037/stl0000136

Hodges, C., Moore, S., Lockee, B., Trust, T., & Bond, A. (2020). The difference between emergency remote teaching and online learning. *EDUCAUSE Review, 27,* 1–12.

Hudson, D. L. (2021). Evidence-based teaching and course design: Using data to develop, implement, and refine university courses. In S. A. Nolan, C. M. Hakala, & R. E. Landrum (Eds.), *Assessing undergraduate learning in psychology: Strategies for measuring and improving student performance* (pp. 127–139). American Psychological Association. https://doi.org/10.1037/0000183-010

Hudson, D. L., Whisenhunt, B. L., Shoptaugh, C. F., Rost, A. D., & Fondren-Happel, R. N. (2014). Redesigning a large enrollment course: The impact on academic performance, course completion and student perceptions in introductory psychology. *Psychology Learning & Teaching, 13*(2), 107–119. https://doi.org/10.2304/plat.2014.13.2.107

Hudson, D. L., Whisenhunt, B. L., Shoptaugh, C. F., Visio, M. E., Cathey, C., & Rost, A. D. (2015). Change takes time: Understanding and responding to culture change in course redesign. *Scholarship of Teaching and Learning in Psychology, 1*(4), 255–268. https://doi.org/10.1037/stl0000043

Hyun, J., Ediger, R., & Lee, D. (2017). Students' satisfaction on their learning process in active learning and traditional classrooms. *International Journal on Teaching and Learning in Higher Education, 29*(1), 108–118.

Kreiner, D. S. (2009). Problem-based activities for a sensation & perception course. *Teaching of Psychology, 36*(4), 253–256. https://doi.org/10.1080/00986280903173157

Kretchmar, M. D. (2001). Service learning in a general psychology class: Description, preliminary evaluation, and recommendations. *Teaching of Psychology, 28*(1), 5–10. https://doi.org/10.1207/S15328023TOP2801_02

Lawson, T. J., & Brown, M. (2018). Using pseudoscience to improve introductory psychology students' information literacy. *Teaching of Psychology, 45*(3), 220–225. https://doi.org/10.1177/0098628318779259

Leder-Elder, S., Good, J. J., Afful, S., Keely, J., & Stiegler-Balfour, J. J. (2015). *Introductory psychology primer: A guide for new teachers of psych 101.* (2nd ed.). Society for the Teaching of Psychology. http://teachpsych.org/Resources/Documents/ebooks/STPIntroPsychPrimer2.pdf

Mui, M. L. S., Carpio, G. A. C., & Ong, C. M. (2019). Evaluation of engagement in learning within active learning classrooms: Does novelty make a difference? *Journal of Learning Spaces, 8*(2). http://libjournal.uncg.edu/jls/article/view/1791

Muir, G. M., & van der Linden, G. J. (2009). Students teaching students: An experiential learning opportunity for large introductory psychology classes in collaboration with local elementary schools. *Teaching of Psychology, 36*(3), 169–173. https://doi.org/10.1080/00986280902960018

Newcomb, A. F., & Bagwell, C. L. (1997). Collaborative learning in an introduction to psychological science laboratory: Undergraduate teaching fellows teach to learn. *Teaching of Psychology, 24*(2), 88–95. https://doi.org/10.1207/ s15328023top2402_2

Nichols, S., & Stahl, G. (2019). Intersectionality in higher education research: A systematic literature review. *Higher Education Research & Development, 38*(6), 1255–1268. https://doi.org/10.1080/07294360.2019.1638348

Nicol, A. A., Owens, S. M., Le Coze, S. S., MacIntyre, A., & Eastwood, C. (2018). Comparison of high-technology active learning and low-technology active learning classrooms. *Active Learning in Higher Education, 19*(3), 253–265. https://doi.org/ 10.1177/1469787417731176

Nikolaus, C. J., An, R., Ellison, B., & Nickols-Richardson, S. M. (2020). Food insecurity among college students in the United States: A scoping review. *Advances in Nutrition, 11*(2), 327–348. https://doi.org/10.1093/advances/nmz111

Norcross, J. C., Hailstorks, R., Aiken, L. S., Pfund, R. A., Stamm, K. E., & Christidis, P. (2016). Undergraduate study in psychology: Curriculum and assessment. *American Psychologist, 71*(2), 89–101. https://doi.org/10.1037/a0040095

Oyserman, D., & Lewis, N. A., Jr. (2017). Seeing the destination AND the path: Using identity-based motivation to understand and reduce racial disparities in academic achievement. *Social Issues and Policy Review, 11*(1), 159–194. https://doi.org/ 10.1111/sipr.12030

Peterson, J. J., & Sesma, A., Jr. (2017). Introductory psychology: What's lab got to do with it? *Teaching of Psychology, 44*(4), 313–323. https://doi.org/10.1177/ 0098628317727643

Richmond, A. S. (2017, February 22). Scratch and win or scratch and lose? Immediate feedback assessment technique. *Improve with Metacognition.* http://www. improvewithmetacognition.com/scratch-win-scratch-lose-immediate-feedback-assessment-technique/

Richmond, A. S., Bacca, A. M., Becknell, J. S., & Coyle, R. P. (2017). Teaching metacognition experientially: A focus on higher versus lower level learning. *Teaching of Psychology, 44*(4), 298–305. https://doi.org/10.1177/0098628317727633

Richmond, A. S., Boysen, G. A., Hudson, D. L., Gurung, R. A. R., Naufel, K. Z., Neufeld, G., Landrum, R. E., Dunn, D. S., & Beers, M. (2021). The Introductory Psychology Census: A national study. *Scholarship of Teaching and Learning in Psychology.* Advance online publication. https://doi.org/10.1037/stl0000277

Richmond, A. S., Fleck, B., Heath, T., Broussard, K. A., & Skarda, B. (2015). Can inquiry-based instruction promote higher-level learning? *Scholarship of Teaching and Learning in Psychology, 1*(3), 208–218. https://doi.org/10.1037/ stl0000032

Richmond, A. S., Gurung, R. A. R., & Boysen, G. (2016). *An evidence-based guide to college and university teaching: Developing the model teacher.* Routledge. https:// doi.org/10.4324/9781315642529

Richmond, A. S., & Hagan, L. K. (2011). Promoting higher level thinking in psychology: Is active learning the answer? *Teaching of Psychology, 38*(2), 102–105. https://doi.org/10.1177/0098628311401581

Sansone, D. (2019). LGBT students: New evidence on demographics and educational outcomes. *Economics of Education Review, 73,* 101933. Advance online publication. https://doi.org/10.1016/j.econedurev.2019.101933

Saville, B. K., Bureau, A., Eckenrode, C., Fullerton, A., Herbert, R., Maley, M., Porter, A., & Zombakis, J. (2014). Interteaching and lecture: A comparison of long-term recognition memory. *Teaching of Psychology, 41*(4), 325–329. https://doi.org/10.1177/0098628314549704

Saville, B. K., Zinn, T. E., & Elliott, M. P. (2005). Interteaching versus traditional methods of instruction: A preliminary analysis. *Teaching of Psychology, 32*(3), 161–163. https://doi.org/10.1207/s15328023top3203_6

Sawyer, J., & Obeid, R. (2017). Cooperative and collaborative learning: Getting the best of both words. In R. Obeid, A. Schartz, C. Shane-Simpson, & P. J. Brooks (Eds.), *How we teach now: The GSTA guide to student-centered teaching.* Society for the Teaching of Psychology. https://teachpsych.org/ebooks/howweteachnow

Sheldon, J. P. (2000). A neuroanatomy teaching activity using case studies and collaboration. *Teaching of Psychology, 27*, 126–128.

Shields, C., & Gredler, M. (2003). A problem-solving approach to teaching operant conditioning. *Teaching of Psychology, 30*(2), 114–116. https://doi.org/10.1207/S15328023TOP3002_06

Silva, M. R., Kleinert, W. L., Sheppard, A. V., Cantrell, K. A., Freeman-Coppadge, D. J., Tsoy, E., Roberts, T., & Pearrow, M. (2017). The relationship between food security, housing stability, and school performance among college students in an urban university. *Journal of College Student Retention, 19*(3), 284–299. https://doi.org/10.1177/1521025115621918

Slavich, G. M., & Zimbardo, P. G. (2012). Transformational teaching: Theoretical underpinnings, basic principles, and core methods. *Educational Psychology Review, 24*(4), 569–608. https://doi.org/10.1007/s10648-012-9199-6

Sternberg, R. J. (1998). The dialectic as a tool for teaching psychology. *Teaching of Psychology, 25*(3), 177–180. https://doi.org/10.1207/s15328023top2503_2

Stewart, D. L. (2013). Racially minoritized students at US four-year institutions. *The Journal of Negro Education, 82*(2), 184–197. https://doi.org/10.7709/jnegroeducation.82.2.0184

Thieman, T. J., Clary, E. G., Olson, A. M., Dauner, R. C., & Ring, E. E. (2009). Introducing students to psychological research: General psychology as a laboratory course. *Teaching of Psychology, 36*(3), 160–168. https://doi.org/10.1080/00986280902959994

Vo, H. M., Zhu, C., & Diep, N. A. (2017). The effect of blended learning on student performance at course-level in higher education: A meta-analysis. *Studies in Educational Evaluation, 53*, 17–28. https://doi.org/10.1016/j.stueduc.2017.01.002

Walker, J. D., & Baepler, P. (2017). Measuring social relations in new classroom spaces: Development and validation of the social context and learning environments (SCALE) survey. *Journal of Learning Spaces, 6*(3), 34–41.

Warren, C. S. (2006). Incorporating multiculturalism into undergraduate psychology courses: Three simple active learning activities. *Teaching of Psychology, 33*(2), 105–109. https://doi.org/10.1207/s15328023top3302_5

Weaver, R. R., Vaughn, N. A., Hendricks, S. P., McPherson-Myers, P. E., Jia, Q., Willis, S. L., & Rescigno, K. P. (2020). University student food insecurity and academic performance. *Journal of American College Health, 68*(7), 727–733. https://doi.org/10.1080/07448481.2019.1600522

Whisenhunt, B. L., Cathey, C., Visio, M. E., Hudson, D. L., Shoptaugh, C. F., & Rost, A. D. (2019). Strategies to address challenges with large classes: Can we exceed student expectations for large class experiences? *Scholarship of Teaching and Learning in Psychology, 5*(2), 121–127. https://doi.org/10.1037/stl0000135

Wiggins, G. P., & McTighe, J. (2005). *Understanding by design* (2nd ed.). Association for Supervision and Curriculum Development.

Young, K. E., Young, C. H., & Beyer, A. (2017). Does the classroom matter? How the physical space affects learning in introductory undergraduate science courses. *Journal of College Science Teaching, 46*(6), 80–87. https://doi.org/10.2505/4/jcst17_046_06_80

Zayac, R. M., Ratkos, T., Frieder, J. E., & Paulk, A. (2016). A comparison of active student responding modalities in a general psychology course. *Teaching of Psychology, 43*(1), 43–47. https://doi.org/10.1177/0098628315620879

6

THE SUCCESSFUL PSYCHOLOGY COURSE

Transformative Skills in Introductory Psychology

STEPHEN L. CHEW, GUY A. BOYSEN, KAREN Z. NAUFEL, KATHERINE WICKES, AND JERRY RUDMANN

KEY RECOMMENDATIONS

1. Emphasize the ways that students can improve their study skills by applying psychology concepts.

2. Design introductory psychology so that it models the use of effective study techniques for students and makes a clear connection between the course design and psychological principles.

3. Emphasize the ways students can improve their health and wellness by applying psychology concepts.

4. Use introductory psychology as a developmental step in fostering students' cultural competency.

5. Emphasize the ways that students can overcome popular misconceptions and inaccuracies about psychology.

(continues)

https://doi.org/10.1037/0000260-007
Transforming Introductory Psychology: Expert Advice on Teacher Training, Course Design, and Student Success, R. A. R. Gurung and G. Neufeld (Editors)

KEY RECOMMENDATIONS (*Continued*)

6. Embed workplace-relevant examples in course design and delivery.

7. Point out to colleagues the value of introductory psychology in promoting and sustaining the academic success of many students.

Because of its immense popularity and placement in undergraduate curricula, introductory psychology is positioned to be a transformational experience for the majority of students. Sixty percent of all students who earn 10 or more college credits complete introductory psychology (Adelman, 2006). Furthermore, students likely complete the course during their first year, often in their first semester of college, which allows it to influence the rest of their academic career.

wow!

Introductory psychology is well suited for this transformative role because it can equip students with knowledge and skills to help them succeed academically, prosper in their careers, and thrive personally. In this chapter, we first discuss the knowledge and skills learned in introductory psychology that can help students succeed academically. We focus on effective study skills, self-regulation, and self-efficacy. Next, we discuss life skills that introductory psychology students can learn, such as healthy behaviors, ethics, and cultural competency, that will help them grow personally and be more successful. Finally, we discuss how introductory psychology can start to prepare students for career success. We summarized our key recommendations for teaching transformative skills in introductory psychology at the start of the chapter.

INTRODUCTORY PSYCHOLOGY TRANSFORMS STUDENTS ACADEMICALLY

Study Skills

Introductory psychology provides a unique opportunity to transform academic skills by having students learn how to learn (see also Chapter 2). The science of learning and memory is a core component of introductory psychology covered by virtually all instructors (Richmond et al., 2021) that should lead to a basic understanding of information processing and memory storage. Students may generalize this content to their academic lives on their own, but intentional integration of study skills content into the course increases the chance of transforming students academically.

Surveys indicate that although students report using some effective study techniques, they also use some ineffective techniques due to mistaken belief in their usefulness (Blasiman et al., 2017; Gurung, 2005; Hartwig & Dunlosky, 2012; Karpicke et al., 2009; Kornell & Bjork, 2007; McCabe, 2011; Morehead et al., 2016; Wissman et al., 2012). For example, rereading material, although not very effective, is students' most-used study technique (Blasiman et al., 2017), and students tend to cram their studying in near deadlines rather than using distributed practice (Kornell & Bjork, 2007). Studies also document the near universality of multitasking. Students listen to music, text, and use social media most of the time while studying (David et al., 2015). In fact, in one study of students' preparation for an introductory psychology test, they used an average of 4.88 different electronic devices during 2 hours of studying (Patterson, 2017). In general, there is ample room for college students to make psychology-informed improvements to their study skills.

Cognitive science has established the practices that increase students' learning in the laboratory and in the classroom (e.g., Agarwal & Bain, 2019; Benassi et al., 2014; Bjork et al., 2013; Brown et al., 2014; Dunlosky et al., 2013; Miyatsu et al., 2018; Putnam et al., 2016). Techniques such as spaced practice, self-testing, interleaving, elaborative processing, and mnemonics are academic tools that every teacher and student should understand and be able to implement. Cognitive science has also documented the detrimental effects of attempting to learn with divided attention. Both attention and working memory have limited capacities, and switching attention between tasks has significant costs on efficiency (Monsell, 2003). Multitasking reliably harms performance in the lab and the classroom (Bellur et al., 2015; Burak, 2012; Carrier et al., 2015; Gingerich & Lineweaver, 2014). Attention and working memory, along with their limitations, are all standard content for introductory psychology. Learning about them should be more than just memorizing concepts; it should empower students to make effective choices about what to do and what not to do when attempting to learn new material in academic settings and beyond.

Standard introductory psychology content provides students with information about effective study strategies, but research indicates that students need help implementing that knowledge. The majority of introductory psychology instructors cover study skills such as distributed practice, testing, and elaborative rehearsal (Richmond et al., 2021). However, the most frequently used teaching technique is to lecture on the skills, which might not be effective. Despite college teachers' assertions that they frequently provide study skills instruction, relatively few students report that they base their studying on teachers' instructions (Kornell & Bjork, 2007; Morehead et al., 2016). Furthermore, even when students understand the most effective learning techniques, they may use ineffective strategies out of habit, poor planning, or because they are usually less effort than effective ones. Research has documented the disconnect between the type of studying students know to be effective for learning, their predictions of how they will study in the future, and their actual study practices (Blasiman et al., 2017; Hartwig & Dunlosky, 2012; Kornell & Bjork, 2007; Susser & McCabe, 2013). For example, cramming works in the short term, and students may rely on it even if they know that distributed practice is beneficial in the long term. Similarly, when asked to assess the effects of multitasking, students recognize that it impairs learning, but they continue to multitask while studying (David et al., 2015; Gingerich & Lineweaver, 2014). Considering the disconnect between students' knowledge and their study practices, teachers of introductory psychology must do more than cover attention, learning, and memory to be transformational. They must model practices such as spacing, retrieval practice, and interleaving; show students how to employ effective study skills; and persuade them of the importance of using them.

To foster student transformation, introductory psychology instructors should follow some best practices in course design and delivery (Agarwal & Bain, 2019; Weinstein et al., 2019). The course should include explicit instruction on study skills (Chew, 2014). Rather than assuming students connect course topics such as attention and memory to their academic behaviors, teachers should explicitly point out the connection. Students should learn study skills early in the semester. Some introductory psychology textbooks include study skills in the first chapter, and teachers should take advantage of this placement to conduct an early study-skills intervention. Furthermore, coverage of core topics such as attention and memory in later chapters provides an opportunity to reemphasize study skills.

In addition to course content, course design should require students to use effective study techniques, and teachers should explain the connection between the course design and psychological principles to students in class and the syllabus. Course designs based on teaching effective study skills might include active learning inside and outside of class (deep processing), frequent evaluations (testing effect), and cumulative evaluations (distributed practice, interleaving). Instructors might also avoid design features that reinforce poor study skills. For example, course designs with few tests (massed practice), recognition testing only (shallow processing), and delivery of all content via passive lecture do not reinforce effective study techniques. To help instructors teach study skills in an explicit, active way, Appendix C of this volume provides a study skills module. The module includes a lesson plan, presentation slides, activities, resources, and assessments. The module can be taught separately or as part of the memory chapter.

Self-Regulation

Self-regulation is a broad concept that refers to a person's taking purposeful actions to make progress toward a desired goal or standard (Baumeister, 2020; Carver & Scheier, 2011). Psychologists have studied three types of self-regulation: self-regulation of learning, behavior, and emotion. All three are linked to successful coping and achievement (Vohs & Baumeister, 2011), and all three can be incorporated into introductory psychology. For example, students with better self-regulation of learning show better academic achievement. At the same time, few students develop effective self-regulation on their own and many students benefit from interventions to develop self-regulation (Zumbrunn et al., 2011).

Self-regulation of behavior involves modifying a particular behavior to become more adaptive. In other words, it is behavior modification through learning. When teaching learning, teachers can use self-regulation of behavior as an application of the principles of learning that is directly relevant to students. When teaching operant conditioning, teachers can describe ways to use positive reinforcement to increase desired study behaviors. A number of techniques exist that make an enjoyable but counterproductive activity contingent on first performing a productive but less enjoyable activity. For example, say a student received a poor exam grade and wants to improve their score on the next exam. The student could identify certain desirable study behaviors and use operant conditioning to increase those behaviors. The student might choose to attend class more frequently. The student could set up a contingency so that if they attended class for six consecutive meetings, they would treat themselves to a special treat of some kind.

The Center for Academic Success (2015) at Louisiana State University developed a self-regulation technique for improving study behavior that they called Focused Study Sessions (FSS). The Office of Academic and Learning Resources (n.d.) at Rhodes College has elaborated on the FSS to give students more concrete suggestions about how to implement them (https://sites.rhodes.edu/academic-and-learning-resources/learning-tips/study-cycle-focused-study-sessions). In an FSS, students first set a study goal for

Just the pomodoro method?

the session, such as reading a section of the textbook. Next, the students study without interruption or distraction for a specified period of time, say 30 minutes. Once they have accomplished that, they are allowed a brief break of about 5 to 10 minutes. After the break, they review or recap what they studied. Students can then start a new FSS. The FSS makes taking a break contingent upon accomplishing the study goal with full focus, as opposed to studying with distractions present. Focused Study Sessions also have the advantage of spacing out learning which increases retention. An FSS is flexible and adaptable. Students trying FSS for the first time can start with shorter study sessions, such as 10 minutes, and work their way up to longer sessions, which is an example of shaping.

Self-regulation of learning focuses specifically on improving learning strategies as opposed to more general behaviors that support learning, like going to class. Baumeister (2020) has written a brief overview of self-regulation of learning for teachers. There are three components. First, there must be a standard or goal that a person wants to achieve, such as learning assigned material to such a degree that they will do well on an exam. Students must plan strategies to meet this goal. For example, Chen et al. (2017) described an effective student intervention that helps students identify learning resources and how best to use them in their courses. The second component is monitoring. A person must accurately monitor their progress toward the desired standard. This awareness of one's own learning is an example of metacognition.

Accurate metacognitive awareness is important for learning (McCabe, 2011; Susser & McCabe, 2013). Students must evaluate whether their current study strategies are helping them learn effectively. The final step involves assessing progress toward the desired goal. If students have not yet reached their goal, then the process is repeated with any needed modifications. For example, if the learning strategies are deemed sufficiently effective, then those strategies are retained. If they are deemed ineffective or inefficient, then the student makes changes that might improve learning. Students must have the ability and resources to adjust their behavior if they are not making adequate progress toward the standard. A substantial body of research supports the value of self-regulated learning (Pintrich, 2004; Zimmerman, 1990; Zumbrunn et al., 2011). There are multiple models and strategies for teaching students how to practice self-regulation of learning (Lapan et al., 2002; Zumbrunn et al., 2011).

Self-regulation of emotion involves maintaining a functional level of emotional responsiveness in the face of emotion-provoking events. Self-regulation helps a person cope with extremes of emotion that can interfere with effective thought and behavior (McRae & Gross, 2020). This topic can easily fit into a discussion of emotions in introductory psychology. Teaching students how to cope with extreme emotions and anxiety has obvious benefits for both learning and physical and mental health (Gross, 2013).

Consistent with other forms of self-regulation, people must set a goal for emotion regulation, they must have strategies for regulating their emotion, and they must be able to assess their success in accomplishing their goal. A person first identifies a discrepancy between their current emotional state and the desired state as a situation where emotion regulation is needed (Gross, 2013; McRae & Gross, 2020). The person then selects and employs emotion regulation strategies. Then they evaluate whether their strategies have been successful. Depending on that evaluation, the cycle may repeat, end, or be repeated with different emotion regulation strategies. Learning about emotion regulation is directly relevant to students. Say a student receives a lot of critical feedback on a draft of a major research paper for a class, and they become angry and upset. They realize that anger will not help them revise the paper for a good grade, and thus they set a goal to calm down and focus on using the comments, unpleasant though they may be, to revise the paper. The student may calm themselves down by emotion regulation strategies, such as distracting themselves for a while or by exercising. They may also reappraise the feedback as not being personally critical but as the professor's attempt to help the student improve their writing. The student then returns to the comments to see if they can accept them and use them constructively. If not, the cycle is repeated, perhaps with different strategies, until emotion regulation is achieved.

One emotion regulation strategy that is directly relevant to students is cognitive reappraisal. In reappraisal, people reconsider what is normally considered a negative emotion as a resource for helping to improve performance (McRae & Gross, 2020). Extreme test anxiety is an obstacle to optimal exam performance. In cognitive reappraisal, students are prompted to think of anxiety as a means of helping them do their best on exams. Brady et al. (2018) used a simple cognitive reappraisal intervention to reduce test anxiety in first-year college students in introductory psychology. The day before the first exam, students received an email message that contained either a cognitive reappraisal message or a control message of encouragement. Here is an excerpt from the cognitive reappraisal message:

> People think that feeling anxious while taking a test will make them do poorly on the test. However, recent research suggests that arousal doesn't generally hurt performance on tests and can even help performance. People who feel anxious during a test might actually do better. This means that you shouldn't

feel concerned if you do feel anxious while studying for or taking tomorrow's exam. If you find yourself feeling anxious, simply remind yourself that your arousal could be helping you do well. (p. 6)

The first-year students who received the reappraisal message showed significantly reduced worry and higher exam scores than students who received the control message. Teaching students how to use cognitive reappraisal to regulate their anxiety is another example of a skill that can be taught in introductory psychology that has important applications in students' lives.

Academic Self-Efficacy

Self-efficacy, first described by Bandura in 1977, refers to a person's beliefs about having the ability to perform the tasks needed to acquire a valued goal (Bandura, 1977; Maddux & Kleiman, 2019). It is independent of skill. Academic self-efficacy involves a person's beliefs about having the ability to complete educational challenges successfully. It is strongly related to academic achievement (Pajares, 1996; Schunk, 1990, 1991). Students may have differing levels of self-efficacy within specific academic subjects, such as writing and math. Still, overall academic self-efficacy is a useful level of analysis. Students high in overall academic self-efficacy participate in class more readily, work harder, persist longer in the face of challenging work, and are more emotionally resilient when they encounter setbacks. They are more likely to take on challenging tasks and put more effort into their work (Usher & Pajares, 2008; Zimmerman, 2000).

A personal example illustrates the properties and impact of academic self-efficacy. Several years ago, one of the authors was assisting the dean of student affairs at a community college. The dean was struggling to identify measurable student learning outcomes for students served by her staff. After thinking about it for several days, the dean exclaimed, "I don't know whether you can measure it, but the bottom line is we give students the confidence needed to persist and succeed." The dean went on to describe a young student, "Maria," who had arrived at the college as a single mom on public assistance with a poor academic record from high school. Maria had placed into developmental math and writing courses and had not thought about a major. At her graduation several years later, Maria was honored as the class valedictorian. During her graduation speech, Maria, in tears, thanked the college, her teachers, and especially the support service staff who had "given her the confidence she needed."

For teachers of introductory psychology, Maria's story is about a student who developed the academic self-efficacy needed to meet the challenges and setbacks faced when navigating through college. A motivational construct such as self-efficacy can be helpful for understanding and predicting academic success (Rudmann et al., 2008). Among general samples of college students, academic self-efficacy predicts outcomes such as adaptation to college, GPA, and graduation (Chemers et al., 2001; Larsen et al., 2015; Richardson et al., 2012). Academic self-efficacy is relevant to introductory psychology because it predicts course performance (Burlison et al., 2009; Jackson, 2002). Jackson (2002) found that sending an efficacy-enhancing communication to a randomly selected set of introductory psychology students significantly increased their efficacy beliefs and led to a small but significant increase in exam scores.

Teachers should work to increase academic self-efficacy in introductory psychology. Bandura specified five influences that contribute to the development of general self-efficacy (Bandura, 1977; Maddux & Kleiman, 2019; Zimmerman, 2002). The leading contributor is mastery experiences. Self-efficacy increases when a student succeeds and does well on a task leading to eventual mastery of a valued goal. Vicarious performances increase self-efficacy when a student witnesses another student similar to themself succeed at the task. Other, less influential sources of efficacy include verbal persuasion by others, imagined performance success, and positive affect states and physical sensations linked to task success (Korgan et al., 2013; Margolis & McCabe, 2006).

Within the academic context, verbal persuasion by both peers and teachers can have powerful, enduring effects. Verbal messages from teachers are especially powerful, for better and for worse. Affirming messages can have positive effects on academic self-efficacy beyond a particular class, especially when coupled with mastery experiences. Negative messages from teachers can likewise have long-term adverse effects. For example, reinforcement of negative stereotypes, like the belief that women are not good at math, can result in lowered academic self-efficacy. Introductory psychology teachers should keep academic self-efficacy in mind when designing pedagogy. Margolis and McCabe (2006) made the following recommendations for building academic self-efficacy:

- Try to make assignments moderately challenging for students.
- Teach students effective learning strategies.
- Stress student control and autonomy in how they approach assignments.
- Reinforce student effort and not just outcomes.
- Give frequent, constructive, task-specific feedback to students.
- Emphasize student successes achieved through their effort.

Teachers who implement these suggestions are likely to increase both student learning and self-efficacy.

INTRODUCTORY PSYCHOLOGY TRANSFORMS STUDENTS PERSONALLY

Health and Wellness

Introductory psychology has the potential to transform students' physical and psychological health through coverage of topics such as sleep, stress, mental disorders, psychotherapy, and drugs. Perhaps more than any other course content, students will be able to connect health-related topics to their everyday lives. One example is sleep. The level of sleep deprivation among college students reflects a widespread disregard for this basic human need (Lund et al., 2010). Introductory psychology is a unique opportunity in the undergraduate curriculum for students to learn about the sleep cycle, sleep hygiene, and the effects of sleep deprivation. Coverage of sleep can include standard reading and writing assignments (Marek et al., 2005), but experiential learning may be more impactful. In one study, students receiving an assignment to sleep 8 hours a night showed significantly increased sleep and test scores (Scullin, 2019). Thus, convincing introductory psychology students to get a full night's sleep could transform both their health and their academic performance.

Sleep disturbance often coincides with stress, and college students consider themselves to be highly stressed (American College Health Association, 2019). Introductory psychology is an opportunity for them to learn basic facts about stress and effective coping methods. Students can complete the College Student Stress Scale to get a sense of the positive and negative events that impact their stress levels (Renner & Mackin, 1998). Although many students will have major stress-related events in their life, most will be happy to learn that the stress they feel is a normal human response that is not harmful to physical or psychological health unless it is extreme or chronic. For students looking to reduce stress, introductory psychology can also offer helpful information about the positive effects of factors such as social engagement, exercise, positive thinking, relaxation, and meditation.

Many students enroll in psychology excited to learn about mental illness, and doing so can be transformative in several ways. Rates of mental illness are high among college students, and it is a significant predictor of college attrition (Auerbach et al., 2016). Also, virtually all students know a person with a mental illness, and the person is often a member of their own family

(Connor-Greene, 2001). Thus, introductory psychology may represent students' first opportunity to learn about the scientific approaches to describing and explaining the mental health problems they encounter in themselves and others. Such knowledge can open people up to seeking help. Courses about mental illness lead students to show increased willingness to seek psychotherapy (Curtin et al., 2004; Kendra et al., 2012), and introductory psychology could have the same effect.

Introductory psychology lessons about psychotherapy should increase students' perceptions of mental health treatment as legitimate and effective. The course can cover numerous psychotherapeutic approaches to the treatment of mental disorders. Many students come to introductory psychology with misconceptions about what psychotherapy entails, and the course provides them with a more accurate picture (McCarthy & Frantz, 2016). The course is an opportunity for instructors to introduce students to the modern, empirically supported methods of psychotherapy, which has little resemblance to portrayals on movies and television. Lessons about psychotherapy can include engaging demonstrations of techniques such as systematic desensitization (Lawson & Reardon, 1997; Sprecher & Worthington, 1982) and the instruction of counseling microskills that students can implement in nontherapeutic settings (Hughes et al., 2011). Students may be transformed by learning that psychological problems they and others face can be treated through safe, effective applications of psychological theory.

In addition to psychotherapy, students in introductory psychology learn about pharmacological treatments for mental illness and about drugs in general. Biopsychology sections of the course allow students to understand how the effects of psychoactive drugs are directly tied to their impact on brain chemistry. Teachers who want to emphasize this content can even assign students to research specific types of drugs and their effects (Goodwin, 2007). Drug use is common among young adults, and students entering college often try drugs for the first time (Johnston et al., 2015). As such, students may use the information from introductory psychology to make informed choices about their drug use for medical and recreational purposes.

Ethics

Introductory psychology is usually the first exposure that students have to research methods, and this introduction should emphasize that psychological research is governed by ethical principles such as informed consent and maintaining the dignity and well-being of participants. Furthermore, these ethical protections are especially important for vulnerable populations such as children and are extended to nonhuman animals used in research. Students should understand that some historic studies that they will learn about, such as the case of fear conditioning in Little Albert or Milgram's studies of obedience, could not be conducted today without extensive protections for the participants, if they could be done at all. Students in introductory psychology should learn about procedural safeguards that ensure that psychological research is both meaningful and ethical.

The American Psychological Association (APA) *Ethical Principles for Psychologists and Code of Conduct* (APA, 2017; hereinafter referred to as the Ethics Code) contains information that should be interwoven into introductory psychology (APA, 2014; see Appendix B for specific examples). Additionally, direct instruction of the Ethics Code leads to better knowledge of it. For instance, students who had intentional instruction pertaining to the Ethics Code for areas of research, teaching, and clinical practice showed greater knowledge of ethics than those who did not have this intentional instruction (Zucchero, 2008).

It is also important for introductory-level students to realize the extent that the Ethics Code matters outside of psychology—and it too can help foster their own success. For instance, academic integrity is essential to schools and higher educational systems (Walker, 1998). Without high standards of academic integrity, student degrees and coursework become worthless. Walker (1998) outlined several types of plagiarism that can threaten academic integrity. These include specific types of plagiarism such as taking credit for someone else's work without citing (illicit or sham citing or verbatim copying), not completing the assignment one's self (ghost writing or purloining), or using the same paper for multiple sources (recycling; Walker, 1998, see p. 3). When students take introductory psychology, they also can learn about how the Ethics Code discusses plagiarism (Ethics Code Section 8.11), publication credit for worthy contributions (Ethics Code Section 8.12), and publishing the same data multiple times (Ethics Code Section 8.13), all which parallel these forms of academic dishonesty. First year psychology students who receive explicit training about plagiarism are also more likely to understand different kinds of plagiarism (Curtis et al., 2013). Thus, students could see salient application of the APA Ethics Code if it is explicitly linked to these policies.

Additionally, the Ethics Code can also transform students to be successful beyond academics. In the workforce, for instance, integrity seems highly desirable. O*Net (https://www.onetonline.org) identifies *integrity* as a work style that affects how well someone does their job, and when "integrity" was entered as a search term for jobs on Monster.com, the search yielded more than 192,000 jobs consisting of that term.

How can instructors make the Ethics Code more salient to their students' personal and professional lives? Handelsman (2006) suggested several techniques for incorporating ethics into introductory psychology, one of which includes discussing "every day ethics" in which students consider the ethics of dilemmas, such as if a person should inform a superior about their coworker using work time for recreational activities (p. 164). Such a discussion could then apply the principles of the Ethics Code to discuss potential answers to this real-world situation.

Similarly, students in introductory psychology could also read Handelsman's (2011) *Sailing the 7 C's of Ethics*, which outlines how the ethics used by psychologists include competency, confidentiality, conflict of interest, consent, character, consultation, and codes. Students could then discuss how these principles would also fit into a profession that they wish to pursue or find interesting. For instance, a student who goes into graphic design may need to maintain *confidentiality* of a client's new product before its unveiling. Similarly, a student who desires to serve in a public office may also discuss how conflict of interest can play a role. This exercise therefore can extend the importance of knowing about ethics beyond psychology.

Ruiz and Warchal (2013) compiled a list of activities for integrating ethics across various topics in introductory psychology. Their guide is freely available through the Office of Teaching Resources in Psychology.

Cultural Competency

Human diversity is a core component of psychology education (APA, 2013). However, multiculturalism is the least commonly covered core topic in introductory psychology (Richmond et al., 2021). This is unfortunate because learning about diversity benefits students in several ways (Kowalski, 2000). Diversity is central to the understanding of individual differences, which is one of psychology's core concepts, and a full scientific understanding of mind and behavior must account for diversity. Furthermore, students who understand diversity are better equipped to have positive interactions with people who are different from themselves. Fortunately, diversity topics occur throughout introductory psychology (Trimble et al., 2003), and this gives teachers ample opportunity to work toward increasing students' cultural competency, which experts define in terms of knowledge, awareness, and skill (Sue, 2001). Specifically, being culturally competent includes having knowledge about diverse groups and their experiences, awareness of personal values and biases, and the skills necessary to work effectively with people from diverse backgrounds.

Cultural competency requires students to develop knowledge about human diversity, and introductory psychology can start this learning process. Virtually any form of human diversity can fit into the course, but discussion of some groups is standard. For example, aging is part of the main content of developmental psychology. Also, culture is a standard introductory psychology topic, especially variations between individualistic and collectivistic cultures. There are many ways teachers can demonstrate the pervasive influence of culture on psychology (Tomcho & Foels, 2002; Warren, 2006), and students can debate the cultural universality of any psychology concept. Gender and sexual orientation are also basic concepts in psychology. Students may enter introductory psychology believing that gender and sexual orientation are simple, dichotomous categories, and teachers can include lessons to illustrate the psychological complexity of these identities (Case et al., 2009; Madson, 2001). Moreover, gender and sexual orientation relate to a wide range of topics, including biopsychology, development, motivation, personality, mental health, and social psychology (Case et al., 2009; Trimble et al., 2003). For both gender and sexual orientation, introductory psychology can help students transition to a fuller recognition of and respect for the complex biopsychosocial factors that affect people's identities.

Other diverse groups are relevant to introductory psychology, but there has been less integration of them into the standard content of the course. For example, although textbook coverage of disability tends to be limited and stereotypical (Goldstein et al., 2010), it is connected to topics such as biopsychology, sensation, development, memory, intelligence, and mental illness (Dunn, 2016; Rosa et al., 2019). In addition, there are entire areas of psychology devoted to racial groups (Whitten, 1993) and social class (Tablante & Fiske, 2015). Introductory psychology courses do not typically address these topics as distinct psychological concepts. Nonetheless, teachers can ask students to think about the importance of race and social class in psychological experiences, as well as the ways that traditional psychology has exhibited bias by discounting such experiences (APA, 2002).

Introductory psychology can transform students' cultural competency by making them aware of the ongoing existence of cultural and personal bias. Students may come to the course with the misinformed belief that stereotypes, prejudice, and discrimination are interchangeable concepts that are largely irrelevant in modern society. However, coverage of social psychology will increase students' ability to differentiate among types of bias, as well as their awareness of the ongoing influence of bias in social relations. Teachers looking for engaging activities and demonstrations will find many related to stereotypes (Goldstein, 1997; Junn et al., 2001; Wurtele & Maruyama,

2013) and prejudice (Ford et al., 1997; Hillman & Martin, 2002; Junn et al., 2001). Perhaps most important, there are many methods for making students aware of the subtle ways that they exhibit bias, even if they do not identify as being prejudiced (Adams et al., 2014; Casad et al., 2013; Isbell & Tyler, 2003; K. A. Morris & Ashburn-Nardo, 2010). In general, diversity education has a positive impact on students' cultural competency (Denson, 2009; Smith et al., 2006), and there is some evidence that introductory psychology can have a similar effect (Matteo & You, 2012). As such, introductory psychology provides opportunities to transform students' cultural awareness.

The final component of cultural competency is skill in working with people of diverse backgrounds. Introductory psychology can provide the foundational knowledge and awareness for students to begin developing this skill. Psychology students should possess the basic skills of recognizing bias and the effects of culture on interpersonal interactions (APA, 2013). The goal for advanced psychology students is for them to effectively use their knowledge to improve intercultural communication. Introductory psychology instructors can start the learning process by developing students' knowledge and awareness. Students should recognize common forms of bias in others and in themselves and understand that psychology can vary between cultures. Achievement of these goals will increase students' potential for having skillful intercultural interactions and set them up for later skill development.

Recognizing the Inaccuracy of Intuitive Psychology

People generally perceive their subjective mental experiences to be rational and under their control. However, one of the fundamental lessons of psychology is that the human mind is governed by processes that fall mostly outside of conscious introspection and that frequently ignore reason, and one of the Introductory Psychology Initiative (APA, 2020) student learning outcomes is for students to provide examples of how "our perceptions filter our experiences of the world through an imperfect personal lens." Despite people's naive assumptions about how the mind works, intuition about human behavior will never lead to full understanding or mastery of psychological science. Recognizing the inaccuracy and irrationality of intuitions about psychology is yet another potential area of transformation for introductory psychology students.

Mental processes are largely automatic and inaccessible to introspection (Bargh & Chartrand, 1999; Wilson, 2004), and the pervasiveness of unconscious mental processes is one of the most surprising lessons of psychology.

The unconscious is a theme that can tie together a wide array of disparate psychology topics (Boysen, 2010). Although textbooks cover the psychoanalytic perspective on the unconscious in chapters on dreaming, personality, and psychotherapy, modern conceptualizations of the unconscious as automatic mental processes are even more pervasive. For example, split-brain research provides an opportunity for students to learn about, and even experience, the cognitive conflicts that can happen outside of awareness and develop a greater appreciation for the fact that conscious explanations of behaviors may not match up with causes occurring outside of awareness (E. J. Morris, 1991; Rasmussen, 2006). They can also learn that such effects are not isolated to split-brain patients because the cognitive processes behind sensation and perception occur outside conscious awareness. Furthermore, priming illustrates the automatic influence of implicit memory associations, and automatic stereotyping and prejudice illustrate the power of these implicit associations over social behavior. These are just a few examples, and teachers will find content related to the unconscious throughout introductory psychology.

Although learning about the unconscious in the abstract is interesting, students can also experience dramatic demonstrations of the power of the unconscious. For example, having students engage in a Stroop task allows them to feel the conflict between conscious and unconscious mental processes. Similarly, teachers can illustrate the influence of automatic cognitive associations by demonstrating priming effects in class (Kite, 1991). Also, having students complete implicit association tests can illustrate how those implicit associations lead to automatic bias toward various social groups (Adams et al., 2014; Casad et al., 2013; Eberhardt, 2019; K. A. Morris & Ashburn-Nardo, 2010). Finally, there are many vivid perceptual illusions that teachers can share with students (e.g., Cavalier & Wesp, 1997; Horner & Robinson, 1997; Klopfer & Doherty, 1992). Illusions are a useful tool in demonstrating the power of the unconscious because they show that conscious knowledge that perception is being tricked cannot override the automatic mental processes that cause the illusion. Overall, what these lessons about the unconscious have in common is their transformative power in changing students' naive views of the human mind and how it functions.

Another failure of intuitive psychology that students learn about in introductory psychology is the unreasonable confidence people have in the accuracy of memories. Few students enter the course understanding that memory is a construction rather than an accurate replaying of past events, but that is one of the enduring findings of memory research. To learn about constructive memory, students can read about classic studies documenting errors in eyewitness testimony and flashbulb memories, but they can also directly experience the fallibility of memory when teachers re-create these studies in class (Gee & Dyck, 1998; Hoyert & O'Dell, 2000; Miller, 1997). In addition, teachers can use the Deese–Roediger–McDermott paradigm to create false memories of hearing a lure word that was not part of a list of to-be-remembered words (Stadler et al., 1999). By learning about and experiencing the constructive nature of memory, introductory psychology students will have a more accurate perspective on how memory works, and this should influence their perspective on the fallibility of memory in their later personal and professional lives.

Students can also be transformed by learning about the biases behind many of their judgments. One of psychology's most influential ideas is that people engage in heuristic thinking when forced to make quick, uncertain judgments (Kahneman, 2011). Although using heuristics saves cognitive energy and can lead to reasonable decisions, they can also systematically lead to irrational mistakes. Students can be led into making many of these mistakes using classroom demonstrations (Morrow, 2002; Swinkels, 2003). For example, students will reliably estimate that people are more likely to die from car accidents than heart attacks and that someone who owns a pickup truck is more likely to be a farmer than a teacher. Students who understand the systematic biases caused by availability, representativeness, and anchoring heuristics can try to avoid the common mistakes they cause in real life.

PREPARING STUDENTS FOR CAREER SUCCESS IN INTRODUCTORY PSYCHOLOGY

Psychology has long suffered from the unwarranted stigma that the undergraduate psychology major teaches students little if any marketable skills, and earning a psychology degree is of little value on the job market (Halonen, 2019). In recent years, the percentage of students who state that their primary reason for attending college is to get a well-paying job has increased (Appleby, Appleby, et al., 2019) Taken together, some students may never consider psychology to be a viable major for themselves regardless of their interest in the field due to unjustified concerns about employment potential (Lin & Stamm, 2018). Thus, it is important to address the relevance of psychology to workplace success in introductory psychology.

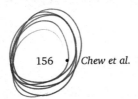
Understanding how people think, feel, and act is critical for success in most any career. Even though information about job and career skills are usually taught later in the psychology major (Ciarocco, 2018; Ciarocco et al., 2016; Halonen, 2019; Halonen & Dunn, 2018), many concepts relevant to career and workplace success are presented in introductory psychology. Introductory psychology students should learn how psychology uniquely contributes to all disciplines and workplace effectiveness. For example, concepts such as conformity, attitude change, groupthink, and group polarization are directly relevant to the workplace, and skills such as measuring attitudes and critically analyzing research are valuable job skills. Teachers do not necessarily have to change what they teach, they just need to point out the relevance of what they are teaching to work and career success. When covering social psychology and presenting the concept of groupthink, for example, students can be asked to reflect on the workplace and other venues that rely heavily on group decision-making to develop policy, products, promotional campaigns, decide a defendant's guilt or innocence, and so on. The teacher can prompt students to think of situations in which they've participated in groups at work, school, or in volunteer organizations and to share experiences in which the group performed well or not so well and relate those experiences to the factors known to contribute to groupthink. Table 6.1 lists introductory psychology topics that can be tied to workplace skills,

Naufel et al. (2019; also see Appleby, Young, et al., 2019) identified 17 career-related skills embedded within five domains that are taught in the course of a psychology major, which are shown in Table 6.2. Introductory psychology teachers often address career-related skills (Richmond et al., 2021). In fact, the majority of instructors address critical thinking, diversity, ethics, and self-regulation in some form in the course. These skills mesh well with the most commonly desired skills sought by employers (Appleby, 2018). Naufel et al. and Appleby, Appleby, et al. (2019) have both suggested that teachers identify these skills on the course syllabus and explain how they are being taught in the course. State the skills in a way that the students might list on their resume. Instead of listing "Research Skills," state that "Students will learn to evaluate the strengths and weaknesses of data collected through various research designs." Appleby, Appleby, et al. (2019) provided specific statements about job and career skills that can be included on the syllabus. Naufel et al. further suggested creating activities that cause students to reflect on the value of what they are learning as applied to the workplace. For example, when discussing the Big Five theory of personality traits, have students reflect on how it might be used to help match students with suitable careers.

TABLE 6.1. Topics Taught in Introductory Psychology and Examples of Their Workplace Applications

General area of course	Skills necessary for future success[a]	Examples of workplace applications
Research methods foundation	Judgment and decision making (making logical decisions)	Biases and heuristics, such as the representative heuristic, can harm one's ability to make logical judgments.
	Integrity	Review of classic, but unethical, studies that led to the American Psychological Association's Ethics Code and an overview of the institutional review board process can lead to discussions of workplace integrity (Cialdini et al., 2004).
	Critical thinking	Awareness that correlation does not mean causation is important for thinking critically.
Biological: neuroscience	Adaptability	Plasticity refers to how neural connections within the brain can change or adapt. Students who understand the various conditions and experiences that promote plasticity (e.g., Dahlin et al., 2008) can apply this knowledge to enhance their personal adaptability.
Biological: sensation	Inclusivity (demonstrating sensitivity to cultural and individual differences)	Sensation explains color blindness and that 8% of the male population and .5% of the female population are colorblind. Materials using color to communicate information may confuse individuals with color blindness. Understanding the physical causes of color blindness when communicating with different audiences promotes inclusivity.
Biological: consciousness	Analytical thinking (attention to details)	Process and quality assurance engineers use analytical thinking to design manufacturing and quality assurance processes. Engineers can benefit from a knowledge of inattentional bias in which people may not notice events, even major events when focusing their attention.
Cognitive: perception	Critical thinking (display proficiency in interpreting statistics and research design)	*Critical thinking* frequently relies on the correct interpretation of statistics. Several psychological theories encompass factors that influence accurate interpretation. For instance, Gestalt principles, often covered in sensation and perception, can predict how people will interpret graphed data. Data points that are grouped together on a line graph make it appear that those points are "one," and people infer that data are related. Data points shown in bar graphs appear separate, and people assume that data points are unrelated (Weissgerber et al., 2015; Zacks & Tversky, 1999). Awareness of ways in which graphs convey information and avoiding factors that can mislead people is helpful knowledge in many fields. Many jobs require knowledge about how to interpret statistical information effectively. With an understanding of some of these biases and principles, students can be proficient in interpreting statistics.

(continues)

TABLE 6.1. Topics Taught in Introductory Psychology and Examples of Their Workplace Applications (*Continued*)

General area of course	Skills necessary for future success[a]	Examples of workplace applications
Cognitive: memory	Management	False memories can hamper the ability of people working in management to coordinate projects. Questions that managers ask, or merely a way a group discusses a task, can sometimes produce false memories about what has been completed and what remains to be done. By knowing that memory can be imperfect, even collectively, as in the case of the Mandela Effect, managers can create an environment that minimizes such errors (Kiisel, n.d.).
Cognitive: cognition	Creativity	Innovation is a form of creativity that involves the implementation of novel, beneficial products or procedures (Rank et al., 2004). The introductory psychology course can present barriers to innovation, such as functional fixedness when people "fixate" on an object's primary purpose (e.g., seeing a paperclip as only useful for holding papers together and not something else).
		Additionally, a cognitive psychology section of the course could cover ways to overcome functional fixedness, such as the generic parts technique. For this technique, people consider the composition of parts of an object. By doing so, they are more likely to overcome functional fixedness (McCaffrey, 2012).
Development: learning	Management	Assembly-line supervisors can, for example, use reinforcement contingencies to encourage higher rates of production.
		Mental health workers and K-8 educators can design token economy systems to encourage adaptive rather than disruptive behavior.
Development: lifespan	Integrity	Discussions of Kohlberg's stages of moral development can include ethical dilemmas that are common in the workplace.
		Present strategies that can foster growth to a later stage of moral development.
		Discussions of moral development, ethics, and integrity can include recent research on unethical practices found to plague organizations and threaten their very survival (Cialdini et al., 2004).

Social and personality: social	Collaboration (on teams) Leadership Management	Group processes such as groupthink, social loafing, and risky shift are factors that emerge and threaten group performance and can lead to poor group decisions. Workplace setting examples will reinforce the importance of group leadership and teamwork skills.
Social and personality: personality	Self-efficacy Adaptability Self-regulation	Assignments and discussions introducing the growth mindset (Dweck, 2008), grit (Duckworth et al., 2007), and academic self-efficacy (Bandura, 1997) can foster attitudes that prepare students to adapt and persevere despite the rapid change frequent in many workplaces.
Social and personality: emotion	Service orientation	The teacher can offer an optional service project in which student teams present psychological topics to K-12 classes or community groups.
Health: stress and health	Self-regulation (manage time and stress by completing assigned tasks with little or no supervision)	Self-regulation strategies (e.g., Oettingen, 2014) acquired for managing time and healthy habits (exercise, diet, sleep) and coping with stress for academic success will continue to be applicable after entering the workforce.
Health: psychological disorders	Service orientation (display empathy)	There are various ways to help introductory psychology students develop a service orientation. Many community-based volunteer programs provide students with opportunities to interact and experience individuals struggling with mental health challenges (e.g., National Alliance on Mental Illness, food banks for homeless). These organizations offer speakers (program leaders and former patients) who visit classes to inform the public and recruit volunteers.
Health: helping	Oral communication (active listening skills)	Carl Rogers and Richard Farson (1987) discussed the concept of active listening in their aptly named book, Active Listening. The idea of active listening, therefore, has strong roots in psychology. Psychology majors may learn about active listening early on in a therapies section in introductory psychology. This skill is essential for effective interpersonal communication.

a Valued postbaccalaureate skills found in Naufel et al. (2019) and on O*Net.

TABLE 6.2. The Skillful Psychology Student: Skill Domains and Skills Taught in Psychology

Skill domain	Skills
Cognitive	Analytic thinking, critical thinking, creativity, information management, judgment and decision making
Communication	Oral communication, written communication
Personal	Adaptability, integrity, self-regulation
Social	Collaboration, inclusivity, management, service orientation
Technological	Flexibility/adaptability to new systems, familiarity with hardware

Note. Adapted from "The Skillful Psychology Student: How to Empower Students With Workforce-Ready Skills by Teaching Psychology," by K. Z. Naufel, S. M. Spencer, D. C. Appleby, A. S. Richmond, J. Rudmann, J. Van Kirk, J. Young, B. J. Carducci, and P. Hettich, 2019, *Psychology Teacher Network*, 29(1), para. 4 (https://www.apa.org/ed/precollege/ptn/2019/03/workforce-ready-skills). Copyright 2019 by the American Psychological Association.

CONCLUSION

A successful introductory psychology course can have a positive impact on students well beyond the class itself. Students can learn knowledge and skills to help them succeed in other courses, make it more likely that they will complete their college degree, and help them thrive in their lives and careers. Part of the reason is because of the course's popularity among first-year college students, but a larger part is because the knowledge and skills that students learn in introductory psychology are both applicable and helpful to students' lives (Gurung et al., 2016). The impact can only happen if the course is taught well. That means that the students do more than learn information; they are transformed by what they learn. They gain new insights and ways of thinking that they will use to their advantage after the class is over. They see the value of psychological knowledge and the importance of psychological research. They use the knowledge to avoid common pitfalls in problem solving and biases in reasoning. This impact can occur regardless of whether students choose to take more psychology courses or, like the majority of students, introductory psychology is the only psychology course they ever take.

Introductory psychology should be taught with the goal of student success and transformation. This goal entails emphasizing knowledge and skills that students need for academic success, such as self-regulation and effective learning strategies, and personal growth, such as healthy behaviors and cultural competence. It also entails teaching psychology so students see its value as a useful scientific field that can help them make better choices and decisions. In this way, introductory psychology can play a unique role in imbuing students with knowledge and skills that are critical for academic, career, and personal success.

REFERENCES

Adams, V. H., III, Devos, T., Rivera, L. M., Smith, H., & Vega, L. A. (2014). Teaching about implicit prejudices and stereotypes: A pedagogical demonstration. *Teaching of Psychology, 41*(3), 204–212. https://doi.org/10.1177/0098628314537969

Adelman, C. (2006). *The toolbox revisited: Paths to degree completion from high school through college*. U.S. Department of Education. https://www2.ed.gov/rschstat/research/pubs/toolboxrevisit/toolbox.pdf

Agarwal, P. K., & Bain, P. M. (2019). *Powerful teaching: Unleash the science of learning*. Jossey-Bass. https://doi.org/10.1002/9781119549031

American College Health Association. (2019). *American College Health Association-National College Health Assessment II: Undergraduate student reference group data report Fall 2019*. American College Health Association. https://www.acha.org/NCHA/ACHA-NCHA_Data/Publications_and_Reports/NCHA/Data/Reports_ACHA-NCHAIIc.aspx

American Psychological Association. (2002). Ethical principles of psychologists and code of conduct. *American Psychologist, 57*(12), 1060–1073. https://doi.org/10.1037/0003-066X.57.12.1060

American Psychological Association. (2013). *APA guidelines for the undergraduate psychology major: Version 2.0*. https://www.apa.org/ed/precollege/about/psymajor-guidelines.pdf

American Psychological Association. (2014). *Strengthening the common core of the introductory psychology course*. American Psychological Association, Board of Educational Affairs. https://www.apa.org/ed/governance/bea/intro-psych-report.pdf

American Psychological Association. (2017). *Ethical principles of psychologists and code of conduct* (2002, Amended June 1, 2010, and January 1, 2017). https://www.apa.org/ethics/code/index.aspx

American Psychological Association. (2020). *The APA Introductory Psychology Initiative*. https://www.apa.org/ed/precollege/undergrad/introductory-psychology-initiative

Appleby, D. C. (2018). Preparing psychology majors to enter the workforce: Then, now, with whom, and how. *Teaching of Psychology, 45*(1), 14–23. https://doi.org/10.1177/0098628317744944

Appleby, D. C., Appleby, K. M., Wickline, V. B., Apple, K. J., Bouchard, L. M., Cook, R., Erickson, L. V., Halpern, D. F., & Kelly, S. M. (2019). A syllabus-based strategy to help psychology students prepare for and enter the workforce. *Scholarship of Teaching and Learning in Psychology, 5*(4), 289–297. https://doi.org/10.1037/stl0000161

Appleby, D. C., Young, J., Van Kirk, J., Rudmann, J., Naufel, K. Z., Spencer, S. M., Hettich, P., Carducci, B. J., & Richmond, A. S. (2019, February). The skillful psychology student: Skills you will need to succeed in the 21st-century workplace. *Psychology Teacher Network*. American Psychological Association. https://www.apa.org/ed/precollege/psn/2019/02/skillful-student

Auerbach, R. P., Alonso, J., Axinn, W. G., Cuijpers, P., Ebert, D. D., Green, J. G., Hwang, I., Kessler, R. C., Liu, H., Mortier, P., Nock, M. K., Pinder-Amaker, S., Sampson, N. A., Aguilar-Gaxiola, S., Al-Hamzawi, A., Andrade, L. H., Benjet, C., Caldas-de-Almeida, J. M., Demyttenaere, K., Florescu, S., de Girolamo, G., Gureje, O., Haro, J. M., Karam, E. G., Kiejna, A., Kovess-Masfety, V., Lee, S., McGrath, J. J., O'Neill, S., Pennell, B.-E., Scott, K., Ten Have, M., Torres, Y., Zaslavsky, A. M., Zarkov, Z., & Bruffaerts, R. (2016). Mental disorders among college students in the World Health Organization World Mental Health Surveys. *Psychological Medicine*, *46*(14), 2955–2970. https://doi.org/10.1017/S0033291716001665

Bandura, A. (1977). Self-efficacy: Toward a unifying theory of behavioral change. *Psychological Review*, *84*(2), 191–215. https://doi.org/10.1037/0033-295X.84.2.191

Bandura, A. (1997). *Self-efficacy: The exercise of control*. W. H. Freeman.

Bargh, J. A., & Chartrand, T. L. (1999). The unbearable automaticity of being. *American Psychologist*, *54*(7), 462–479. https://doi.org/10.1037/0003-066X.54.7.462

Baumeister, R. F. (2020). Self-regulation and conscientiousness. In R. Biswas-Diener & E. Diener (Eds.), *Noba textbook series: Psychology*. DEF Publishers. http://noba.to/3j96qxwr

Bellur, S., Nowak, K. L., & Hull, K. S. (2015). Make it our time: In class multitaskers have lower academic performance. *Computers in Human Behavior*, *53*, 63–70. https://doi.org/10.1016/j.chb.2015.06.027

Benassi, V., Overson, C., & Hakala, C. (Eds.). (2014). *Applying science of learning in education: Infusing psychological science into the curriculum*. American Psychological Association. http://teachpsych.org/ebooks/asle2014/index.php

Bjork, R. A., Dunlosky, J., & Kornell, N. (2013). Self-regulated learning: Beliefs, techniques, and illusions. *Annual Review of Psychology*, *64*(1), 417–444. https://doi.org/10.1146/annurev-psych-113011-143823

Blasiman, R. N., Dunlosky, J., & Rawson, K. A. (2017). The what, how much, and when of study strategies: Comparing intended versus actual study behaviour. *Memory*, *25*(6), 784–792. https://doi.org/10.1080/09658211.2016.1221974

Boysen, G. A. (2010). An integrative undergraduate capstone course on the unconscious. *Teaching of Psychology*, *37*(4), 237–245. https://doi.org/10.1080/00986283.2010.510972

Brady, S. T., Hard, B. M., & Gross, J. J. (2018). Reappraising test anxiety increases academic performance of first-year college students. *Journal of Educational Psychology*, *110*(3), 395–406. https://doi.org/10.1037/edu0000219

Brown, P. C., Roediger, H. L., & McDaniel, M. A. (2014). *Make it stick: The science of successful learning*. The Belknap Press of Harvard University Press. https://doi.org/10.4159/9780674419377

Burak, L. (2012). Multitasking in the university classroom. *International Journal for the Scholarship of Teaching and Learning*, *6*(2), 8. https://doi.org/10.20429/ijsotl.2012.060208

Burlison, J. D., Murphy, C. S., & Dwyer, W. O. (2009). Evaluation of the motivated strategies for learning questionnaire for predicting academic performance in college students of varying scholastic aptitude. *College Student Journal*, *43*(4), 1313–1323.

https://link.gale.com/apps/doc/A217511792/AONE?u=naal_sam&sid=AONE&x-id=3eaec87f

Carrier, L. M., Rosen, L. D., Cheever, N. A., & Lim, A. F. (2015). Causes, effects, and practicalities of everyday multitasking. *Developmental Review, 35*, 64–78. https://doi.org/10.1016/j.dr.2014.12.005

Carver, C. S., & Scheier, M. F. (2011). Self-regulation of action and affect. In K. D. Vohs & R. F. Baumeister (Eds.), *Handbook of self-regulation: Research, theory, and applications* (2nd ed., pp. 3–21). Guilford Press.

Casad, B. J., Flores, A. J., & Didway, J. D. (2013). Using the implicit association test as an unconsciousness raising tool in psychology. *Teaching of Psychology, 40*(2), 118–123. https://doi.org/10.1177/0098628312475031

Case, K. A., Stewart, B., & Tittsworth, J. (2009). Transgender across the curriculum: A psychology for inclusion. *Teaching of Psychology, 36*(2), 117–121. https://doi.org/10.1080/00986280902739446

Cavalier, R., & Wesp, R. (1997). The garbage-can illusion as a teaching demonstration. *Teaching of Psychology, 24*(2), 125–127. https://doi.org/10.1207/s15328023top2402_10

Center for Academic Success. Louisiana State University (2015). *The study cycle: Focused study sessions.* https://www.lsu.edu/cas/earnbettergrades/vlc/CAS_VLC_StudyCycleFSS.pdf

Chemers, M. M. Hu, Li-tze, & Garcia, B. F. (2001). Academic self-efficacy and first year college student performance and adjustment. *Journal of Educational Psychology, 93*(1), 55–64. https://psycnet.apa.org/doi/10.1037/0022-0663.93.1.55

Chen, P., Chavez, O., Ong, D. C., & Gunderson, B. (2017). Strategic resource use for learning: A self-administered intervention that guides self-reflection on effective resource use enhances academic performance. *Psychological Science, 28*(6), 774–785. https://doi.org/10.1177/0956797617696456

Chew, S. L. (2014). Helping students to get the most out of studying. In V. A. Benassi, C. E. Overson, & C. M. Hakala (Eds.), *Applying science of learning in education: Infusing psychological science into the curriculum.* Society for the Teaching of Psychology. http://teachpsych.org/ebooks/asle2014/index.php

Cialdini, R., Petrova, P., & Goldstein, N. (2004). The hidden cost of organizational dishonesty. *MIT Sloan Management Review, 45*(3), 67–73.

Ciarocco, N. J. (2018). Traditional and new approaches to career preparation through coursework. *Teaching of Psychology, 45*(1), 32–40. https://doi.org/10.1177/0098628317744963

Ciarocco, N. J., Dinella, L. M., Hatchard, C. J., & Valosin, J. (2016). Integrating professional development across the curriculum: An effectiveness study. *Teaching of Psychology, 43*(2), 91–98. https://doi.org/10.1177/0098628316636217

Connor-Greene, P. A. (2001). Family, friends, and self: The real-life context of an abnormal psychology class. *Teaching of Psychology, 28*(3), 210–212.

Curtin, L., Martz, D. M., Bazzini, D. G., & Vicente, B. B. (2004). They're not "abnormal" and we're not making them "abnormal": A longitudinal study. *Teaching of Psychology, 31*(1), 51–53.

Curtis, G. J., Gouldthorp, B., Thomas, E. F., O'Brien, G. M., & Correia, H. M. (2013). Online academic-integrity mastery training may improve students' awareness of, and attitudes toward, plagiarism. *Psychology Learning & Teaching, 12*(3), 282–289. https://doi.org/10.2304/plat.2013.12.3.282

Dahlin, E., Neely, A. S., Larsson, A., Bäckman, L., & Nyberg, L. (2008). Transfer of learning after updating training mediated by the striatum. *Science, 320*(5882), 1510–1512. https://doi.org/10.1126/science.1155466

David, P., Kim, J., Brickman, J. S., Ran, W., & Curtis, C. M. (2015). Mobile phone distraction while studying. *New Media & Society, 17*(10), 1661–1679. https://doi.org/10.1177/1461444814531692

Denson, N. (2009). Do curricular and cocurricular diversity activities influence racial bias? A meta-analysis. *Review of Educational Research, 79*(2), 805–838. https://doi.org/10.3102/0034654309331551

Duckworth, A. L., Peterson, C., Matthews, M. D., & Kelly, D. R. (2007). Grit: Perseverance and passion for long-term goals. *Journal of Personality and Social Psychology, 92*(6), 1087–1101. https://doi.org/10.1037/0022-3514.92.6.1087

Dunlosky, J., Rawson, K. A., Marsh, E. J., Nathan, M. J., & Willingham, D. T. (2013). Improving students' learning with effective learning techniques: Promising directions from cognitive and educational psychology. *Psychological Science in the Public Interest, 14*(1), 4–58. https://doi.org/10.1177/1529100612453266

Dunn, D. S. (2016). Teaching about psychosocial aspects of disability: Emphasizing person–environment relations. *Teaching of Psychology, 43*(3), 255–262. https://doi.org/10.1177/0098628316649492

Dweck, C. S. (2008). *Mindset: The new psychology of success.* Ballantine Books.

Eberhardt, J. L. (2019). *Biased: Uncovering the hidden prejudice that shapes what we see, think, and do.* Penguin Books.

Ford, T. E., Grossman, R. W., & Jordan, E. A. (1997). Teaching about unintentional racism in introductory psychology. *Teaching of Psychology, 24*(3), 186–188. https://doi.org/10.1207/s15328023top2403_8

Gee, N. R., & Dyck, J. L. (1998). Using a videotape clip to demonstrate the fallibility of eyewitness testimony. *Teaching of Psychology, 25*(2), 138–140. https://doi.org/10.1207/s15328023top2502_18

Gingerich, A. C., & Lineweaver, T. T. (2014). OMG! Texting in class = u fail: Empirical evidence that text messaging during class disrupts comprehension. *Teaching of Psychology, 41*(1), 44–51. https://doi.org/10.1177/0098628313514177

Goldstein, S. B. (1997). The power of stereotypes: A labeling exercise. *Teaching of Psychology, 24*(4), 256–258. https://doi.org/10.1207/s15328023top2404_5

Goldstein, S. B., Siegel, D., & Seaman, J. (2010). Limited access: The status of disability in introductory psychology textbooks. *Teaching of Psychology, 37*(1), 21–27. https://doi.org/10.1080/00986280903426290

Goodwin, K. A. (2007). Peer-taught drug awareness in the introductory psychology course. *Teaching of Psychology, 34*(1), 34–37. https://doi.org/10.1177/009862830703400107

Gross, J. J. (2013). Emotion regulation: Taking stock and moving forward. *Emotion, 13*(3), 359–365. https://doi.org/10.1037/a0032135

Gurung, R. A. R. (2005). How do students really study (and does it matter)? *Teaching of Psychology, 32*(4), 239–241.

Gurung, R. A. R., Hackathorn, J., Enns, C., Frantz, S., Cacioppo, J. T., Loop, T., & Freeman, J. E. (2016). Strengthening introductory psychology: A new model for teaching the introductory course. *American Psychologist, 71*(2), 112–124. https://doi.org/10.1037/a0040012

Halonen, J. S. (2019, March 25). Defending the major: Exploiting the workforce advantage of the psychology degree. *American Psychological Association's Psych Learning Curve: Where Psychology and Education Connect.* American Psychological Association. http://psychlearningcurve.org/defending-the-psychology-major/

Halonen, J. S., & Dunn, D. S. (2018). Embedding career issues in advanced psychology major courses. *Teaching of Psychology, 45*(1), 41–49. https://doi.org/10.1177/0098628317744967

Handelsman, M. (2011). Sailing the 7 C's of ethics. *Eye on Psi Chi, 15*(2). https://www.psichi.org/page/152EyeWin11fHandelsm#.XuZq7S2ZNYg

Handelsman, M. M. (2006). Teaching ethics in introductory psychology. In D. Dunn & S. Chew (Eds.), *Best practices for teaching introduction to psychology* (pp. 159–175). Lawrence Erlbaum Associates.

Hartwig, M. K., & Dunlosky, J. (2012). Study strategies of college students: Are self-testing and scheduling related to achievement? *Psychonomic Bulletin & Review, 19*(1), 126–134. https://doi.org/10.3758/s13423-011-0181-y

Hillman, J., & Martin, R. A. (2002). Lessons about gay and lesbian lives: A spaceship exercise. *Teaching of Psychology, 29*(4), 308–311. https://doi.org/10.1207/S15328023TOP2904_12

Horner, D. T., & Robinson, K. D. (1997). Demonstrations of the size–weight illusion. *Teaching of Psychology, 24*(3), 195–197. https://doi.org/10.1207/s15328023top2403_12

Hoyert, M. S., & O'Dell, C. D. (2000). Examining memory phenomena through flashbulb memories. *Teaching of Psychology, 27*(4), 272–273. https://doi.org/10.1207/S15328023TOP2704_06

Hughes, J. S., Gourley, M. K., Madson, L., & Le Blanc, K. (2011). Stress and coping activity: Reframing negative thoughts. *Teaching of Psychology, 38*(1), 36–39. https://doi.org/10.1177/0098628310390852

Isbell, L. M., & Tyler, J. M. (2003). Teaching students about in-group favoritism and the minimal groups paradigm. *Teaching of Psychology, 30*(2), 127–130. https://doi.org/10.1207/S15328023TOP3002_10

Jackson, J. W. (2002). Enhancing self-efficacy and learning performance. *Journal of Experimental Education, 70*(3), 243–254. https://doi.org/10.1080/00220970209599508

Johnston, L. D., O'Malley, P. M., Bachman, J. G., Schulenberg, J. E., & Miech, R. A. (2015). *Monitoring the Future national survey results on drug use, 1975–2015: Vol. 2. College students and adults ages 19–55.* Institute for Social Research, The University of Michigan. http://monitoringthefuture.org/pubs.html#monographs

Junn, E. N., Grier, L. K., & Behrens, D. P. (2001). Playing "Sherlock Holmes": Enhancing students' understanding of prejudice and stereotyping. *Teaching of Psychology, 28*(2), 121–124. https://doi.org/10.1207/S15328023TOP2802_12

Kahneman, D. (2011). *Thinking, fast and slow.* Macmillan.

Karpicke, J. D., Butler, A. C., & Roediger, H. L., III. (2009). Metacognitive strategies in student learning: Do students practise retrieval when they study on their own? *Memory, 17*(4), 471–479. https://doi.org/10.1080/09658210802647009

Kendra, M. S., Cattaneo, L. B., & Mohr, J. J. (2012). Teaching abnormal psychology to improve attitudes toward mental illness and help-seeking. *Teaching of Psychology, 39*(1), 57–61. https://doi.org/10.1177/0098628311430315

Kiisel, T. (n.d.). Are you familiar with the Mandela Effect? It can hurt your business. *OnDeck.* https://www.ondeck.com/resources/familiar-mandela-effect-can-hurt-business

Kite, M. E. (1991). Observer biases in the classroom. *Teaching of Psychology, 18*(3), 161–164. https://doi.org/10.1207/s15328023top1803_7

Klopfer, D., & Doherty, M. E. (1992). The Janus illusion. *Teaching of Psychology, 19*(1), 37–40. https://doi.org/10.1207/s15328023top1901_8

Korgan, C., Durdella, N., & Stevens, M. (2013). The development of academic self-efficacy among first-year college students in a comprehensive public university. *Higher Education, 10,* 11–37.

Kornell, N., & Bjork, R. A. (2007). The promise and perils of self-regulated study. *Psychonomic Bulletin & Review, 14*(2), 219–224. https://doi.org/10.3758/BF03194055

Kowalski, R. M. (2000). Including gender, race, and ethnicity in psychology content courses. *Teaching of Psychology, 27*(1), 18–24. https://doi.org/10.1207/S15328023TOP2701_3

Lapan, R. T., Kardash, C. M., & Turner, S. (2002). Empowering students to become self-regulated learners. *Professional School Counseling, 5*(4), 257–265.

Larsen, L. M., Pesch, K. M., Surapaneni, S., Bonitz, V. S., Wu, T. F., & Werbel, D. (2015). Predicting graduation: The role of mathematics/science self-efficacy. *Journal of Career Assessment, 23*(3), 399–409. https://doi.org/10.1177/1069072714547322

Lawson, T. J., & Reardon, M. (1997). A humorous demonstration of in vivo systematic desensitization: The case of eraser phobia. *Teaching of Psychology, 24*(4), 270–271. https://doi.org/10.1207/s15328023top2404_12

Lin, L., & Stamm, K. (June 4, 2018). Graduating with a degree in psychology? Check out what the data say about careers, workforce demographics, salaries and more! *Psychology Learning Curve: Where Psychology and Education Connect.* APA Center for Workforce Studies, American Psychological Association. https://psychlearningcurve.org/data-on-psychology-workforce/

Lund, H. G., Reider, B. D., Whiting, A. B., & Prichard, J. R. (2010). Sleep patterns and predictors of disturbed sleep in a large population of college students. *The Journal of Adolescent Health, 46*(2), 124–132. https://doi.org/10.1016/j.jadohealth.2009.06.016

Maddux, J. E., & Kleiman, E. (2019). Self-efficacy. In R. Biswas-Diener & E. Diener (Eds.), *Nova textbook series: Psychology.* DEF Publishers. http://noba.to/bmv4hd6p

Madson, L. (2001). A classroom activity exploring the complexity of sexual orientation. *Teaching of Psychology, 28*(1), 32–35. https://doi.org/10.1207/S15328023TOP2801_08

Marek, P., Christopher, A. N., Koenig, C. S., & Reinhart, D. F. (2005). Writing exercises for introductory psychology. *Teaching of Psychology, 32*(4), 244–246.

Margolis, H., & McCabe, P. P. (2006). Improving self-efficacy and motivation: What to do, what to say. *Intervention in School and Clinic, 41*(4), 218–227. https://doi.org/10.1177/10534512060410040401

Matteo, E. K., & You, D. (2012). Reducing mental illness stigma in the classroom. *Teaching of Psychology, 39*(2), 121–124. https://doi.org/10.1177/0098628312437720

McCabe, J. (2011). Metacognitive awareness of learning strategies in undergraduates. *Memory & Cognition, 39*(3), 462–476. https://doi.org/10.3758/s13421-010-0035-2

McCaffrey, T. (2012). Innovation relies on the obscure: A key to overcoming the classic problem of functional fixedness. *Psychological Science, 23*(3), 215–218. https://doi.org/10.1177/0956797611429580

McCarthy, M. A., & Frantz, S. (2016). Challenging the status quo: Evidence that introductory psychology can dispel myths. *Teaching of Psychology, 43*(3), 211–214. https://doi.org/10.1177/0098628316649470

McRae, K., & Gross, J. J. (2020). Emotion regulation. *Emotion, 20*(1), 1–9. https://doi.org/10.1037/emo0000703

Miller, L. A. (1997). Teaching about repressed memories of childhood sexual abuse and eyewitness testimony. *Teaching of Psychology, 24*(4), 250–255. https://doi.org/10.1207/s15328023top2404_4

Miyatsu, T., Nguyen, K., & McDaniel, M. A. (2018). Five popular study strategies: Their pitfalls and optimal implementations. *Perspectives on Psychological Science, 13*(3), 390–407. https://doi.org/10.1177/1745691617710510

Monsell, S. (2003). Task switching. *Trends in Cognitive Sciences, 7*(3), 134–140. https://doi.org/10.1016/S1364-6613(03)00028-7

Morehead, K., Rhodes, M. G., & DeLozier, S. (2016). Instructor and student knowledge of study strategies. *Memory, 24*(2), 257–271. https://doi.org/10.1080/09658211.2014.1001992

Morris, E. J. (1991). Classroom demonstration of behavioral effects of the split-brain operation. *Teaching of Psychology, 18*(4), 226–228. https://doi.org/10.1207/s15328023top1804_6

Morris, K. A., & Ashburn-Nardo, L. (2010). The Implicit Association Test as a class assignment: Student affective and attitudinal reactions. *Teaching of Psychology, 37*(1), 63–68. https://doi.org/10.1080/00986280903426019

Morrow, J. (2002). Demonstrating the anchoring-adjustment heuristic and the power of the situation. *Teaching of Psychology, 29*(2), 129–132. https://doi.org/10.1207/S15328023TOP2902_11

Naufel, K. Z., Spencer, S. M., Appleby, D. C., Richmond, A. S., Rudmann, J., Van Kirk, J., Young, J., Carducci, B. J., & Hettich, P. (2019, March). The skillful psychology student: How to empower students with workforce-ready skills by teaching psychology. *Psychology Teacher Network, 29*(1). https://www.apa.org/ed/precollege/ptn/2019/03/workforce-ready-skills

Oettingen, G. (2014). *Rethinking positive thinking: Inside the new science of motivation.* Penguin Books.

Office of Academic and Learning Resources, Rhodes College. (n.d.). *The study cycle & focused study sessions.* https://sites.rhodes.edu/academic-and-learning-resources/learning-tips/study-cycle-focused-study-sessions

Pajares, F. (1996). Self-efficacy beliefs in academic settings. *Review of Educational Research, 66*(4), 543–578. https://doi.org/10.3102/00346543066004543

Patterson, M. C. (2017). A naturalistic investigation of media multitasking while studying and the effects on exam performance. *Teaching of Psychology, 44*(1), 51–57. https://doi.org/10.1177/0098628316677913

Pintrich, P. R. (2004). A conceptual framework for assessing motivation and self-regulated learning in college students. *Educational Psychology Review, 16*(4), 385–407. https://doi.org/10.1007/s10648-004-0006-x

Putnam, A. L., Sungkhasettee, V. W., & Roediger, H. L., III. (2016). Optimizing learning in college: Tips from cognitive psychology. *Perspectives on Psychological Science, 11*(5), 652–660. https://doi.org/10.1177/1745691616645770

Rank, J., Pace, V. L., & Frese, M. (2004). Three avenues for future research on creativity, innovation, and initiative. *Applied Psychology, 53*(4), 518–528. https://doi.org/10.1111/j.1464-0597.2004.00185.x

Rasmussen, E. B. (2006). Expanding your coverage of neuroscience: An interview with Michael Gazzaniga. *Teaching of Psychology, 33*(3), 212–215. https://doi.org/10.1207/s15328023top3303_10

Renner, M. J., & Mackin, R. S. (1998). A life stress instrument for classroom use. *Teaching of Psychology, 25*(1), 46–48. https://doi.org/10.1207/s15328023top2501_15

Richardson, M., Abraham, C., & Bond, R. (2012). Psychological correlates of university students' academic performance: A systematic review and meta-analysis. *Psychological Bulletin, 138*(2), 353–387. https://doi.org/10.1037/a0026838

Richmond, A. S., Boysen, G. A., Hudson, D. L., Gurung, R. A. R., Naufel, K. Z., Neufeld, G., Landrum, R. E., Dunn, D. S., & Beers, M. (2021). The Introductory Psychology Census: A national study. *Scholarship of Teaching and Learning in Psychology.* Advance online publication. https://doi.org/10.1037/stl0000277

Rogers, C. R., & Farson, R. E. (1987). Active listening. In R. G. Newman, M. A. Danzinger, & M. Cohen (Eds.), *Communicating in business today.* D. C. Heath & Company. http://www.eqi.org/active_listening_rogers_farson.htm

Rosa, N. M., Bogart, K., Dunn, D. S., & Becker-Blease, K. (2019). *Increasing inclusiveness and awareness: Disability in introductory psychology.* Society for the Teaching of Psychology. https://teachpsych.org/resources/Documents/otrp/resources/Disability%20in%20Intro%20Psych%20Revision%20042419%20-%20Google%20Docs.pdf

Rudmann, J. L., Tucker, K. L., & Gonzalez, S. (2008). Using cognitive, motivational, and emotional constructs for assessing learning outcomes in student services: An exploratory study. *Journal of Applied Research in the Community College, 15*(2), 27–40.

Ruiz, A., & Warchal, J. (2013). *Activities guide: Teaching ethics in the introduction to psychology course.* Office of Teaching Resources in Psychology. http://teachpsych.org/resources/Documents/otrp/resources/ruiz13.pdf

Schunk, D. H. (1990). Goal setting and self-efficacy during self-regulated learning. *Educational Psychologist, 25*(1), 71–86. https://doi.org/10.1207/s15326985ep2501_6

Schunk, D. J. (1991). Self-efficacy and academic motivation. *Educational Psychologist, 26*(3–4), 207–231. https://doi.org/10.1080/00461520.1991.9653133

Scullin, M. K. (2019). The eight hour sleep challenge during final exams week. *Teaching of Psychology, 46*(1), 55–63. https://doi.org/10.1177/0098628318816142

Smith, T. B., Constantine, M. G., Dunn, T. W., Dinehart, J. M., & Montoya, J. A. (2006). Multicultural education in the mental health professions: A meta-analytic review. *Journal of Counseling Psychology, 53*(1), 132–145. https://doi.org/10.1037/0022-0167.53.1.132

Sprecher, P. L., & Worthington, E. L., Jr. (1982). Systematic desensitization for test anxiety as an adjunct to general psychology. *Teaching of Psychology, 9*(4), 232–233. https://doi.org/10.1207/s15328023top0904_15

Stadler, M. A., Roediger, H. L., III, & McDermott, K. B. (1999). Norms for word lists that create false memories. *Memory & Cognition, 27*(3), 494–500. https://doi.org/10.3758/BF03211543

Sue, D. W. (2001). Multidimensional facets of cultural competence. *The Counseling Psychologist, 29*(6), 790–821. https://doi.org/10.1177/0011000001296002

Susser, J. A., & McCabe, J. (2013). From the lab to the dorm room: Metacognitive awareness and use of spaced study. *Instructional Science, 41*(2), 345–363. https://doi.org/10.1007/s11251-012-9231-8

Swinkels, A. (2003). An effective exercise for teaching cognitive heuristics. *Teaching of Psychology, 30*(2), 120–122. https://doi.org/10.1207/S15328023TOP3002_08

Tablante, C. B., & Fiske, S. T. (2015). Teaching social class. *Teaching of Psychology, 42*(2), 184–190. https://doi.org/10.1177/0098628315573148

Tomcho, T. J., & Foels, R. (2002). Teaching acculturation: Developing multiple "cultures" in the classroom and role-playing the acculturation process. *Teaching of Psychology, 29*(3), 226–229. https://doi.org/10.1207/S15328023TOP2903_11

Trimble, J. E., Stevenson, M. R., & Worell, J. (2003). *Toward an inclusive psychology: Infusing the introductory psychology textbook with diversity content.* American Psychological Association.

Usher, E. L., & Pajares, F. (2008). Sources of self-efficacy in school: Critical review of the literature and future directions. *Review of Educational Research, 78*(4), 751–796. https://doi.org/10.3102/0034654308321456

Vohs, K. D., & Baumeister, R. F. (2011). *Handbook of self-regulation: Research, theory, and applications* (2nd ed.). Guilford Press.

Walker, J. (1998). Student plagiarism in universities: What are we doing about it? *Higher Education Research & Development, 17*(1), 89–106. https://doi.org/10.1080/0729436980170105

Warren, C. S. (2006). Incorporating multiculturalism into undergraduate psychology courses: Three simple active learning activities. *Teaching of Psychology, 33*(2), 105–109. https://doi.org/10.1207/s15328023top3302_5

Weinstein, Y., Sumeracki, M., & Caviglioli, O. (2019). *Understanding how we learn: A visual guide.* Routledge.

Weissgerber, T. L., Milic, N. M., Winham, S. J., & Garovic, V. D. (2015, April 22). Beyond bar and line graphs: Time for a new data presentation paradigm. *PLOS Biology, 13*(4), e1002128. https://doi.org/10.1371/journal.pbio.1002128

Whitten, L. A. (1993). Infusing Black psychology into the introductory psychology course. *Teaching of Psychology, 20*(1), 13–21. https://doi.org/10.1207/s15328023top2001_3

Wilson, T. D. (2004). *Strangers to ourselves: Discovering the adaptive unconscious.* Belknap Press/Harvard University Press. https://doi.org/10.2307/j.ctvjghvsk

Wissman, K. T., Rawson, K. A., & Pyc, M. A. (2012). How and when do students use flashcards? *Memory, 20*(6), 568–579. https://doi.org/10.1080/09658211.2012.687052

Wurtele, S. K., & Maruyama, L. (2013). Changing students' stereotypes of older adults. *Teaching of Psychology, 40*(1), 59–61. https://doi.org/10.1177/0098628312465867

Zacks, J., & Tversky, B. (1999). Bars and lines: A study of graphic communication. *Memory & Cognition, 27*(6), 1073–1079. https://doi.org/10.3758/BF03201236

Zimmerman, B. J. (1990). Self-regulated learning and academic achievement: An overview. *Educational Psychologist, 25*(1), 3–17. https://doi.org/10.1207/s15326985ep2501_2

Zimmerman, B. J. (2000). Self-efficacy: An essential motive to learn. *Contemporary Educational Psychology, 25*(1), 82–91. https://doi.org/10.1006/ceps.1999.1016

Zimmerman, B. J. (2002). Becoming a self-regulated learner: An overview. *Theory Into Practice, 41*(2), 64–70. https://doi.org/10.1207/s15430421tip4102_2

Zucchero, R. (2008). Can psychology ethics effectively be integrated into introductory psychology? *Journal of Academic Ethics, 6*(3), 245–257. https://doi.org/10.1007/s10805-009-9070-7

Zumbrunn, S., Tadlock, J., & Roberts, E. D. (2011). *Encouraging self-regulated learning in the classroom: A review of the literature.* Metropolitan Educational Research Consortium (MERC). https://scholarscompass.vcu.edu/cgi/viewcontent.cgi?article=1017&context=merc_pubs

7
CHANGING THE PARADIGM

Support and Development for Teachers of Introductory Psychology

MELISSA J. BEERS, WILLIAM S. ALTMAN, ELIZABETH YOST HAMMER, ERIN E. HARDIN, AND JORDAN D. TROISI

KEY RECOMMENDATIONS

1. Formal training and support for all introductory psychology instructors is necessary to implement the vision for course design and implementation articulated in the Introductory Psychology Initiative (IPI; American Psychological Association, 2020).

   a. Instructors teaching introductory psychology must receive training and support that develops and deepens their content knowledge, encourages sound principles of course design, focuses on strategies to support student skill development and scientific reasoning, and helps them design authentic, equitable assessment strategies aligned with learning outcomes.

   (continues)

https://doi.org/10.1037/0000260-008
Transforming Introductory Psychology: Expert Advice on Teacher Training, Course Design, and Student Success, R. A. R. Gurung and G. Neufeld (Editors)

KEY RECOMMENDATIONS (*Continued*)

    b. Training should employ and model inclusive teaching methods to address the diversity of audiences and purposes among instructors and students and be modifiable to accommodate the varying needs of diverse instructors and institutional contexts.

    c. Training experiences should be guided by a philosophy grounded in educational development. Specifically, all training offered to instructors of introductory psychology should share the following defining characteristics:

        i. be driven by specific outcomes and objectives;

        ii. be regularly assessed and modified;

        iii. provide long-term, sustained training opportunities;

        iv. draw on evidence-based pedagogy;

        v. model evidence-based pedagogical practices;

        vi. allow for the creation of communities of support and innovation; and

        vii. ensure institutional cultural relevance and alignment for equity and inclusion for all.

2. Supplementing formal training opportunities, sustained, collaborative networks and communities of practice are needed to support instructors in implementing their courses after IPI recommendations are adopted.

    a. Change cannot occur without ongoing, collaborative support specific to the IPI recommendations. Without support for change and innovation, instructors may not be able to sustain modifications in their courses.

    b. Formal and informal communities of practice are needed to support instructors as they adopt and implement the recommendations of the IPI and to create an inclusive space for instructors to observe, listen, and share with one another.

Historically, training and support for teachers of psychology—particularly introductory psychology—has been minimal, focusing on elements of course implementation as opposed to principles of course design. A paradigm change is needed in instructor training and support to realize a meaningful shift in the outcomes achieved in introductory psychology courses. This chapter articulates a philosophy to guide decisions about training and support grounded in educational development to achieve this change. We advocate for training and support that is outcome driven and evidence based, models best practices, is culturally aware and aligned, is regularly assessed and modified, creates opportunities for collaboration, and is sustained over time through collaborative peer networks or communities of practice. Transforming course design and student outcomes requires a corresponding transformation in contemporary methods of training and supporting teachers of introductory psychology.

As established in the previous six chapters of this book, the introductory psychology course presents an extraordinary opportunity to introduce students to the discipline of psychology, apply psychological science to improve their lives and communities (Chapter 3), and develop transformative skills (Chapter 6). Fortunately for the field of psychology, the introductory course is ubiquitous, which means it is taught in every possible format (e.g., online, in-person, hybrid) and institutional contexts, including high schools, community colleges, public and private institutions, historically Black colleges and universities and Hispanic-serving institutions, small liberal arts colleges, large research-intensive universities, and educational programs in prisons. This single course engages an enormous and diverse population of students. The instructors who teach it embody incredible diversity as well, in training and background within psychology and its related fields and in the contexts in which they teach.

Given the importance of the introductory psychology course in representing the discipline and in laying a strong foundation for students who want to pursue future study, one might expect that teachers of introductory psychology would receive training and support commensurate with the significance of the task. Despite training specific to teaching introductory psychology being a recommendation for strengthening the introductory course (e.g., American Psychological Association [APA], 2014), evidence has suggested this is not yet the case. Introductory Psychology Initiative (IPI) Census data revealed that only 33% of individuals had one of what we view as primary training experiences (e.g., taking a credit-bearing course or seminar on college teaching, teaching observations by a supervisor or peer, a conference with a teaching component) before teaching for the first time (Richmond et al., 2021). Furthermore, 16% of our Census respondents had received no training whatsoever before teaching the course for the first time. While there has been significant growth in the range and variety of instructional methods and techniques instructors can use in their courses in the last 20 years (see Chapter 6), and many of our Census respondents report a greater amount of training experiences in the last 5 years, there is clearly still much room for improvement in how teachers of introductory psychology are trained, mentored, and supported.

The purpose of this chapter is to turn a critical lens on training and development for instructors of introductory psychology. As discussed throughout this book, teachers of introductory psychology have a vast array of options to consider in the design of their courses, as well as the instructional techniques they may employ. Training and support for teachers of psychology is essential if they are to implement evidence-based practices and grow personally and professionally. Further, opportunities for instructor development benefit students and can have measurable impacts on their learning (e.g., Condon et al., 2016). Perhaps most critically, training and development create an opportunity for teachers to critically examine their practice with an eye to inclusion, equity, and culturally responsive pedagogy (cf. Montenegro & Jankowski, 2020). Given the complexity involved in supporting teachers and the enormity of the consequences for students, it is impossible to propose a specific format for training or even to prescribe content for training programs. Rather, our goal in this chapter is to describe a philosophy of practice grounded in educational development to guide decisions about training and support for instructors of introductory psychology. Teachers of introductory psychology can draw on this framework to inform their decisions about ongoing development, but training cannot be entirely self-directed. Thus, we identify practical considerations to support developers, local leaders, and administrators in developing a robust system of support and development for teachers of the introductory psychology course at their institutions.

WHY A NEW APPROACH TO TRAINING IS NEEDED

As our Census data show, it seems that most introductory psychology instructors have learned how to be teachers by either observing their own teachers or through some sort of basic training. Also, most instructors of introductory psychology who responded to the Census have not been provided with sufficient training or opportunities for development to enable them to engage in the most successful approaches to course design, assessment, or student development. This has long been a problem for instructors of psychology, including graduate student instructors (Meyers et al., 1998; Williams & Richman, 1971), who often teach the introductory psychology class.

Introductory psychology is frequently taught at the postsecondary level by instructors new to college teaching with little or no training in the most effective, evidence-based forms of pedagogy (Jensen, 2011). Moreover, opportunities for training are often based on one-shot workshops (e.g., at conferences), although longer and more tailored training programs of many different kinds have long been shown to be more effective (Amburgey, 2006; Ebert-May et al., 2015; Johnston et al., 1994; Knight et al., 2006; Postareff et al., 2008; Rabalais & Perritt, 1983; Romano et al., 2004). When not taught by novice instructors, the course is often taught by more experienced subject-area experts whose background may be insufficient in many areas covered by the course. Although some of these features of "typical" instructor preparation may not be ideal, an important question is the extent to which these current models are nonetheless effective; in other words, is a new approach to training instructors actually needed? Unfortunately, there seems to be ample evidence that the answer is yes and that the existing training paradigm has not been working for some time.

If the current training paradigm worked, instructors would feel well-prepared and confident, but more important, students would demonstrate achievement of key learning outcomes. However, our current training paradigm does not yield these results. Although some students may retain some memories of particular demonstrations or stories (VanderStoep et al., 2000), students have not been achieving our long-term objectives, such as becoming more scientific thinkers or better consumers of scientific information or news (Arnold et al., 1985). We have long known that most students do not retain the information from the course itself over the long term (Eurich, 1934; Gustav, 1969), and this seems to have changed little in more contemporary studies (Herman, 2010; Landrum & Gurung, 2013)—regardless of what students believe about their learning (Hard et al., 2019). Similarly, students who complete the class seem only slightly more knowledgeable about psychology than others who have not even taken the class (Rickard et al., 1988). Also, consistent with findings from other fields (e.g., Hooper & Butler, 2008), broader goals such as improved study skills, writing, approaches to thinking, or problem solving seem unable to transfer to other classes, even within the major, or to scientific reading outside of what was learned in class (Hard et al., 2019; McFarland et al., 1974).

Given such long-standing evidence that our current paradigm for training instructors is not working optimally, why does it persist? To be sure, there have been some excellent attempts to create the sort of training that would enable full- and part-time instructors at all levels to excel in teaching (e.g., Bergquist & Phillips, 1975; Burnstad, 2002; Feldhusen et al., 1998; Holtzclaw et al., 2005; Johnston et al., 1994; Whooley, 1991); however, these training models have not taken hold, and a true paradigm shift has not occurred.

THE NATURE OF PARADIGM SHIFTS

As described by Thomas Kuhn (1970), the nature of science is to work within a "set of received beliefs" (p. 4) about how the world works. These paradigms generally result from the practitioners' own educations and serve as their models for how to engage in their work. These paradigms are extremely useful in that they guide the work of a field's practitioners in practical ways. However, when enough anomalies or novel results appear, showing that the current paradigm does not predict outcomes of our efforts accurately, then the paradigm under which we are operating must undergo a shift (or in Kuhn's terms, a *scientific revolution*) to a new set of underlying principles (Kuhn, 1970).

Unfortunately, however, such scientific revolutions do not occur quickly. Initially, when some of the work in a field begins to contradict the dominant paradigm, it is often dismissed or disregarded as anomalous due to errors or mismeasurement. For instance, instructors may see particular problems in their courses from time to time and put that down to a particular class or cohort of students or a few bad days. But when we look across the field, what we see are not isolated anomalies, and the inadequacies of traditional teaching methods have been evident for quite some time. Thus, given the mounting evidence that the current way we teach is not working, we must acknowledge that it is time for a paradigm shift in training teachers of introductory psychology.

In this chapter, we propose just such a paradigmatically different model of training. In re-imagining how instructors of introductory psychology should optimally be trained, we begin with the overarching philosophical and theoretical considerations that underlie the proposed model, bringing together research and theory from the faculty and educational development literature and applying them specifically to introductory psychology. Next, we consider the unique challenges faced by introductory psychology instructors that must be incorporated into any successful model of training. Finally, we summarize and integrate these considerations to make specific recommendations for training introductory psychology instructors.

PROPOSED MODEL FOR TRAINING

Instructor training can and should look different in different contexts. It should be relevant to the specific institution, including the student population and the institutional mission. While there is no one-size-fits-all model of training, there are themes and characteristics common to successful instructor training. We propose a training philosophy based on effective practices from the faculty development literature (e.g., Beach et al., 2016; Gillespie & Robertson, 2010). While it is important to note that this training philosophy can be applied to any pedagogical training, we recommend these practices be applied specifically to support instructors implementing the framework for teaching introductory psychology outlined in the previous chapters. We present the philosophy here and subsequently discuss how it can be applied to the design of an introductory psychology course. As shown in Figure 7.1, this model is based on an educational development approach and identifies the critical components that trainers should consider in developing instructor training.

Historically, the term *faculty development* has been used to describe programs or initiatives "designed to improve faculty performance in all aspects of their professional lives" (Nelsen, 1983, p. 70), with a focus on pedagogical instruction. Millis (1994) distinguished between *faculty development* (which

FIGURE 7.1. Proposed Training Philosophy

Note. This model illustrates the components necessary for effective training for introductory psychology instructors.

focuses on improving the skills of individual faculty members), *instructional development* (which supports curricular design), and *organizational development* (which enhances the resources of the institution). More recently, there is a movement to use the term *educational development* as a way to capture the breadth of the impact of training in all three contexts, as well as the variety of audiences (e.g., graduate students, high school teachers, adjunct instructors, as well as administrative leaders; Little, 2014). Centering the proposed training philosophy around this broad approach takes the focus off the traditional tenure-track faculty member and allows for applicability to the variety of contexts in which introductory psychology is taught.

Be Driven by Specific Objectives

Just as any course should be designed by beginning with a determination of what students should be able to demonstrate in terms of learning at the end of the course (see the discussion of backward design in Chapter 2), so too should training have well-defined, specific, realistic, and measurable objectives. Macfarlane (2014) argued that well-considered objectives will not only make the purpose of the training clear for participants but it will also help in planning more meaningful experiences and with evaluating (with an eye toward improving) the training. Further, he suggested communicating training objectives before the training through the promotional or invitational announcements.

Regularly Assess and Modify Training

As educational development matures into what Beach and colleagues (2016) referred to as an "age of evidence," educational developers and trainers are being called on to help instructors with student and curricular assessment and are also required to assess their own programming. While this may feel like "pressure to demonstrate the return on investment in their own programs" (Beach et al., 2016, p. 13), we should embrace assessing our programs to ensure we are meeting our intended objectives and offering instructors what they need. As with other types of assessments, trainers should be sure to close the loop, using the data to inform and enhance future programming (Plank & Kalish, 2010).

Have Sustained Opportunities for Development

It has been established that sustained, strategic educational development opportunities are more effective for lasting change than one-shot workshops

(Darling-Hammond et al., 2009; Vega, 2015). Instead of these "one-shot-wonders" (Ferlazzo, 2018), instructors need well-planned opportunities with clearly developed objectives that are appropriate for the context of the institution and the student population. This kind of sustained development allows instructors to implement and assess strategies and methods that work for their teaching style. In addition, sustained, systematic opportunities support the notion that educational development is not an "event" but a "process" that is relevant throughout an instructor's career (Harwell, 2003), fostering an attitude of continuous improvement.

Teach Evidence-Based Pedagogical Practices

To be truly effective, instructor training should draw from evidence-based knowledge of how students learn (see Chapter 6). Cognitive scientists have much to offer here, and indeed many educational developers have written books applying cognitive science to student learning (see Ambrose et al., 2010; McGuire et al., 2015; Schwartz & Gurung, 2012). In fact, Richmond and colleagues (2016) included "possess[ing] knowledge of basic pedagogical and learning theory" and "maintaining current knowledge about effective pedagogical practices" (p. 7) as criteria for being a model teacher. To develop and support model teachers, pedagogical training should draw on evidence-based resources to train teachers to use effective strategies to enhance their students' learning.

Model Evidence-Based Pedagogical Practices

Similarly, educational developers themselves should model evidence-based practices when training (i.e., teaching) instructors (Diaz et al., 2009). In other words, we should practice what we preach (Chew et al., 2018; Nunn-Ellison et al., 2015). Modeling evidence-based practices should be integrated into every stage of training, including the planning (e.g., include active learning activities instead of straight lecture presentation), promotion (e.g., include clear, thoughtful objectives), implementation (e.g., activate prior knowledge of instructor participants), and assessment (e.g., use clear, informative rubrics for evaluation) stages. Trainers should then use the assessment data to go through the cycle again. [handwritten margin note: this all seems like Gagne's g events of instruction]

In addition to better pedagogical practices, trainers should model inclusive pedagogical practices by being participant centered, allowing participants to be authentic, and validating (in fact, encouraging) diverse perspectives (Linder et al., 2015). Trainers should also attend to issues of accessibility, ensuring that offerings accommodate instructors with hearing, visual, or other limitations. By doing so, trainers should create inclusive educational development to model inclusive pedagogical practices.

Create Communities of Support and Innovation

Just as the most effective educational development is sustained, so too is it collaborative (Graziano & Kahn, 2013). Diaz et al. (2009) encouraged developing collaborative programs as one of the main suggestions for educational developers in the 21st century. Communities of support or communities of practice allow learning to continue outside of the formal instructions or training, as instructors turn to each other for information (Beers et al., 2020). In addition, these communities serve as advocates for evidence-based teaching and learning in their own units, stretching the reach of the original programming. By creating diverse communities of innovative instructors, educational development can begin to have impacts or shift institutional culture. Designing communities with diversity in mind at the outset enhances the ideas discussed and can improve all instructors' cultural competence.

Be Culturally Aware and Aligned

After considering the characteristics of training detailed earlier, educational developers should adapt strategies to meet the needs of their institutional culture, mission, and student populations. When designing programs (and choosing which literature to review in preparation), trainers should ask themselves, What is the current student population like, and how do we want it to grow? What is the standard class size or course level for instructor participants? In what stages of their careers are the participants? What is the campus climate with regard to innovative teaching? What are the institutional priorities in terms of education? What is the overarching institutional mission, or is there one? The answers to these questions should underlie the planning and implementation of any educational programming.

Matching training to an institution's culture does not imply that training should simply seek to maintain the status quo. Cultural awareness and responsiveness involve critically examining how some students may be underserved by dominant models of teaching and learning in place throughout courses at an institution, including introductory psychology. Institutions have the potential to make meaningful shifts in inclusion and equity by engaging teachers in training, support, development, and critical self-reflection.

As shown in Figure 7.1, we recommend a set of common characteristics for any professional learning opportunity. However, for the present purpose, we recommend applying this training philosophy as program leaders and developers work with instructors to implement the outcomes and recommendations detailed in other chapters of this book and as individual instructors engage in self-reflection and seek training experiences for their own growth and development as educators. For the vision of introductory psychology presented in this book to be fully realized, instructors must have access to relevant, high-quality training and feel empowered to act on it. This philosophy is relevant to training instructors of any course across multiple disciplines. However, teaching introductory psychology presents unique and distinctive challenges for both instructors and those who train them that require the consideration of both teachers and developers.

CHALLENGES UNIQUE TO INTRODUCTORY PSYCHOLOGY

Scope and Amount of Content

One of the challenges present in training instructors of introductory psychology is the sheer amount of content that is included. The typical introductory psychology textbook includes 16 separate chapters in an average of 700 pages (Griggs & Jackson, 2013). Our Census data indicated that about 77% of instructors rely on their introductory psychology textbook between "a moderate amount" and "a great deal" to know what content to cover. This means the majority of instructors are relying on near-encyclopedic textbooks to guide their decisions about content coverage. Even attempts to distill these divergent topics into foundational pillars (Gurung et al., 2016) mean that instructors still are expected to cover research methods and ethics; biological, developmental, cognitive, social, and personality psychology; and mental health and well-being. Given the specialized nature of graduate training in psychology, even the most highly trained introductory psychology instructor will have expertise in only one or a few of the major topics of the course. Indeed, only 26% of respondents to the IPI Census said that the wide range of topics covered in the introductory course was "not challenging at all"—the other 74% acknowledged, to varying extents, the difficulty of teaching such diverse topics. Similarly, staying current regarding new findings in the discipline was also a common challenge, with 20% indicating staying current was extremely or very challenging and 55% indicating staying current is slightly or moderately challenging. Consequently, instructors often need training on the specific content areas that they will be expected to teach and ongoing access to training and support to keep current in new developments.

Instructors of introductory psychology do not just need training in content, however. They also need training in pedagogy so that they know how best to integrate, as opposed to simply covering, that content. Without unifying integrative themes, attempts to "cover" the breadth of content most often results in surface-level instruction on a series of disconnected topics, perhaps at best allowing students to achieve a basic understanding of the concepts. Indeed, we know that these attempts to cover content are largely unsuccessful. Two years after taking the introductory course, nonmajors retain just over half of the content (Landrum & Gurung, 2013). The same study showed that even psychology majors retain less than two thirds of the content from their introductory course.

Unfortunately, making the connections and themes articulated in the IPI learning objectives explicit is not easy. Traditional introductory textbooks rarely provide truly integrative themes, relying instead on standard 16-chapter models in a modular approach, organized around content. Furthermore, few instructors are familiar with the ideas of backward course design (Fink, 2003; McTighe & Wiggins, 1999), and even fewer have been trained to implement backward design principles in their courses (see Chapter 2 for a detailed discussion of backward design). Thus, the basic pedagogical principles of backward design are not only especially important for introductory psychology because of the breadth of content in the course but they are also especially hard to implement because of (a) the lack of support provided by traditional textbooks and other publisher resources, (b) the inherent difficulty of identifying unifying themes across such ostensibly divergent topics, and (c) instructors' lack of awareness and training.

Finally, instructors need training in how to cover and integrate the breadth of content in the introductory course. They also need training in how to decide what content not to cover. As noted previously, the typical introductory psychology student does not retain large portions of the content to which they are exposed (Landrum & Gurung, 2013), leading many scholars to argue that introductory psychology instructors should worry less about covering content and more about teaching students how to think scientifically about and apply whatever content they are learning (e.g., Jhangiani & Hardin, 2015). However, this still leaves instructors with the difficult task of deciding what content to emphasize and what content to minimize or even omit. The Pillar Model (Gurung et al., 2016, as discussed in Chapter 3, this volume) is a start in that it provides guidance about minimum content coverage (at least two topics from each of the five pillars); however, instructors likely still need guidance in making decisions about content coverage within selected topics (does covering "personality" require covering the entire chapter, for example?). This may be especially true for instructors in contexts in which administrators require all instructors to cover a similar (and often exhaustive) body of content. Here again, understanding principles of backward course design are likely to be essential, helping instructors distinguish content that supports the acquisition of enduring understandings from content that is important for students to know and do from content that is worth being familiar with.

Thus, whereas the philosophy of training articulated earlier is relevant to training instructors of any course, across multiple disciplines, those who train introductory psychology instructors must also attend to these instructors' unique needs for (a) training in specific content (e.g., how to teach neuroscience or cognition), (b) training in how to integrate the breadth of content, and (c) training in how to decide what content to de-emphasize or omit.

Assessment Strategies

A central tenet of backward design is to start planning a course by envisioning what students should know and be able to do at the end of the course. Thus, the first step in course design should be to consider how student learning will be assessed. Unfortunately, without training in course design and assessment, instructors are likely to prioritize content knowledge and fail to consider other objectives of the course and how best to assess them. Indeed, learning objectives too often appear on a syllabus but are not visible anywhere else in a course.

Assignments and exams are often the aspects of a course in which instructors have the most individual discretion, according to IPI Census data, yet there is little variation in the types of assessment strategies used in introduction to psychology. Multiple-choice exams and quizzes are the most common strategy to assess student learning, even though few instructors have ever received explicit training on writing multiple-choice questions or know the evidence behind writing effective questions (cf. Rodriguez & Albano, 2017). Objective examinations offer economy of scale for large courses and are often well-suited for assessing foundational knowledge, but as was discussed in Chapter 3, content knowledge is just one component of the recommended IPI student learning objectives. Other strategies may be more useful to assess objectives such as "describe the advantages and limitations of various research strategies," or "apply psychological principles to personal growth and other aspects of everyday life." Yet, instructors are rarely, if ever, given explicit training or guidance on what to assess in their courses or how best to do it (Dunn et al., 2020).

Contemporary approaches to assessment encourage instructors to consider the "authenticity" of assignments. If intentionally aligned with course objectives, assessments can create an opportunity for students to grapple with realistic, contemporary problems and encourage students to rely on higher level thinking and application. In a traditional framework, papers or assignments are generated by students, reviewed by an instructor, and never looked at or used again beyond the student–instructor dyad. In a sense, this practice generates work that is "disposable." In contrast, assignments could be an opportunity to create products students use and share outside the context of a particular course. Such "nondisposable" assignments can address contemporary problems and have an impact beyond the limitations of the classroom (Seraphin et al., 2019). For example, students could create materials that help their local community by generating a tutorial, public service announcement, or teaching tool for future semesters. They might also apply what they are learning to communicate to a wider audience (e.g., write a letter to a policymaker, create a YouTube video, or develop an informational pamphlet for a local nonprofit). Such ideas may be both exciting and intimidating to instructors seeking to expand the range of assessment strategies in their courses.

To be culturally responsive in our assessment techniques, our methods of assessment must be as diverse as the population we reach with introductory psychology. The first step in developing culturally responsive assessments is to recognize that assessment can systematically privilege some students and marginalize others (cf. Montenegro & Jankowski, 2020). The methods we use to assess learning have important implications for diversity, equity, and inclusion (DEI). Training and development can help instructors recognize the importance of assessment in DEI, see the value in alternatives to traditional forms of assessment, and develop new ways to integrate such ideas into their courses.

Finally, introductory psychology is often taught within the context of general education curricula, and for that reason, can be subject to specific assessment demands based on university or legislative requirements. Many external forces exert pressure on what constitutes "good" curricula and evidence of student learning and can potentially undermine assessment efforts (Halonen et al., 2020). Training and support for assessment can help balance the need to provide evidence of student learning to accreditors and administrators with the intended purpose of improving student learning.

Diversity of Audiences and Purposes

Beyond challenges produced by the amount and breadth of the content included in introductory psychology and how best to assess student learning, another challenge is that students, even within the same section of a class, often have very different reasons for taking the course. Further, at the administrative level, the course itself often serves different purposes. In most departments, the course serves as a prerequisite to other psychology courses and thus is expected to impart foundational content knowledge for majors and nonmajors who will take additional psychology courses. In addition, our Census data show that the course also serves as a general education course for at least 65% of colleges and universities responding; as such, the course is expected to impart broad knowledge and skills for students who may never take another psychology course. Such students may perceive being asked to learn psychology-specific content as irrelevant to their own major or longer term goals.

Here again, however, training in principles of backward course design is likely to be especially useful in helping instructors of introductory psychology to meet these challenges. By identifying unifying themes and tying the course content to a bigger picture, often skills-based learning outcomes, introductory psychology instructors can help students see the relevance of the course beyond the content. Indeed, the learning goals for majors and general education can align quite well. Jhangiani and Hardin (2015) mapped the APA learning outcomes for the psychology major onto outcomes commonly linked to general education throughout the United States (see American Association of Colleges and Universities, 2008) and found considerable overlap. They recommended that a universal focus on applying content-based knowledge and using scientific reasoning and critical thinking in all introductory courses would meet the needs of the widest variety of students. These two skills-focused student outcomes are clearly reflected in all three IPI learning goals (see Chapter 3).

To meet the psychology content goal (Goal 1), students should be able to apply the basic concepts and knowledge they are learning of psychology to their own personal growth and other aspects of everyday life, not just memorize static content. To meet the scientific thinking goal (Goal 2), students should develop skills to use empirical evidence to draw logical and objective conclusions about behavior and mental processes; evaluate, design, or conduct psychological research; and examine how psychological science can be used to counter unsubstantiated statements, opinions, or beliefs.

The third and final goal incorporates both scientific reasoning and application in the context of integrative themes, specifically stating that students should be able to apply psychological principles to change their lives and communities in positive ways and recognize that perceptions filter our experiences of the world through an imperfect personal lens. Thus, by focusing on principles of backward design to prioritize the kinds of skills-based, enduring understandings articulated in the recommended student learning outcomes (see Chapter 3), those who train and support introductory psychology instructors can better address the challenges unique to teaching a course with such a diversity of audiences and purposes.

Contextual Factors

Thus far, we have focused on challenges created by the breadth of content and diversity of audiences within a single course section. However, the diversity of contexts across which the course is taught creates another set of challenges in understanding how to train and develop instructors of introductory psychology. As noted elsewhere, the course is taken by approximately 1.6 million students annually (Gurung et al., 2016) across high school, 2- and 4-year college, and university settings. High schools differ from one another. Colleges differ from one another. High schools and colleges differ from each other. Thus, any attempt to design common models for training introductory psychology instructors must consider a wide range of contextual factors relevant to the course.

For example, course section sizes vary greatly based on institution type. Some students at large universities take introductory psychology in courses with 200, 300, or 1,000 students; in contrast, students at high schools and smaller colleges, including liberal arts colleges and community colleges, will likely have fewer classmates, perhaps 20, 30, or 40 individuals. Our Census data indicate that most responding instructors teach introductory psychology sections with 40 or fewer students. But some sections are much larger, bringing the overall mean section size to about 67 total individuals among those Census responders. Indeed, just among this chapter's authors, typical section sizes range from 25 (Altman and Troisi) to 380 (Hardin).

In addition to the size of each course section, which affects the type of pedagogy and activities possible, institution type can influence how introductory psychology is taught. We have already discussed how students within a single course section often have very different motivations and goals for the course; such differences also occur systematically across institutions. Due to features associated with their idiosyncratic mission, population of students, religious affiliation, and so on, different institutions may have different goals and learning objectives for introductory psychology. For example, at some colleges, the introductory psychology course may be split into sections that differ according to whether students anticipate majoring in psychology. These factors can orient what the introductory psychology course should look like and, as such, how to train individuals to teach it.

Features of the institution often have a direct bearing on course-related decisions as well. As our Census data show (see Table 7.1), institutions vary in how much autonomy is given to instructors to make choices in the course (e.g., what textbook to use, what information to include in syllabi, what assessments of learning to use). Data from our Census indicate decisions about course design are frequently shared; instructors are generally given the most liberty to make decisions about course assessments (e.g., assignments and exams) and supplemental materials used in the course (85% and 74%, respectively) but less liberty with regard to the choice of their textbook or the topics covered in the course (58% and 54%, respectively). Limiting the autonomy of instructors, of course, limits the choices they may make in teaching introductory psychology. If decisions about content, learning assessment, and syllabi are made by someone other than the instructor, there is the potential for one's creativity in teaching to be stifled. But in such a broad and comprehensive course as introductory psychology, limiting instructors' autonomy can also help guide their decision making. This might be especially valuable in the areas where the instructor has fewer background experiences, and less training, or expertise. Reducing the number of course design decisions can help instructors set and maintain focus on specific educational priorities.

Institutions also vary in the pathways through which introductory psychology is taught. For example, students who take introductory psychology in high school will likely have many more hours of in-class instruction time than will individuals taking it at the college level. The same is true of the

TABLE 7.1. Elements of Course Design and Individual or Collaborative Decision Making in Introductory Psychology

	Decision is completely up to the instructor	Decision is shared	Decision is made by someone else
Choosing the textbook	58.1%	31.4%	10.6%
Choosing topics covered in the course	53.5%	36.3%	10.2%
Course syllabus	61.4%	34.5%	4.1%
Materials used in the course	74.1%	23.9%	2.0%
Assignments and exams	84.8%	12.8%	2.4%

Note. Data from Richmond et al. (2021).

10% of our Census respondents who teach the course over two terms. Moreover, the proliferation of web-based tools has led many institutions of higher education to develop online or hybrid versions of introductory psychology, either instead of or in addition to face-to-face versions of the course. Nevertheless, among those who responded to the IPI Census, in a typical semester, 84% of introductory courses are taught face to face, whereas only 12% are taught online, and 4% are taught in a hybrid fashion. These different pathways have direct implications for the training of instructors for these courses and the skills they need to be able to deliver and assess the course effectively.

Clearly, there are specific aspects of training to teach introductory psychology—both before teaching for the first time and in an ongoing way—that depend a great deal on the specific institutional context in which one will be teaching. Instructors teaching large classes will need training in classroom management, creative approaches to active pedagogy, and methods of assessment that differ from those used by instructors who will teach small classes. As another example, instructors with limited autonomy in course-related decisions will need less training in choosing which topics to omit. Thus, those involved in training introductory psychology instructors must carefully assess and respond to relevant contextual factors to ensure an appropriate training focus within the broader training goals.

Instructor Variables

Finally, beyond these contextual factors, we must also remember that the characteristics of individuals teaching introductory psychology vary within and between institutions. Although not a consideration unique to introductory psychology, this diversity of instructors does create unique challenges for training and development. Drawing specifically from information at the college level, our Census data reveal that larger universities have a higher proportion of graduate students teaching introductory psychology than 4-year colleges (of our 18 graduate student respondents, 78% taught at doctoral-granting institutions). In addition to role, these patterns suggest different levels of experiences as well. Some institutions also are more likely to have novice instructors or more experienced instructors, which can also be factors in instructors' feelings of expertise, efficacy, and decision making in courses. Moreover, some colleges and universities are more likely to employ adjunct instructors (and perhaps especially at the introductory level within disciplines). For example, our Census data found that instructors who are part time and not tenure track were more likely to be employed at 2-year associate's granting colleges than other institution types.

Training should also take to heart the aspects of the course that seem challenging to instructors. Our Census data point out that class size was not perceived as a major challenge but that getting students to read and think critically were much more likely to pose challenges to instructors of introductory psychology. As such, training approaches should target the specific challenges that teachers of the course face.

TWO ESSENTIAL RECOMMENDATIONS

Throughout this entire volume, each chapter has explored methods to strengthen the structure, design, and implementation of introductory psychology to prioritize key learning objectives, employ sound course design strategies, and support student development and success. Yet, to take action, teachers must be aware of these resources, understand how to implement them, and be supported in their teaching. Taking into consideration the recommendations of the IPI, the training philosophy we have presented in this chapter, and the challenges unique to teaching introductory psychology, we conclude by recommending that all introductory psychology instructors receive two essential things: formal training and ongoing support.

Formal Training

As we have established, the art and science of teaching introductory psychology is a skill that is learned and developed. To implement the framework presented in this volume, instructors teaching introductory psychology must receive training and support. This training may be developed locally within an institution, as part of a conference, or as a stand-alone training offered by experts in this domain. We recommend training focus on these objectives:

- supplementing instructors' content knowledge in the varied topics covered in the introductory course;

- understanding principles of backward course design, so instructors are more skilled at

  - integrating content around themes,

  - deciding what content not to cover,

  - focusing on skills of applying and thinking scientifically about that content, and

  - developing authentic, equitable assessment strategies aligned with desired learning outcomes;

- promoting inclusive teaching strategies to support the diversity of audiences and purposes among instructors of introductory psychology and model such strategies for adoption in their classrooms; and
- being modifiable to accommodate the varying needs of diverse instructors and institutional contexts.

For example, in some of the pilot workshops our team has developed through IPI, we begin by having participants reflect on the challenges and opportunities specific to their unique contexts. This sets the stage before engaging them in a backward-design process of identifying "enduring understandings" for a particular topic in their course, as well as for the entire course. Next, our participants engage in activities to create or identify assessments of these outcomes and link them to specific IPI student learning outcomes. Then, in terms of the course-level outcomes and integrative themes, we ask participants to link key content from across core areas of the course to these themes to begin to see those connections across topics before identifying specific inclusive teaching strategies for that content. Included in these activities are discussions of topics within a chapter that could be de-emphasized in service of the larger learning goals. Integrating break-out sessions focused on helping instructors acquire content knowledge of topics for which they have less expertise ensures that all the recommendations would be included.

Beyond these specific recommendations regarding the content of the training offered to introductory psychology instructors, we recommend training should adopt an educational development approach and adhere to the following practices:

- be driven by specific outcomes and objectives;
- be regularly assessed and modified;
- provide long-term, sustained training opportunities;
- draw on evidence-based pedagogy;
- model evidence-based pedagogical practices;
- allow for the creation of communities of support and innovation; and
- ensure institutional cultural relevance and alignment for equity and inclusion for all.

Although these objectives can be met in a variety of training formats (e.g., graduate-level pedagogy classes, conference sessions, workshops), there is a unique advantage to developing training specific to the teaching of introductory psychology. In the Census, only between 10% and 20% of respondents identified training experiences they had that were specific to teaching introductory psychology; despite the significance of the course and its unique challenges, few instructors receive training and development specific to the demands of the course.

In light of the many unique challenges involved in designing, assessing, and implementing the introductory psychology course, we recommend establishing an Introductory Psychology Course Design Institute. Such an institute should be designed to meet the objectives described in this chapter and be composed of training modules, materials, and social supports to give participants a sense of the importance of the issues discussed in this chapter and volume. The institute would culminate in a fully designed course with a syllabus, assessment plan, and course portfolio. Sample modules for the institute may include, but not be limited to, topics such as the following:

- Understanding and Applying the IPI Goals and Student Learning Outcomes (SLOs)
- Course Design 101: Principles of Backward Design
- Appreciating Diverse Learners and Course Contexts: Opportunities and Constraints
- Supporting Student Skill Development for Transformation and Success
- Designing Authentic and Equitable Assignments Aligned With the IPI SLOs
- Creating a Learning Environment: Inclusive Teaching Strategies for Introductory Psychology
- Applying the APA Five-Pillar Model to Focus Your Course Content
- Teaching Your Course: Strategies for Classroom and Time Management
- Ongoing Course Assessment: The IPI Course Portfolio

An Introductory Psychology Course Design Institute would help instructors understand, internalize, and implement the IPI SLOs (see Chapter 3) and models for assessment (Chapter 4), backward course design approach (Chapter 2), and student transformational outcomes (Chapter 6). We envision an institute that combines presentations and opportunities to model effective teaching strategies, breakout sessions with a menu of specific content areas from which instructors could choose to supplement their content expertise, and active workshops in which smaller groups of instructors work together to (re)design activities, class sessions, assessments, and course syllabi that they can take back to their specific institutions. It would also incorporate ongoing and follow-up assessments.

The institute itself should be modeled on the backward course design philosophy so that each seminar (or activity or session) would be designed to meet a particular objective and would itself model the overall approach of objective-setting, design, and assessment in which instructors are being trained. Ideally, we believe that the resources and materials employed in the institutes could be created, tested, and shared by the participants, ultimately building up a vast repository of information and approaches over time.

These institutes could take many forms. For example, they could be stand-alone institutes held in central locations, such as regional venues, to make them more accessible to participants. They could be conference-associated institutes that are held the day before or after the conference ends. Alternatively, institutes could be virtual and delivered fully online or locally developed and held at one's own institution. Regardless of the setting and format, we envision a model institute would adopt the educational development approach described in this chapter, simultaneously serving three levels of participants:

- educational administrators, who need to understand the need and importance of the issues set forth in this volume;

- educational development and training professionals, who would learn to implement the recommendations for training at their own institutions; and

- introductory psychology teachers, who would benefit directly from the information, materials, and training opportunities provided by the institute.

Finally, to produce a lasting impact, the institutes should be available and accessible on a regular basis and should be publicized in ways that draw the attention of their constituents. As noted previously in this volume, there have been many attempts to assist instructors in improving the introductory psychology course. These initiatives have yielded some excellent information; however, they have not resulted in extensive or long-lasting change. As we learned from the IPI Census and from the listening sessions we conducted throughout 2018 and 2019, many introductory psychology instructors seem to have been unaware of many of the previous efforts to strengthen the introductory psychology course, leading to our second recommendation.

Ongoing Support

We must provide not only formal training for instructors of introductory psychology but also a mechanism that will sustain and extend the benefits of this training beyond a formal institute. Formal and informal communities for teachers of psychology are already thriving in the Society for the Teaching of Psychology (STP), on social media, and in teaching conferences such as the National Institute for the Teaching of Psychology, STP's Annual Conference on Teaching, and the Psych One conference. Yet, we see a critical need to develop an ongoing community specific to introductory psychology, structured to support the principles of educational development we have described in this chapter. Improving our practice through inclusive, development-oriented methods is essentially a social process (Bandura, 1977; Dobozy, 2012; Wenger et al., 2002). Newman (2017) argued that one-time workshops (such as institutes) do not allow for the reinforcement necessary to successfully implement and sustain teaching innovations, and ongoing support is needed for instructors when the actual work is being done. In addition, if we view the work of this volume as shifting a paradigm, then educational developers and instructors must commit the time to make that shift happen. To that end, we propose training and support are followed by participation in communities of practice.

Communities of practice are effective ways to build relationships and share knowledge, tools, and techniques (Abigail, 2016; Hoadley, 2012). A *community of practice* is a model of social learning whereby individuals begin to identify with a community by adopting the practices shared by its members. The type of learning experienced in a community of practice is not always intentional; rather, it is a function of the activity, context, and culture in which it is situated (Beers et al., 2020). Communities of practice encourage and sustain development as members develop knowledge independently through authentic practice in the community and rely less on "experts" or authorities transmitting information.

In their work on developing and sustaining communities of practice, Fraser and colleagues (2017) found that the top-ranked factors were skilled leadership; personal value; mutual respect, understanding, and trust; establishing informal relationships and communication links; and having concrete, attainable goals and objectives. For communities of practice to work most effectively, members need to feel engagement and identification with the group (Daly, 2011). Indeed, McCormack and colleagues (2017) recommended that for communities of practice to be sustainable, members should view themselves as both facilitators and members of the community.

As with the training itself, a community of practice can take many forms, from nationally organized groups with members from many institutions to locally organized groups from a single institution—for example, an instructional team teaching introductory psychology in one program or a group of new teachers from many different institutions. Regardless of format, de Carvalho-Filho and colleagues (2020) provided the following 12 tips for successful, long-lasting, and impactful communities of practice:

- Begin with a core group of interested, committed individuals. Start small with a core group and let the reputation build.

- Develop clear, shared goals. Again, use the backward design model and begin with clear objectives.

- Begin with a specific task or problem to solve. A problem-solving approach ensures that the group has a focus and can aid in developing group cohesion.

- Be inclusive and value others' perspectives. The community should be welcoming to a variety of ideas and perspectives.

- Intentionally invite members with varying levels of experience with the topic. To have diverse perspectives, members should come from a variety of career stages and experiences.

- Utilize a facilitator. Select a facilitator who can ensure that all voices are heard and that the group stays on track to meet its goals and objectives.

- Make good use of your time together. Everyone is busy, so ensure that the time committed to the community is worthwhile. Being problem focused and having clear goals helps facilitate this.

- Establish the support of your institution or organization. Having institutional support is critical not only in implementing communities of practice but also in getting participant buy-in.

- Work to keep it alive. Communities of practice by definition should be sustainable. So, have a plan to keep the momentum and energy going.

- Promote the successes of the community members. By doing so, the community will be more vibrant, more visible, and more likely to gain institutional support.

- Consider virtual options. Even if your community meets face to face, use technology to enhance attendance and allow for more flexibility from members.

- Assess and improve. Finally, regularly assess the community of practice to evolve and meet ever-changing needs.

We piloted such a community of practice in fall 2019 for instructors exploring the new IPI SLOs. Participants from all over the United States represented a variety of schools and disciplines. We began by establishing a shared repository for resources, to which any member of the community of practice could contribute, and a listserv so members could ask one another questions and share their experiences. We conducted monthly online meetings, each centered on a discussion of how each instructor was addressing a specific SLO. Communities like this could be developed within and across institutions, depending on members' needs. Unlike a formal team, participation in a community of practice is voluntary, and the goals of the community are shaped by those who engage (Wenger et al., 2002). In this sense, there is no "right" or "best" way to manage a community other than by creating an inclusive space for members to observe, listen, and share with one another.

CONCLUSION

We have presented our key recommendations for teacher training and development. To realize the revolutionary changes to introductory psychology envisioned by the IPI and described in this volume, it will not be enough to implement recommended actions haphazardly or opportunistically. A true paradigm shift requires slow, sustained, intentional change at multiple levels and across an entire discipline, the kind of paradigmatic change that requires patience and persistence. The fact that we see similar attempts to change instructor education in general (Gaff & Simpson, 1994; Travis, 1995; Whooley, 1991) and in fields as diverse as biology (Jensen, 2011), business (Roach et al., 2015), chemistry (Coppola, 2016), economics (Allgood et al., 2018), English (Marting, 1987), engineering (Fink et al., 2005), and nursing (James, 2004) suggests a groundswell of support for the kinds of changes for which we are advocating.

To achieve this revolution in instructor training, we must confront a number of challenges. One is the need to overcome some instructors' resistance to any sort of training or evaluation of their teaching (McCrickerd, 2012; Strachan et al., 1980). Beyond these instructor-level challenges loom institutional barriers. Many instructors lack the independent decision making required to engage in the most productive forms of course design, teaching, and assessment because they are constrained by institutional requirements and policies. These might include institutional demands for particular content, assessment strategies, course designs, or syllabi.

Moreover, although all institutions claim to value high-quality teaching, they do not always prioritize it with regard to how they reward instructors— at least in terms of instructor perceptions (Ginns et al., 2010). For example, in many institutions, instructors continue to be rewarded primarily for research publication and the successful acquisition of grant funding (Brewster, 1967; Clifton & Buskist, 2005). While they may wish to become more effective instructors, it is perfectly rational for them to prioritize these other areas instead (Perlman et al., 1996). Similarly, there are many reasons why full- and part-time non-tenure-stream instructors may not participate in professional development and training. These include lack of tangible (e.g., time, money) and intangible (e.g., respect) institutional support, a real or perceived lack of time, disrespect or disregard by their full-time or tenure-stream colleagues or administrators, or the fact that teaching is not their primary occupation (Knight et al., 2007; Sandford et al., 2011). These long-lived, ongoing difficulties indicate the need for a paradigm shift at the institutional level. Although such change will not happen easily or quickly, such institution-level change is essential and will require persuading institutions of the benefits of supporting the kind of instructor training laid out in this chapter. There is already mounting evidence that more effective pedagogy is associated with a number of outcomes about which institutions care deeply (see Jankowski, 2017): increased retention of students, increased student success and satisfaction, and ultimately, happier alumni more willing to support their development efforts.

It will be essential to rigorously evaluate the outcomes of our proposed training model to provide the evidence needed to convince institutions of its value. At least as important, rigorous evaluation is needed to convince ourselves and our students of the value of these efforts. The need for a new model of training is clear, as are the benefits to students, instructors, institutions, the discipline, and—should the kind of transformation outlined in this book be achieved—the greater good.

REFERENCES

Abigail, L. K. M. (2016). Do communities of practice enhance faculty development? *Health Profession Education*, *2*(2), 61–74. https://doi.org/10.1016/j.hpe.2016.08.004

Allgood, S., Hoyt, G., & McGoldrick, K. (2018). Teacher training for PhD students and new faculty in economics. *The Journal of Economic Education*, *49*(2), 209–219. https://doi.org/10.1080/00220485.2018.1438947

Ambrose, S. A., Bridges, M. W., DiPietro, M., Lovett, M. C., & Norman, M. K. (2010). *How learning works: Seven research-based principles for smart teaching*. Jossey-Bass.

Amburgey, V. (2006). One model of professional development for higher education faculty. *Computers in the Schools*, *23*(3–4), 105–113. https://doi.org/10.1300/J025v23n03_07

American Association of Colleges and Universities. (2008). *College learning for the new global century*. https://www.aacu.org/sites/default/files/files/LEAP/GlobalCentury_final.pdf

American Psychological Association. (2014). *Strengthening the common core of the introductory psychology course.* https://www.apa.org/ed/governance/bea/intro-psych-report.pdf

American Psychological Association. (2020). *The APA Introductory Psychology Initiative.* https://www.apa.org/ed/precollege/undergrad/introductory-psychology-initiative

Arnold, J. D., Cunningham, T. F., Makosky, V. P., McGrevy, D. F., Ross, J. A., & Searleman, A. (1985). Students' long-term evaluation of introductory psychology: How psychology compares with other introductory courses. *Teaching of Psychology, 12*(3), 139–142. https://doi.org/10.1207/s15328023top1203_6

Bandura, A. (1977). *Social learning theory.* Prentice Hall.

Beach, A., Sorcinelli, M. D., Austin, A., & Rivard, J. (2016). *Faculty development in the age of evidence.* Stylus.

Beers, M., Dell'Armo, K., & Plate, A. (2020). The other side of the podium: Supporting graduate student teaching development. In T. M. Ober, E. Che, J. E. Brodsky, C. Raffaele, & P. J. Brooks (Eds.), *How we teach now: The GSTA guide to transformative teaching* (pp. 30–41). Society for the Teaching of Psychology. http://teachpsych.org/ebooks/howweteachnow-transformative

Bergquist, W. H., & Phillips, S. R. (1975). Components of an effective faculty development program. *The Journal of Higher Education, 46*(2), 177–211. https://doi.org/10.2307/1980880

Brewster, B. (1967). The lost art of teaching. *Journal of Education for Librarianship, 8*(2), 71–77. https://doi.org/10.2307/40322319

Burnstad, H. M. (2002). Part-time faculty development at Johnson County Community College. *New Directions for Community Colleges, 2002*(120), 17–26. https://doi.org/10.1002/cc.85

Chew, S. L., Halonen, J. S., McCarthy, M. A., Gurung, R. A. R., Beers, M. J., McEntarffer, R., & Landrum, R. E. (2018). Practice what we teach: Improving teaching and learning in psychology. *Teaching of Psychology, 45*(3), 239–245. https://doi.org/10.1177/0098628318779264

Clifton, J., & Buskist, W. (2005). Preparing graduate students for academic positions in psychology: Suggestions from job advertisements. *Teaching of Psychology, 32*(4), 265–267.

Condon, W., Iverson, E. R., Manduca, C. A., Rutz, C., & Willett, G. (2016). *Faculty development and student learning: Assessing the connections.* Indiana University Press.

Coppola, B. P. (2016). Broad & capacious: A new norm for instructional development in a research setting. *Change: The Magazine of Higher Learning, 48*(2), 34–43. https://doi.org/10.1080/00091383.2016.1163206

Daly, C. J. (2011). Faculty learning communities: Addressing the professional development needs of faculty and the learning needs of students. *Currents in Teaching and Learning, 4*(1), 3–16.

Darling-Hammond, L., Chung Wei, R., Andree, A., Richardson, N., & Orphanos, S. (2009). *Professional learning in the learning profession: A status report on teacher development in the U.S. and abroad.* National Staff Development Council. https://edpolicy.stanford.edu/sites/default/files/publications/professional-learning-learning-profession-status-report-teacher-development-us-and-abroad_0.pdf de Carvalho-Filho, M. A., Tio, R. A., & Steinert, Y. (2020). Twelve tips for implementing a community of practice for faculty development. *Medical Teacher, 42*(2), 143–149. https://doi.org/10.1080/0142159x.2018.1552782

Diaz, V., Garrett, P. B., Kinley, E., Moore, J., & Schwartz, C. (2009, May 28). Faculty development for the 21st Century. *EDUCAUSE Review, 44*(3), 46–55.

Dobozy, E. (2012). Learning in higher education symposia: A new professional development model for university educators. *Issues in Educational Research, 22*(3), 228–245.

Dunn, D. S., Troisi, J. D., & Baker, S. C. (2020). Faculty receptivity to assessment: Changing the climate for evaluating teaching and learning in psychology. *Scholarship of Teaching and Learning in Psychology, 6*(3), 244–253. https://doi.org/10.1037/stl0000247

Ebert-May, D., Derting, T. L., Henkel, T. P., Middlemis Maher, J., Momsen, J. L., Arnold, B., & Passmore, H. A. (2015). Breaking the cycle: Future faculty begin teaching with learner-centered strategies after professional development. *CBE Life Sciences Education, 14*(2). https://doi.org/10.1187/cbe.14-12-0222

Eurich, A. C. (1934). Retention of knowledge acquired in a course in general psychology. *Journal of Applied Psychology, 18*(2), 209–219. https://doi.org/10.1037/h0071566

Feldhusen, J. F., Ball, D., Wood, B. K., Dixon, F. A., & Larkin, L. (1998). A university course on college teaching. *College Teaching, 46*(2), 72–75. https://doi.org/10.1080/87567559809596240

Ferlazzo, L. (2018, June 11). Response: Professional development does not need 'one-shot wonders.' *Education Week.* https://blogs.edweek.org/teachers/classroom_qa_with_larry_ferlazzo/2018/06/response_professional_development_does_not_need_one-shot_wonders.html

Fink, L. D. (2003). *Creating significant learning experiences: An integrated approach to designing college courses.* Jossey-Bass.

Fink, L. D., Ambrose, S., & Wheeler, D. (2005). Becoming a professional engineering educator: A new role for a new era. *Journal of Engineering Education, 94*(1), 185–194. https://doi.org/10.1002/j.2168-9830.2005.tb00837.x

Fraser, C., Honeyfield, J., Breen, F., Protheroe, M., & Fester, V. (2017). From project to permanence: Growing inter-institutional collaborative teams into long-term, sustainable communities of practice. In J. McDonald & A. Cater-Steel (Eds.), *Communities of practice: Facilitating social learning in higher education* (pp. 567–598). Springer. https://doi.org/10.1007/978-981-10-2879-3_27

Gaff, J. G., & Simpson, R. D. (1994). Faculty development in the United States. *Innovative Higher Education, 18*(3), 167–176. https://doi.org/10.1007/BF01191111

Gillespie, K. J., & Robertson, D. L. (2010). *A guide to faculty development* (2nd ed.). Jossey-Bass.

Ginns, P., Kitay, J., & Prosser, M. (2010). Transfer of academic staff learning in a research-intensive university. *Teaching in Higher Education, 15*(3), 235–246. https://doi.org/10.1080/13562511003740783

Graziano, J., & Kahn, G. (2013). Sustained faculty development in learning communities. *Learning Communities Research and Practice, 1*(2), Article 5. https://washingtoncenter.evergreen.edu/lcrpjournal/vol1/iss2/5

Griggs, R. A., & Jackson, S. L. (2013). Introductory psychology textbooks: An objective analysis update. *Teaching of Psychology, 40*(3), 163–168. https://doi.org/10.1177/0098628313487455

Gurung, R. A. R., Hackathorn, J., Enns, C., Frantz, S., Cacioppo, J. T., Loop, T., & Freeman, J. E. (2016). Strengthening introductory psychology: A new model for teaching the introductory course. *American Psychologist, 71*(2), 112–124. https://doi.org/10.1037/a0040012

Gustav, A. (1969). Retention of course material after varying intervals of time. *Psychological Reports, 25*(3), 727–730. https://doi.org/10.2466/pr0.1969.25.3.727

Halonen, J. S., Beers, M. J., & Brown, A. N. (2020). Assessment at the crossroads: How did we get here and what should we do? *Scholarship of Teaching and Learning in Psychology, 6*(3), 254–268. https://doi.org/10.1037/stl0000243

Hard, B. M., Lovett, J. M., & Brady, S. T. (2019). What do students remember about introductory psychology, years later? *Scholarship of Teaching and Learning in Psychology, 5*(1), 61–74. https://doi.org/10.1037/stl0000136

Harwell, S. H. (2003). *Teacher professional development: It's not an event, it's a process.* CORD. http://citeseerx.ist.psu.edu/viewdoc/download?doi=10.1.1.111.9200&rep=rep1&type=pdf

Herman, W. E. (2010, March 19–20). *How much do students remember from an introductory psychology course?* [Paper presentation]. Farmingdale State College Annual Conference on the Teaching of Psychology: Ideas & Innovations, Tarrytown, NY.

Hoadley, C. (2012). What is a community of practice and how can we support it? In D. Jonassen & S. Land (Eds.), *Theoretical foundations of learning environments* (2nd ed., pp. 286–299). Routledge.

Holtzclaw, J. D., Morris, L. G., & Pyatt, R. (2005). FIRST: A model for developing new science faculty. *Journal of College Science Teaching, 34*(6), 24–29.

Hooper, R. I., & Butler, S. (2008). Student transfer of general education English skills to a social work diversity course: Is it happening? *Journal of the Idaho Academy of Science, 44*(2), 1–10.

James, K. M. G. (2004). Bridging the gap: Creating faculty development opportunities at a large medical center. *Journal of Continuing Education in Nursing, 35*(1), 24–26. https://doi.org/10.3928/0022-0124-20040101-09

Jankowski, N. A. (2017). *Unpacking relationships: Instruction and student outcomes.* American Council on Education. https://www.acenet.edu/Documents/Unpacking-Relationships-Instruction-and-Student-Outcomes.pdf

Jensen, J. L. (2011). Higher education faculty versus high school teacher: Does pedagogical preparation make a difference? *Bioscene, 37*(2), 30–36.

Jhangiani, R., & Hardin, E. E. (2015). Skill development in introductory psychology. *Scholarship of Teaching and Learning in Psychology, 1*(4), 362–376. https://doi.org/10.1037/stl0000049

Johnston, J. A., Kerr, B. A., Bondeson, W. B., Hansen, R. N., & Claiborn, C. D. (1994). The Wakonse conference on college teaching. *Journal of Counseling and Development, 72*(5), 480–484. https://doi.org/10.1002/j.1556-6676.1994.tb00977.x

Knight, P., Baume, D., Tait, J., & Yorke, M. (2007). Enhancing part-time teaching in higher education: A challenge for institutional policy and practice. *Higher Education Quarterly, 61*(4), 420–438. https://doi.org/10.1111/j.1468-2273.2007.00350.x

Knight, P., Tait, J., & Yorke, M. (2006). The professional learning of teachers in higher education. *Studies in Higher Education, 31*(3), 319–339. https://doi.org/10.1080/03075070600680786

Kuhn, T. S. (1970). *The structure of scientific revolutions.* University of Chicago Press.

Landrum, R. E., & Gurung, R. (2013). The memorability of introductory psychology revisited. *Teaching of Psychology, 40*(3), 222–227. https://doi.org/10.1177/0098628313487417

Linder, C., Harris, J. C., Allen, E. L., & Hubain, B. (2015). Building inclusive pedagogy: Recommendations from a national study of students of color in higher education and student affairs graduate programs. *Equity & Excellence in Education, 48*(2), 178–194. https://doi.org/10.1080/10665684.2014.959270

Little, D. (2014). Reflections on the state of the scholarship of educational development. *To Improve the Academy, 33*(1), 1–13.

Macfarlane, J. P. (2014, September 22). Articulating learning outcomes for faculty development workshops. *Faculty Focus.* https://www.facultyfocus.com/articles/faculty-development/articulating-learning-outcomes-faculty-development-workshops/

Marting, J. (1987). *An historical overview of the training of teaching assistants.* (ED285511). ERIC. https://eric.ed.gov/?id=ED285511

McCormack, C., Kennelly, R., Gilchrist, J., Hancock, E., Islam, J., Northcote, M., & Thomson, K. (2017). From dream to reality: Sustaining a higher education community of practice beyond initial enthusiasm. In J. McDonald & A. Cater-Steel (Eds.), *Communities of practice: Facilitating social learning in higher education* (pp. 599–622). Springer. https://doi.org/10.1007/978-981-10-2879-3_28

McCrickerd, J. (2012). Understanding and reducing faculty reluctance to improve teaching. *College Teaching, 60*(2), 56–64. https://doi.org/10.1080/87567555.2011.633287

McFarland, D. J., Jacobus, K. A., & Hines, K. M. (1974). Transfer of instruction in introductory psychology. *Psychological Reports, 34*(1), 147–150. https://doi.org/10.2466/pr0.1974.34.1.147

McGuire, S. Y., Angelo, T., & McGuire, S. (2015). *Teach students how to learn: Strategies you can incorporate into any course to improve student metacognition, study skills, and motivation.* Stylus.

McTighe, J., & Wiggins, G. P. (1999). *Understanding by design handbook.* Association for Supervision and Curriculum Development.

Meyers, S. A., Reid, P. T., & Quina, K. (1998). Ready or not, here we come: Preparing psychology graduate students for academic careers. *Teaching of Psychology, 25*(2), 124–126. https://doi.org/10.1207/s15328023top2502_11

Millis, B. (1994). Faculty development in the 1990s: What it is and why we can't wait. *Journal of Counseling and Development, 72*(5), 454–464. https://doi.org/10.1002/j.1556-6676.1994.tb00974.x

Montenegro, E., & Jankowski, N. A. (2020, January). *A new decade for assessment: Embedding equity into assessment praxis* (Occasional Paper No. 42). University of Illinois and Indiana University, National Institute for Learning Outcomes Assessment.

Nelsen, W. (1983). Faculty who stay: Renewing our most important resource. In R. Baldwin & R. Blackburn (Eds.), *College faculty: Versatile human resources in a period of constraint* (pp. 67–83). Jossey-Bass. https://doi.org/10.1002/ir.37019834008

Newman, T. (2017). Making an impact: Utilising faculty learning communities to enhance teaching and learning. In J. McDonald & A. Cater-Steel (Eds.), *Communities of practice: Facilitating social learning in higher education* (pp. 423–435). Springer. https://doi.org/10.1007/978-981-10-2879-3_20

Nunn-Ellison, K., Kapka, L., Myers, J., McGrew, H., Bernheisel, J., & Cutler, J. (2015). *Practice what you preach!* National Institute for Learning Outcomes Assessment. https://www.learningoutcomeassessment.org/documents/Nunn-Ellison%20et%20al_Assessment_in_Practice.pdf

Perlman, B., Konop, K., McFadden, S. H., & McCann, L. (1996). New faculty do want to teach. *Teaching of Psychology, 23*(4), 232–234. https://doi.org/10.1207/s15328023top2304_6

Plank, K. M., & Kalish, A. (2010). Program assessment. In K. J. Gillespie, D. L. Robertson, & Associates. (Eds.), *A guide to faculty development: Practical advice, examples, and resources* (2nd ed., pp. 135–150). Jossey-Bass.

Postareff, L., Lindblom-Ylänne, S., & Nevgi, A. (2008). A follow-up study of the effect of pedagogical training on teaching in higher education. *Higher Education, 56*(1), 29–43. https://doi.org/10.1007/s10734-007-9087-z

Rabalais, M. J., & Perritt, J. E. (1983). Instructional development for part-time faculty. *Community College Review, 11*(2), 20–22. https://doi.org/10.1177/009155218301100204

Richmond, A. S., Boysen, G. A., & Gurung, R. A. R. (2016). *An evidence-based guide to college and university teaching: Developing the model teacher.* Routledge. https://doi.org/10.4324/9781315642529

Richmond, A. S., Boysen, G. A., Hudson, D. L., Gurung, R. A. R., Naufel, K. Z., Neufeld, G., Landrum, R. E., Dunn, D. S., & Beers, M. (2021). The Introductory Psychology Census: A national study. *Scholarship of Teaching and Learning in Psychology.* Advance online publication. https://doi.org/10.1037/stl0000277

Rickard, H. C., Rogers, R., Ellis, N. R., & Beidleman, W. B. (1988). Some retention, but not enough. *Teaching of Psychology, 15*(3), 151–152. https://doi.org/10.1207/s15328023top1503_14

Roach, J., Milkman, M., & McCoy, J. (2015). Recent business doctorates' teacher training and perceptions of their preparedness to teach business courses. *Academy of Educational Leadership Journal, 19*(1), 1–14.

Rodriguez, M. C., & Albano, A. D. (2017). *The college instructor's guide to writing test items: Measuring student learning.* Routledge. https://doi.org/10.4324/9781315714776

Romano, J. L., Hoesing, R., O'Donovan, K., & Weinsheimer, J. (2004). Faculty at mid-career: A program to enhance teaching and learning. *Innovative Higher Education, 29*(1), 21–48. https://doi.org/10.1023/B:IHIE.0000035365.92454.a5

Sandford, B. A., Dainty, J. D., Belcher, G. G., & Frisbee, R. L. (2011). Perceptions of the willingness of part-time instructors in community colleges in the U.S. to engage in professional development opportunities and the best method(s) of delivering these experiences. *Journal of Career & Technical Education, 26*(1), 48–61. https://doi.org/10.21061/jcte.v26i1.514

Schwartz, B. M., & Gurung, R. A. R. (Eds.). (2012). *Evidence-based teaching for higher education.* American Psychological Association. https://doi.org/10.1037/13745-000

Seraphin, S. B., Grizzell, J. A., Kerr-German, A., Perkins, M. A., Grzanka, P. R., & Hardin, E. E. (2019). A conceptual framework for non-disposable assignments:

Inspiring implementation, innovation, and research. *Psychology Learning & Teaching, 18*(1), 84–97. https://doi.org/10.1177/1475725718811711

Strachan, A., Welch, V. O., Barker, C., Compas, B., & Ferguson, M. L. (1980). A framework for training college-level teachers of psychology: Five basic processes. *Teaching of Psychology, 7*(3), 180–182. https://doi.org/10.1207/s15328023top0703_17

Travis, J. E. (1995). *Models for improving college teaching: A faculty resource* (ED403811). ERIC. https://eric.ed.gov/?id=ED403811

VanderStoep, S. W., Fagerlin, A., & Feenstra, J. S. (2000). What do students remember from introductory psychology? *Teaching of Psychology, 27*(2), 89–92. https://doi.org/10.1207/S15328023TOP2702_02

Vega, V. (2015, November 1). Teacher development research review: Keys to educator success. *Edutopia.* https://www.edutopia.org/teacher-development-research-keys-success

Wenger, E., McDermott, R., & Snyder, W. M. (2002). *Cultivating communities of practice: A guide to managing knowledge.* Harvard Business School Press.

Whooley, J. E. (1991, March). A program to increase teaching effectiveness of college faculty. *College Student Journal, 25,* 487–491.

Williams, J. E., & Richman, C. L. (1971). The graduate preparation of the college professor of psychology: A survey. *American Psychologist, 26*(11), 1000–1009. https://doi.org/10.1037/h0032257

PART **II** OPERATIONALIZING
RECOMMENDATIONS
ACROSS DIVERSE
CONTEXTS

8 TEACHING INTRODUCTORY PSYCHOLOGY AS A HIGH SCHOOL ELECTIVE

Davis High School

KRISTIN H. WHITLOCK

- Context: High school
- Student enrollment: 2,600
- Grades: 10-12
- Enrollment type: Public
- Underrepresented minoritized students: 8%
- Term: 2 semesters, 4 quarters
- Schedule: Traditional block (A/B days)
- Introductory psychology class sizes: 30

CONTEXT

Davis High School is a large suburban public high school in Kaysville, Utah. Davis High School is one of 10 high schools in the Davis County School District. As a comprehensive high school, Davis High offers a wide range of courses for both college-bound and non-college-bound students.

https://doi.org/10.1037/0000260-009
Transforming Introductory Psychology: Expert Advice on Teacher Training, Course Design, and Student Success, R. A. R. Gurung and G. Neufeld (Editors)

Ninety-seven percent of the student body graduates from Davis High. Students have many opportunities to earn college credit while at school because Davis High offers 37 Concurrent Enrollment (CE) and 18 Advanced Placement (AP) courses. Fifty-two percent of Davis High School's student body participates in AP courses.

Four psychology courses are offered at Davis High School: Introductory Psychology (1 semester), Sport Psychology (1 semester), CE Sport Psychology (1 semester), and AP Psychology (2 semesters). These are elective social studies courses, which means that they are not required for graduation. Psychology courses are primarily taught by those trained to teach social studies. The Utah State Office of Education (USOE) offers a psychology credential, but it is not required to teach psychology courses.

UNIQUE CHALLENGES OF TEACHING INTRODUCTORY PSYCHOLOGY

The designation of psychology as an elective social studies course presents several challenges, including finding sufficient funding, a general lack of teacher training, and developing cohesive curriculum standards. Elective courses, in general, do not receive the same attention that core classes do. Funding for teacher training, textbook adoption, and classroom materials may be harder to obtain. In addition to this general oversight, the traditional placement of psychology courses in the social studies department makes little sense. Psychology course content and skills share little in common with other social studies courses. Department meetings rarely provide relevant information or training opportunities for psychology teachers.

Teachers vary widely in their knowledge of psychology when they begin teaching the course. The USOE provides a psychology credential, but it is not required to teach the course. That means that you can teach a high school course in psychology without having ever taken a psychology course. Many teachers are trained to teach history or government. Few colleges and universities in the state of Utah offer a teaching major or minor in psychology. This leaves many teachers without the knowledge or skills necessary to teach the science of psychology.

While course curriculum in CE and AP courses are dictated by outside sources, there are no specific state curriculum standards for introductory psychology. This is not to say that Utah teachers do not have guidelines to help in their curricular decisions. Luckily, the USOE suggests that Utah teachers follow the American Psychological Association's (APA's) *National*

Standards for High School Psychology Curricula (2011). Utah is one of a handful of states that follows these important standards. Currently, 34 states have no curriculum standards for psychology. In the state of Utah, individual school districts may still implement their own requirements for the course.

CURRENT AND FUTURE IMPLEMENTATIONS OF THE INTRODUCTORY PSYCHOLOGY INITIATIVE RECOMMENDATIONS

Student Learning Outcomes and Assessment

The student learning outcomes (SLOs) of the introductory course at Davis High School are aligned with the APA's (2011) *National Standards for High School Psychology Curricula*. These guidelines are divided into seven broad content domains: Scientific Inquiry, Biopsychology, Development and Learning, Sociocultural Context, Cognition, Individual Variations, and Applications of Psychological Science. It is recommended that teachers begin with research and focus on one content area from each domain.

Because I enjoy some flexibility in designing my course, I recently introduced an overarching theme to organize the content, namely, around the common myths of psychology. My students begin each unit with a question focused on a myth, such as "Can you really be left- or right-brained?" While debunking myths is the central unifying theme to my course, I still satisfy the content standards outlined in the *National Standards*.

When the integrative themes of the Introductory Psychology Initiative (IPI; APA, 2020) were introduced, I was immediately interested in incorporating them because I had already been taking a thematic approach. At the same time, the social studies standards in my district were being updated. At the request of our Social Studies Curriculum Director, a colleague and I submitted a proposal incorporating the IPI SLOs into our district standards, with the expected release being fall 2021.

Course Models and Design

The teachers in our professional learning community began working to implement the IPI SLOs in our psychology curriculum. We have wrestled with the best way to organize around the themes while satisfying the content requirements of the APA's *National Standards*. We are considering teaching in traditional content units while weaving the themes throughout them. Table 8.1 provides a sample format for teaching the Memory unit.

TABLE 8.1. Sample Format for Teaching Memory

Introductory Psychology Initiative theme	Course content
Theme 3A: Psychological science relies on empirical evidence and adapts as new data develop.	How does human memory work?
Theme 3B: Psychology explains general principles that govern behavior while recognizing individual differences.	How much information can individuals hold in their sensory, short-term, and long-term memory?
Theme 3C: Psychological, biological, social, and cultural factors influence behavior and mental processes.	How is memory physically stored?
Theme 3D: Psychology values diversity, promotes equity, and fosters inclusion in pursuit of a more just society.	Can eyewitness testimony be trusted?
Theme 3E: Our perceptions and biases filter our experiences of the world through an imperfect personal lens.	Do our memories work like a computer?
Theme 3F: Applying psychological principles can change our lives, organizations, and communities in positive ways.	How can we improve our memory?
Theme 3G: Ethical principles guide psychology research and practice.	Can false memories be implanted during therapy?

Teacher Training and Development

Training for high school psychology teachers is limited. In Utah, teachers must seek out professional development opportunities primarily outside of their school districts. The first place to look is the APA's Teachers of Psychology Secondary Schools (TOPSS). TOPSS has programming at the annual APA convention, as well as summer workshops at Clark University and Oregon State University. Many states also have grassroots regional organizations loosely affiliated with TOPSS, such as the organization in our state called Utah Teachers of Psychology in Secondary Schools. These regional organizations provide yearly workshops for teachers and provide resources and networking opportunities. The Society for the Teaching of Psychology also has relevant programming for high school teachers at the Annual Conference on Teaching. High school teachers should take advantage of spring conferences provided by their regional psychological associations, such as the Rocky Mountain Psychological Association. The College Board also provides 1-day workshops in the fall and weeklong AP Summer Institutes for AP teachers, such as the one provided by Davis County School District.

Student Success and Transformation

There is no other class that can immediately impact high school students like psychology. For many students, this may be their only exposure to the field. A well-taught course can dispel many of the psychological myths they will encounter. Students develop scientific literacy because of this course. Students begin to use the language of psychology to explain their experiences and understand others, and they start to see the world differently as they recognize how their own biases influence their perceptions. They learn how to learn. Students also develop skills to help them increase their well-being. They start to see how the principles of psychological science can help solve the problems our communities face. Many students decide, after taking high school psychology, that this is the major for them. High school psychology is an integral first step in the academic pipeline. Implementation of the IPI SLOs at the high school level will help smooth students' transition to college-level psychology courses. Adopting the IPI SLOs will also provide curricular consistency at all levels of psychology education.

REFERENCES

American Psychological Association. (2011). *National Standards for High School Psychology Curricula*. https://www.apa.org/education/k12/national-standards

American Psychological Association. (2020). *The APA Introductory Psychology Initiative*. https://www.apa.org/ed/precollege/undergrad/introductory-psychology-initiative

9

TEACHING INTRODUCTORY PSYCHOLOGY TO STUDENTS OF VARYING AGES

Cascadia College

GARTH NEUFELD

- Context: Community college
- Student enrollment: 5,000 annually, 2,700 full time
- Average student age: 19
- Enrollment type: Open
- Underrepresented minoritized students: 18%
- Term: Quarters
- Introductory psychology class sizes: 33

CONTEXT

Cascadia College is a 2-year institution in Bothell, Washington. The majority (35%) of its enrollment consists of Running Start students (i.e., students from local high schools, dual enrollment). It is the newest community college in the state and shares a campus with the University of Washington

https://doi.org/10.1037/0000260-010
Transforming Introductory Psychology: Expert Advice on Teacher Training, Course Design, and Student Success, R. A. R. Gurung and G. Neufeld (Editors)

Bothell. The college focuses on active and integrative learning, including linked courses and service learning.

Sections of the introductory psychology course are taught by tenured, tenure-track, and adjunct faculty in face-to-face, online, and hybrid formats. Student learning outcomes (SLOs) for the course are aligned with four college-wide outcomes of Learn Actively, Think Critically, Communicate Clearly, and Interact in Diverse Environments. All faculty share the same SLOs for the course, which are reviewed collectively on a 5-year cycle (or sooner) and then submitted to the Student Learning Council for approval. None of the faculty cover the entirety of the course content, but they commonly teach major topics of Research Methods, Learning, Neuroscience, Social Psychology, and Health/Stress in their entirety. Approximately 16 annual sections of the course are taught by two tenured faculty members and two adjunct faculty members.

UNIQUE CHALLENGES OF TEACHING INTRODUCTORY PSYCHOLOGY

There are three unique challenges to teaching introductory psychology at Cascadia College: (a) the variation in student age, (b) the quarter term, and (c) aligning college-wide, division-wide, and course-specific outcomes.

Over one third of the college's student enrollment comprises dual-enrolled students from local high schools. In the introductory psychology course, this number is objectively higher, likely exceeding 50%. Pair this with the existing traditional community college population of students returning to college after job loss or raising a family with particular academic goals in mind, and the diverse student age population in the introductory psychology classroom context becomes quite complex.

The introductory psychology course contains a lot of content, and most instructors would agree that it is too much for students to learn in a single term. Faculty members at Cascadia College have freedom in what they choose to omit from the introductory psychology curriculum. How much a student can meaningfully learn in the course is considered in relation to the 11-week quarter that includes 55 classroom hours in a face-to-face format. And, while the amount of time spent in the classroom does not change when compared with semester-based terms, the content coverage is greatly accelerated. While this is probably the biggest challenge for instructors at Cascadia College, it also has significant implications for students. More than 40% of Cascadia College students work while going to college, and over half (57%)

are state supported. For these and other reasons, our students are vulnerable to conflicts in schedules, financial problems, and transportation issues, as well as numerous other threats to their daily academic responsibilities. Because the quarter is only 11 weeks long, missing even a week of course-work can be difficult to overcome. For this reason, introductory psychology instructors must design a course that can accommodate these situations.

Cascadia College has college-wide outcomes that are meant to trickle down to each division, department, and course. Social science division-wide outcomes seek to align our disciplines, embracing its founding value of integrated learning. At a course level, the psychology department is not permitted to embrace recommendations for introductory psychology directly and comprehensively but must work to integrate new outcomes into an already-existing framework.

CURRENT AND FUTURE IMPLEMENTATIONS OF THE INTRODUCTORY PSYCHOLOGY INITIATIVE RECOMMENDATIONS

SLOs and Assessment

For a number of years, the SLOs of the introductory psychology course at Cascadia College have been aligned with the *APA Guidelines for the Undergraduate Psychology Major: Version 2.0* (American Psychological Association, 2013). One of the major changes to the SLOs since this time was the introduction of the Introductory Psychology Initiative's (IPI's; American Psychological Association, 2020) integrative themes (Outcome 3).

The first iteration of the integrative themes was released in fall 2019 for pilot testing. These themes were introduced in some sections of introductory psychology at Cascadia College, though they were not used as explicit learning outcome indicators. Rather, we sought to see how themes were being perceived in the current course design. In these sections, a survey was given to students at the end of the quarter that asked, for each theme on a scale of 1 (*not confident at all*) to 5 (*very confident*), "How confident are you that you could explain the following theme to someone who has never taken a psychology course?" Students were then asked to explain the theme in their own words without referencing the textbook.

The IPI SLOs will be integrated and used across all sections of Psychology 100 at Cascadia College. This integration will be a collaborative process of full- and part-time faculty members and will be submitted to Cascadia's Student Learning Council for final approval. These updated SLOs will remain in place for a 5-year cycle before the next review period.

Course Models and Design

While the process of backward design (Wiggins & McTighe, 2005; also see IPI Recommendations in Part I of this book) is slowly making its way into common language and practice of instructors at Cascadia College, it is not yet being used widely. Our department plans to work collectively to backward design our courses based on the shared introductory psychology SLOs.

We see backward design of SLOs and student transformation as two sides of the same coin. Using backward design, skills, learning strategies, and inclusion become metacognitive practices for both students and instructors but only after instructors have strategically and successfully leveraged course material to that end. For example, a shared assignment that our department has sometimes used asks students to design experiments. While skills, learning strategies, and inclusion can be purposefully added to and/or identified within the assignment (an IPI recommendation), it is only with that end in mind that this will successfully happen. For this reason, our department will use this shared assignment to address these recommendations explicitly. This collective process will teach us individually not only to backward design an SLO but also to infuse skill development and its recognition into an assessment.

Future work of the introductory psychology course at Cascadia College will be aimed at creating coherence across the curriculum (an IPI recommendation). Organizing themes will allow our faculty members to put their personal touch on the course, according to their own passions or specific expertise. For example, in light of recent cultural acknowledgment of racist and patriarchal systems, a capable and comfortable Cascadia College instructor may take this topic on as a consistent framework to teach myriad introductory psychology concepts (e.g., memory, fight or flight, prejudice, modeling, confirmation bias, history of psychology).

Teacher Training and Development

Faculty at Cascadia College are expected to contribute in three areas: teaching, professional development, and service. There is no alignment among introductory psychology instructors in terms of teacher training. However, there is a strong teaching tradition, and faculty are often hired with a significant emphasis on teaching prowess and experience, specifically as it relates to the college's founding value of active learning. Many teaching-focused professional development opportunities are available for psychology faculty, but there is no requirement for participation. The recommendations in this book for the formal training of graduate students are irrelevant to our undergraduate-only institution. However, there are some principles from these recommendations that we will work to implement, including participating in formal training opportunities as they arise and making a practice of mentoring and training new faculty (i.e., creating communities of practice) around the recommendations of the IPI.

Student Success and Transformation

At Cascadia College, we often tell students that psychology can make your life better, a variation of one of the SLO integrative themes. Increasingly, the introductory psychology course at Cascadia College is being leveraged to accomplish this through skill attainment in students. Some of these skills line up nicely with college-wide learning outcomes (e.g., critical thinking and interacting in diverse and complex environments). More explicitly, Cascadia College introductory psychology instructors address academic and study skills (an IPI recommendation) through chapters on memory and learning. On the basis of the recommendations of the IPI, the department is now considering using or building a shared module specifically related to academic success and study skills based on work by Dunlosky et al. (2013).

Beyond academics, we believe that psychology has a transformational effect on students' lives. We were happy to see recommendations specific to this end. We intend to help students see how learning theories move out of laboratories and into real-life health and wellness decisions (an IPI recommendation)—for example, by using rewards to influence one's own behavior in positive ways. We will go beyond textbook examples of Pavlov's dog or Skinner's rat to make the application of psychology more accessible and meaningful to students' lives. This could help students create better habits or better understand and cope with issues such as panic attacks.

In 2020, Cascadia College made commitments to developing antiracist systems and practices. For our department, this begins with the introductory psychology curriculum. For this reason, the college-wide value will be aligned with fostering cultural competency in students (an IPI recommendation). We will collectively use concepts and theories related to social psychology and critical thinking (e.g., ingroup–outgroup bias, cognitive dissonance, heuristics) to better analyze and understand our current cultural realities (e.g., racism, political divisiveness, ableism).

REFERENCES

American Psychological Association. (2013). *APA guidelines for the undergraduate psychology major: Version 2.0.* https://www.apa.org/ed/precollege/about/psymajor-guidelines.pdf

American Psychological Association. (2020). *The APA Introductory Psychology Initiative.* https://www.apa.org/ed/precollege/undergrad/introductory-psychology-initiative

Dunlosky, J., Rawson, K. A., Marsh, E. J., Nathan, M. J., & Willingham, D. T. (2013). Improving students' learning with effective learning techniques: Promising directions from cognitive and educational psychology. *Psychological Science in the Public Interest, 14*(1), 4–58. https://doi.org/10.1177/1529100612453266

Wiggins, G. P., & McTighe, J. (2005). *Understanding by design* (2nd ed.). Association for Supervision and Curriculum Development.

10

TEACHING INTRODUCTORY PSYCHOLOGY WITH REVISED STANDARDS

Lehigh Carbon Community College

ROBIN MUSSELMAN

- Context: Community College
- Student Enrollment: 6,900 annually
- Average Student Age: 24
- Enrollment Type: Open access
- Underrepresented Minoritized Students: 46%
- Term: 14-week semesters; 5-week winter session; 5- and 10-week summer sessions
- Introductory Psychology Class Sizes: 25 (online), 35 (face-to-face)

CONTEXT

Lehigh Carbon Community College (LCCC) is a comprehensive community college located in northeastern Pennsylvania. The college has a main campus in Schnecksville, which is a suburban site with a sprawling traditional college campus. North of the main campus, in Schuylkill County, is a campus

https://doi.org/10.1037/0000260-011
Transforming Introductory Psychology: Expert Advice on Teacher Training, Course Design, and Student Success, R. A. R. Gurung and G. Neufeld (Editors)

in Tamaqua that was financed by a trust that also provides full scholarships for every local high-school graduate. There is also a full campus in Allentown, in a more urban setting; this represents an unusual circumstance of having three distinctive campuses in suburban, rural, and urban settings. LCCC also offers courses at the Lehigh Valley International Airport, which are specifically targeted for professional pilot majors.

LCCC is designated as a Hispanic-Serving Institution by the U.S. Department of Education. During the 2019–2020 academic year, there were more than 1,300 high school students, from 43 high schools, enrolled at LCCC. A local foundation sponsors an early college program, in which students from the Allentown School District are transported to the Schnecksville campus to attend college classes tuition free. Approximately 45% of the student enrollment consists of Pell Grant recipients.

Approximately 2,000 students are enrolled in introduction to psychology in an academic year. About 50% of these students meet in a face-to-face format, and approximately 35% are online students. The remaining students are dual enrollment—taught in a high-school classroom, on campus, or online. In addition to these designated dual enrollment classes, there are a number of high school students enrolled in college-level classes.

During the 2019–2020 academic year, two full-time faculty members taught sections of introduction to psychology; the remaining 87 sections were taught by part-time and adjunct faculty. There are no prerequisites for the course, and many students are in their first semester of college. All sections use the same course outline and textbook. Online sections of the course use a Quality Matters certified course shell. Assessment of college-wide competencies is conducted on a biannual schedule.

In spring 2020, all face-to-face courses moved to a synchronous remote format. LCCC offered no face-to-face courses in either fall 2020 or spring 2021.

UNIQUE CHALLENGES OF TEACHING INTRODUCTORY PSYCHOLOGY

For years, the major concern in the introduction to psychology course has been a lack of standardization. Although the course has always originated from a common course outline and a common textbook, a review of syllabus for individual courses indicated that the standards for content coverage, assignments, and assessments varied greatly.

During the 2019–2020 academic year, the course outline was modified and approved by the College Curriculum Committee. The course content was consistent with the 2014 recommendations of the American Psychological Association Board of Educational Affairs Working Group on Strengthening the Common Core of the Introductory Psychology Course.

During that academic year, the online presentation of the course was certified through Quality Matters, and now all online sections of the course are offered using that Canvas shell. Individual faculty members may make specific content choices through the guidelines in the course outline and may add individual assignments to those presented in the Canvas course template.

Prior to fall 2019, the Psychology Department was a part of the Division of Social Sciences. As of fall 2019, the Psychology Department was designated a division, and a faculty coordinator for psychology was designated. Each division at LCCC has a faculty coordinator who is a full-time faculty member and receives 9 credits release time during the academic year (full-time faculty are required to teach 15 credits in each of the fall and spring semesters—assignments for winter and summer sessions are considered supplemental). This new designation has been an important change, because it allows for more coordinated planning, course evaluation, and faculty assignments.

CURRENT AND FUTURE IMPLEMENTATIONS OF THE INTRODUCTORY PSYCHOLOGY INITIATIVE RECOMMENDATIONS

Student Learning Outcomes and Assessment

In fall 2019, all sections of the course adopted three student learning outcomes (SLOs):

- Demonstrate a knowledge base in psychology that addresses the breath and diversity of psychology as a hub science.

- Discern differences between personal views and scientific evidence concerning psychological phenomena obtained from research, the general public, and the media.

- Articulate the personal relevance of course material, including an understanding of the importance of ethics and social responsibility in a diverse world.

In addition to these SLOs, courses included assessment of achievement of college-wide competencies that analyze human diversity and apply scientific reasoning.

The assessment for SLOs in this course had been a pretest/posttest design using a multiple-choice assessment incorporated into every Canvas shell. In the first year of using the new course outline, all sections of the course were to conduct three different assessments to address the SLOs and college competencies. The online courses also piloted a written assignment that would be used as a general assessment in the future. All assessments were recorded for fall 2019, but due to the changeover to remote classes in the first week in March 2020, assessments were not completed that spring. On the basis of this evaluation, the division will be incorporating the assessments piloted in the online courses for the next round of assessment (2021–2022).

There was a plan to once again review the course SLOs with an eye to the final recommendations from the Introductory Psychology Initiative (IPI; American Psychological Association, 2020) and to incorporate the use of integrative themes in the course. This was put on hold due to the massive changes in courses necessary for the summer and fall 2020 semesters. A decision was made to continue with the SLOs as stated above until sometime in 2021.

Course Models and Design

There was a plan to first develop the course template for the online course, using the framework of Quality Matters (an evidence-based framework) and then move to the course templates for the face-to-face and hybrid courses. Because the online courses are taught by full-time faculty (including one full-time faculty member who is interdisciplinary), the decision was made to first develop a standardized course template in Canvas for the online course and then to move to the other formats.

During the current academic year, there is a college-wide focus on creating inclusive learning environments. This was the topic for the fall college-wide convocation, available to all faculty. In addition, LCCC offered faculty development sessions monthly on topics such as teaching to empower, rethinking equitable and inclusive classrooms, and supporting the mental health of LGBTQ+ students during uncertain times.

Our division also offered two sections of the course in a learning community format with a college experience section aimed specifically to support Latinx students. These learning communities incorporated the introduction to psychology course with a one credit section that focuses on student learning strategies and resources to support student success. In addition, we worked with part-time and adjunct faculty during the summer to prepare for the fall semester, with a focus on inclusive learning environments.

Plans for the future will include integrated course themes and the inclusion of writing. The goal is to have a complete Canvas course shell, and revised SLOs and assessments ready for the 2021–2022 academic year.

Teacher Training and Development

The Psychology Division is supported by five highly qualified faculty. As of spring 2020, only two full-time psychology faculty members taught the introductory course. After efforts were made to encourage more full-time faculty to teach the course, we have four full-time psychology faculty members and one social science faculty member teaching the introductory course in fall 2020. The faculty demonstrate continued professional growth through conference attendance and continuing education. All full-time psychology faculty are trained and teach distance learning courses—online, hybrid, and enhanced—and are members of the Society for Teaching of Psychology.

All faculty are required to complete a program in Excellence in Instruction and achieve a certification in Canvas before teaching. For the introductory course, we have 20 part-time and adjunct faculty. These 20 faculty members have been fairly constant, with no new faculty added in the past two years. It is difficult to gather all of these faculty members together due to their diverse working schedules but, since the shift to remote classes in March 2020, our Division has met with the part-time and adjunct faculty throughout the spring and summer months. This allowed us to work on the technology needed for the remote classes as well as active learning and inclusive environments within those classes.

There is a need for more training and development, specifically focused on the faculty teaching the introductory course. The shift to remote learning and the closing of the campuses has put many of our plans on hold, but we plan to return to campus for face-to-face classes and continue to offer remote, hybrid, and online classes throughout 2021. Initially, we had hoped to sponsor a regional teacher training conference that would focus on the IPI recommendations. In eastern Pennsylvania, there are many colleges and universities within driving distance, so we had hoped to have a 1-day drive-in conference. Like so many other things, this has been thwarted by the COVID-19 restrictions currently in place, but we have decided that we want to offer a similar opportunity in a virtual setting.

The advantage of working to encompass the "local" institutions is that it will continue to encourage collaboration among them. We have enjoyed the expertise and fellowship of many psychology faculty members working in our regional area. We find that most of us struggle with similar issues and appreciate the sharing of information and expertise.

Student Success and Transformation

One of our SLOs for the introductory course is to stress the personal relevance of psychology to the individual student as well as to the diverse world. This has informed our choices of textbooks, assignments, and assessments. We believe that the value of this course is evidenced by its widespread recommendation and popularity.

During summer 2020, we had a reading and discussion group for the faculty that focused on teaching and learning. The articles focused on teaching in remote settings, inclusive teaching, and specific strategies to encourage student success. These were productive, but it would be important for us to follow through with all our faculty and also to add assessments to determine the efficacy of the incorporated strategies.

We have made a commitment to continue to use the current textbook, which in the upcoming edition, has reinforced the recommendations of the IPI and included a new section on learning to learn through psychology.

REFERENCE

American Psychological Association. (2020). *The APA Introductory Psychology Initiative.* https://www.apa.org/ed/precollege/undergrad/introductory-psychology-initiative

TEACHING INTRODUCTORY PSYCHOLOGY TO STUDENTS WITH VARYING DEGREES OF READINESS

11

Irvine Valley College

JERRY RUDMANN, KARI TUCKER, MICHAEL CASSENS, BENJAMIN MIS, AND YEMMY TAYLOR

- Context: Community College
- Annual Student Enrollment (2018-19): 22,055; 10,093 full-time
- Student Age Categories: Less than 20 years old–31.3%; 21-24 years old–31.8%
- Enrollment Type: Open
- Percentage of First-Generation Students: 23.1%
- Underrepresented Minority Students: 61.9%
- Term: Semesters
- Introductory Psychology Class Size: 45 (some large lecture sections)

CONTEXT

Irvine Valley College is a 2-year institution established in 1985 in Irvine, California. College faculty and support staff focus mainly on preparing students for academic and transfer success by integrating course offerings,

https://doi.org/10.1037/0000260-012
Transforming Introductory Psychology: Expert Advice on Teacher Training, Course Design, and Student Success, R. A. R. Gurung and G. Neufeld (Editors)

cocurricular options, and support services. The college claims to have the state's highest student transfer rate.

Four tenured and five part-time faculty members teach approximately 30 sections of introductory psychology each academic year. Professors teach the course face-to-face and online. The Course Outline of Record (COR) for the introductory course (Psychology 1) includes 11 learning objectives that define, in behavioral terms, what the student can do upon completing the course. We expect all instructors to teach the 11 learning objectives regardless of the textbook they adopt or what they emphasize. The COR and the accompanying learning objectives have undergone articulation with every campus within the University of California and California State University systems and several local private universities.

Faculty periodically meet to discuss, evaluate, and prioritize the Student Learning Outcomes (SLOs) for all courses. The two SLOs for the introductory course are: SLO #1—Compare and contrast the different psychological perspectives; and SLO #2—When provided with examples of explanations and interpretations of human behavior taken from the popular media, students can distinguish between scientific and pseudoscientific explanations. Everyone who teaches the course agrees to assess the same SLOs and submit end-of-term assessment data into a campus-wide tracking system. Although the department's SLO activities satisfy our regional accreditor's expectations, the psychology faculty do not believe our SLO process has been sufficiently informative.

UNIQUE CHALLENGES OF TEACHING INTRODUCTORY PSYCHOLOGY

1. *Student readiness*: Public community colleges follow an open-access policy. It follows that many students arrive without a focused academic plan and have low confidence (i.e., low academic self-efficacy). Many are the first in their family to attend college, or they have emerged from high school with a rather unspectacular academic record. Some students suffer from low academic motivation. Many lack effective time-management habits and have never heard of evidence-based study skills.

2. *Popularity of introductory psychology*: The majority of students enroll in introductory psychology during the first year, if not their first term, in college. In response to this popularity, we are encouraged to offer multiple sections, some in large lecture mode. The course's popularity ensures

having many academically underprepared students enroll in every introductory psychology classroom.

3. *Challenging content*: The introductory course's content challenges teachers and students. Instructors must decide on what chapters to include, as well as the breadth and depth of what they cover. Because introductory psychology is a survey of the discipline, students must grapple with a complex array of concepts, facts, theories, constructs, and principles. Instructors often complain that they "cannot cover it all" in a single term.

4. *Professional development*: It is challenging to provide relevant professional development resources for our psychology teachers. Our full-time professors have heavy teaching loads (15+ units, which include three or more course preparations per semester without the benefit of teaching assistants), committee obligations, and volunteer time to mentor Psi Beta students. Most adjuncts are "freeway flyers" who race between colleges to teach classes. We also experience turnover among the adjunct professors because some go elsewhere to assume tenure track positions, others move away, etc. Although Irvine Valley offers a faculty-driven professional development the week before each fall and spring term, the programming typically has little, if any, direct relevance for psychology teachers.

Despite the challenges just described, the department continually scores at or near the top in terms of the college's productivity metrics (e.g., seat-fill rate). The introductory course is a primary contributor to the department's high productivity.

CURRENT AND FUTURE IMPLEMENTATIONS OF THE INTRODUCTORY PSYCHOLOGY INITIATIVE RECOMMENDATIONS

SLOs and Assessment

Faculty will meet to renew the introductory psychology SLOs and the course model-and-design options covered in Chapters 2 and 3. Our analysis found that the majority of the Introductory Psychology Initiative (IPI; American Psychological Association, 2020) SLOs align somewhat with our introduction to psychology's course learning objectives and our existing SLOs. The department's teachers have agreed to meet in the near future to discuss the recently released IPI SLOs and brainstorm possible assessment tools and strategies. Our Information Technology department recently made it possible to administer SLOs assessment within the course management system (CMS; Canvas) and export the captured SLO data to Tableau for plotting charts that aggregate and disaggregate results. Because we can now conduct SLO assessment inside our CMS and have the IPI SLOs available, we have tentatively planned several research projects as outlined below.

- *Baseline teacher coverage:* Using a 5-point Likert scale, professors will rate the extent they cover each of the IPI SLOs when they teach introductory psychology.

- *Baseline student knowledge*: The department will survey a sample of recent introductory psychology students. We will adapt Cascadia College's study by asking students, on a 1-to-5 Likert scale, to identify "How confident are you that you could explain the following [IPI SLO] to someone who has never taken a psychology course?" Next, we will ask students to write their answers without reference to a textbook. The survey data will provide a baseline for gauging how well introductory psychology prepares students for the IPI SLOs.

Our objective is to develop a local version of the IPI SLOs and integrate them across all introductory psychology sections offered at Irvine Valley College. Doing this will require a collaborative process of full- and part-time faculty members. Once the faculty agree to adopt the IPI SLOs, we will begin to gather teaching resources and corresponding assessment tools and strategies. We will review SLO assessments available on the American Psychological Association's Project Assessment website (pass.apa.org), the October 2020 special issue of *Teaching of Psychology*, and other sources. Although instructors will continue to be free to choose their textbook and determine the content they cover in introduction to psychology, we will expect everyone to teach the newly adopted course SLOs.

Course Models and Design

New tools and strategies can be created or found to measure learning outcomes like skills, learning strategies, and inclusion (which is an IPI recommendation; see Part I of this book). But we must purposefully and intentionally implement them to acquire meaningful and useful assessment information. Faculty will begin to develop an introductory psychology course having coherence (which is an IPI recommendation) across the curriculum. The recommendation to use organizing themes will allow faculty members to continue to personalize the introductory class according to their interests and strengths.

Teacher Training and Development

Although teaching-related professional development options are available for our psychology faculty, there is no requirement to participate. However, we will strongly encourage participation in formal training opportunities as they arise and find new ways to mentor and train less experienced teachers. We will consider forming a faculty interest group designed to strengthen our effort to optimize the introductory course.

Student Success and Transformation

- *Giving away psychology modules*: Introductory psychology attracts many first-year students. Because of this, the course is well-positioned to enhance their academic success. In response to IPI recommendations, we offer the following plan. The department's Psi Beta chapter trains honor students to present Giving Away Psychology (GAP) workshops to their peers. In response to the pandemic, the students and their faculty advisers have chosen PlayPosit software to produce and deliver workshops having an interactive video format. As part of our case study, our goal will be to have all introductory psychology students attend these four workshops: Academic Self-Regulation (i.e., time management, metacognition, mental contrasting with implementation intentions, Mindset, and neuroplasticity), Evidence-Based Learning Strategies (i.e., spaced practice, elaboration, interleaving, etc.), Interpersonal Communication (i.e., supportive listening and networking through small talk), and Careers and Life Skills Developed in Psychology. Introductory psychology instructors will have the option of incorporating the workshops and deciding how much credit they will allocate to students who complete them. The department will use a code to record the extent of workshop completion (none, some, or all) while enrolled in an introductory psychology course. All four workshops will be ready when the fall 2021 semester commences in August 2021.

- *Institutional research study*: We plan to study introductory psychology's positive impact. In collaboration with the college's Office of Research, the psychology faculty will design a longitudinal study. The study will monitor pre- and post–case study outcomes (e.g., persistence rate, units earned, transfer rate) of student cohorts who have completed the introductory course. We will also compare these success metrics to demographically matched equivalent groups composed of students who did not take the introductory course during their first year.

- *Alumni follow-up study*: We will periodically deploy a survey designed to gauge the extent that alumni recall and use any of the academic and life skills (e.g., time management, learning strategies, self-regulation, health and wellness decisions) taught in introductory psychology.

Respect for Human Diversity

In response to the IPI recommendation "Use the Introductory Psychology course as a developmental step in fostering students' cultural competency," and the IPI key theme ("Psychology values diversity, promotes equity, and fosters inclusion in pursuit of a more just society"), we will do the following: We will cover concepts and theories that challenge racism and political divisiveness. Further, we will encourage knowledge of factors that contribute to prejudice, discrimination, and inequity (ingroup–outgroup bias, cognitive dissonance, stereotyping, stereotype threat, and implicit bias, and others).

REFERENCE

American Psychological Association. (2020). *The APA Introductory Psychology Initiative.* https://www.apa.org/ed/precollege/undergrad/introductory-psychology-initiative

12 TEACHING INTRODUCTORY PSYCHOLOGY IN A SMALL UNIVERSITY

McKendree University

GUY A. BOYSEN

- Context: Private 4-Year Undergraduate College
- Student Enrollment: 2,200, with 1,800 undergraduates
- Average Student Age: 75% under 24 years old
- Enrollment Type: Private
- Underrepresented Minoritized Students: 34%
- Term: Semesters
- Introductory Psychology Class Sizes: 15–30

CONTEXT

At McKendree University, Introduction to Psychology is a core component of both general education and the psychology program. The course is one of four options for fulfilling a social science requirement in the general education program. In the psychology major and minor, Introduction to

https://doi.org/10.1037/0000260-013
Transforming Introductory Psychology: Expert Advice on Teacher Training, Course Design, and Student Success, R. A. R. Gurung and G. Neufeld (Editors)

Psychology is a prerequisite for all other psychology courses. In addition, students who major or minor in related programs such as biopsychology, forensic studies, occupational therapy, and sport psychology must also start with Introduction to Psychology, as do students in any program with a required psychology course. Due to the popularity of psychology courses and programs, most students will have taken Introduction to Psychology by their sophomore year.

All sections of Introduction to Psychology at the university have some shared parameters. The course is 3 credit hours and begins with an enrollment cap of 25 students. Typically, there are five sections of the course offered each semester with an average enrollment of 20 students per section. Instructors all have advanced degrees and do not use graduate or undergraduate teaching assistants. Psychology faculty have agreed on a shared textbook and shared learning objectives. The textbook is the briefer version of a comprehensive 16-chapter introductory text. The learning objectives include two goals that are related to the general education program and eight goals that are specific to psychology. In addition, there is a shared behavior-change journal assignment and a critical-thinking paper associated with the general education requirements.

Outside of these shared parameters, instructors have autonomy in course design and instruction. Academic freedom reigns, and there is no direct oversight of instruction during the semester. Teaching styles for the course are as diverse as the instructors. In addition to the instructional variations, there are two course formats: in-person and online. Moreover, the course is also offered as part of the university honors program, and honors sections are aligned with the curricular requirements of the honors program rather than the psychology department.

UNIQUE CHALLENGES OF TEACHING INTRODUCTORY PSYCHOLOGY

The small size of the university affects Introduction to Psychology in several ways. The four full-time psychology faculty teach a 4-4 course load. Given their other instructional responsibilities, there are too many sections of Introduction to Psychology for full-time faculty to cover themselves. As such, responsibility for instruction falls mostly to part-time instructors. Due to the small size of the university, psychology is part of a broad department that includes all social sciences. With no psychology-specific chair, administrators, or staff, no one is directly responsible for overseeing the management, instruction, or curriculum of Introduction to Psychology.

Taken together, the small-college setting leads to some challenges. Due to the small faculty and absence of psychology-specific infrastructure, there is no assurance of consistency across sections. Moreover, there is no organizational structure that brings psychology teachers together to have discussions about curriculum or instruction (e.g., department meetings). University policy dictates that full-time faculty oversee the curriculum, but not all full-time faculty instruct the course, and none of them possess unique authority over the course. As such, curricular changes to Introduction to Psychology tend to be infrequent and reactive. When changes do occur, there is no official mechanism for communicating them to instructors, nor is there a mechanism for determining if the changes have taken place.

CURRENT AND FUTURE IMPLEMENTATIONS OF THE INTRODUCTORY PSYCHOLOGY INITIATIVE RECOMMENDATIONS

SLOs and Assessment

The course learning objectives include two general education goals stemming from the university mission and eight psychology-specific goals stemming from foundational indicators in the *APA Guidelines for the Undergraduate Psychology Major: Version 2.0* (American Psychological Association, 2013). Although the current course learning objectives predate the Introductory Psychology Initiative (IPI; American Psychological Association, 2020) outcomes, alignment is almost perfect with the IPI's Psychology Content objectives 1.1–1.3 and Scientific Thinking objectives 2.1–2.4. However, the IPI recommendations about Key Themes tend to be framed too specifically to align with the course's current learning objectives. Conversely, the McKendree course's learning objectives include goals related to effective collaboration and written communication, and these skills are absent from the IPI outcomes.

Assessment of the general education component of the course follows the IPI recommendations to use backward design and directly align assessment with learning outcomes. For example, one general education goal for the course is for students to "exhibit personal and social responsibility." To accomplish this goal, students complete a semester-long behavior change assignment in which they set goals for personal improvement, operationally define their goals, and implement psychological principles to achieve the goals. Learning is assessed using a shared rubric aligned with each component of the assignment, and instructors report the results as part of the institutional assessment program.

Teacher Training and Development

McKendree University offers extensive opportunities for professional development related to teaching. All new instructors complete an orientation program, and all online instructors complete a self-directed course on the learning management system. Furthermore, a half-day teaching conference occurs at the start of each semester. In addition to basic instructional training, the conference includes rotating content that matches current pedagogical concerns at the university. For example, when the university switched learning management systems, the conference emphasized pedagogy using the new system. In addition to instruction-focused teaching conferences, the university has an annual half-day assessment conference. The conference covers assessment practices and provides faculty with feedback on their program's assessment plans. Although these professional development opportunities are consistent with IPI recommendations that teachers receive training, they are not discipline specific. As such, instructors who want to pursue training related to teaching Introduction to Psychology must do so outside of the university.

Student Success and Transformation

One IPI recommendation related to student success and transformation is to show students how they can apply psychology to improve their study skills. The course textbook outlines effective study skills in the first chapter. Although it is up to instructors to choose how much they emphasize the study skills material, students' primary source of course content does expose them to accurate information about effective study skills in what is likely to be their first assigned reading.

Another transformational component of Introduction to Psychology according to the IPI recommendations is its ability to improve students' health and wellness. Introduction to Psychology students complete a semester-long behavior change assignment. The assignment consists of a series of journals that begin by having them select and operationally define a behavior that they would like to change. Each journal then asks them to apply psychology concepts in the achievement of their behavior change goal. For example, they apply operant conditioning to alter behavior during the learning section of the course. This assignment gives students the opportunity to directly experience the effects psychology can have on their health and wellness.

Goals for Future IPI Implementation

There are several IPI recommendations that should be prioritized when the McKendree University faculty revisit the Introduction to Psychology curriculum. First, the IPI learning objectives should be adopted. The current objectives stem from the APA's goals for the undergraduate major and are not specific to Introduction to Psychology. As such, switching to the IPI objectives would provide better alignment between course content and goals. Second, assessment of student learning should be aligned with IPI's Psychology Content and Scientific Thinking outcomes. Currently, only general education learning outcomes have a shared assessment across sections, and these assessments provide little indication of how well students understand psychological science on completion of the course. A shared assessment of knowledge would aid in determining the effectiveness of instructional strategies within and between sections of the course. Third, all sections of the course should include a shared module on effective study skills that is covered in the first week of class. Not only would covering study skills prime students for later success in the course, it would give them an early appreciation of the value of psychology in their lives. Finally, the Introduction to Psychology instructors should form a professional development group. The group could share evidence-based teaching practices related to the course as well as pedagogical innovations in need of testing in the classroom.

REFERENCES

American Psychological Association. (2013). *APA guidelines for the undergraduate psychology major: Version 2.0.* https://www.apa.org/ed/precollege/about/psymajor-guidelines.pdf

American Psychological Association. (2020). *The APA Introductory Psychology Initiative.* https://www.apa.org/ed/precollege/undergrad/introductory-psychology-initiative

13

TEACHING INTRODUCTORY PSYCHOLOGY TO A HOMOGENOUS STUDENT POPULATION

Samford University

STEPHEN L. CHEW

- Context: Regional Private University
- Student Enrollment: 5,729 total, with 3,576 undergraduates
- Average Student Age: 20
- Enrollment Type: Selective
- Underrepresented Minoritized Students: 12%
- Term: Semesters plus a mini-term
- Introductory Psychology Class Sizes: 50

CONTEXT

Samford University is a private, regional university affiliated with the Alabama Baptist State Convention and located in Birmingham, Alabama. Samford is composed of seven schools, including a law school and a divinity

https://doi.org/10.1037/0000260-014
Transforming Introductory Psychology: Expert Advice on Teacher Training, Course Design, and Student Success, R. A. R. Gurung and G. Neufeld (Editors)
Copyright © 2022 by the American Psychological Association. All rights reserved.

school. A college of health sciences, a business school, and a school of education offer both graduate and undergraduate degrees. The remaining two schools, a school of the arts and the college of arts and sciences, are composed almost exclusively of undergraduate programs. The vast majority of undergraduate students are full-time students of traditional college age who will complete their degrees in 4 years. Samford is a predominantly White institution among students and faculty.

The psychology department is housed in the college of arts and sciences. It has no graduate programs and its focus is on undergraduate liberal arts education. More than half of the psychology majors will pursue some form of advanced education. The department has five tenure-track faculty and two continuing, part-time adjunct faculty. There are typically about 100 psychology majors, although the number fluctuates widely, ranging from 80 to 140 in recent years. Although we often have a large group of students who enter Samford as a psychology major, the majority of our majors declare psychology after taking introductory psychology.

Sections of the introductory psychology course are taught by tenured, tenure-track, and adjunct faculty. Unless there is a pandemic, all sections are taught face-to-face during the fall and spring semesters. Summer courses are likely to be online. Typical introductory psychology class sizes in the regular semester are around 50 students. Introductory psychology is a high-demand course both for the psychology major, as the most popular option for fulfilling the social science general education requirement, and as a service course for various other majors. The department offers eight sections of the course during the regular semester, five in the fall and three in the spring.

Faculty are given wide leeway in how they design their courses, which includes introductory psychology. Quality assurance comes in the hiring and mentoring process for new faculty. The department made huge strides in academic rigor and teaching quality in the last 30 years. The dean at that time hired a new department chair with the intent of transforming a struggling department into a model liberal arts program. That faculty member served as chair for 26 years and hired and mentored all the current psychology faculty. The program is strongly student centered and research based.

Student learning outcomes (SLOs) for the department are based on the *APA Guidelines for the Undergraduate Psychology Major: Version 2.0* (American Psychological Association, 2013). All faculty see excellence in teaching as their primary focus. All are active in the Society for the Teaching of Psychology, engage in pedagogical research, and attend conferences on the teaching of psychology. All faculty are expected to be able to teach introductory psychology, but the chair has recognized that some faculty are better able to cope with the challenges of teaching the course than others. The faculty who regularly teach introductory psychology are highly collegial and share advice, activities, strategies, and resources. There is no formal mechanism for professional development of teaching within the department. The department is on the cusp of hiring a new chair from another college and will likely change with the leadership of the new chair.

There is no centralized control of course content or assessment strategy in different sections of introductory psychology. The course focus and activities can vary depending on the instructor. None of the faculty cover the entirety of a typical introductory psychology textbook, but what is omitted is determined by the instructor. Even so, all faculty cover the topics of research methods, neuroscience, learning, developmental psychology, psychological disorders, psychotherapy, and social psychology in their entirety.

UNIQUE CHALLENGES OF TEACHING INTRODUCTORY PSYCHOLOGY

The unique challenges of teaching introductory psychology at Samford stem from the homogeneity of the student population. Most students do not have much experience with people of different races, religions, cultures, and socioeconomic backgrounds. They may hold views that are maintained by consensus of their friends rather than consideration of evidence, especially for issues that might challenge their worldview. A major goal of the course is to help students see beyond their worldview. Beyond that, introductory psychology carries the same challenges found at other schools, showing students the breadth of topics that psychology encompasses and convincing students of the value of psychological science both to society in general and to the students specifically. Although introductory psychology is required for all further psychology courses, the vast majority of students will take only the one course or perhaps the one course and lifespan development.

CURRENT AND FUTURE IMPLEMENTATIONS OF THE INTRODUCTORY PSYCHOLOGY INITIATIVE RECOMMENDATIONS

SLOs and Assessment

The department has no uniform set of SLOs or assessment strategies for introductory psychology. When the Introductory Psychology Initiative (IPI; American Psychological Association, 2020) produced the July 2020 draft of the SLOs, I distributed them to the rest of the department, but I do not know if they were used by any of the other faculty. I can only speak for how I have used the IPI SLOs when next I taught introductory psychology. The SLOs I had developed for the class were consistent with several of the proposed SLOs from the IPI. Therefore, instead of changing my SLOs wholesale, I modified them to include the parts of the IPI SLOs that were missing from my own. I credit the IPI SLOs in helping crystalize some general beliefs I had about teaching introductory psychology. I already based my course around integrative themes and skills, such as recognizing the biases that shape our judgment and cause us to make flawed decisions, and using research methods to distinguish between valid evidence, pseudoscience, bad science, and wishful thinking. Of the suggested integrative themes in the SLOs (American Psychological Association, 2021), I already emphasize Themes A ("Psychological science relies on empirical evidence . . ."), B ("Psychology explains general principles that govern behavior . . ."), C ("Psychological, biological, social, and cultural factors influence . . ."), E ("Our perceptions and biases filter our experiences . . ."), and G ("Ethical principles guide psychology . . ."). I credit the IPI SLOs with forcing me to modify my introductory course to include the two other themes of D and F, which respectively address diversity and applying psychology to change lives, organizations, and communities in positive ways.

Like many faculty, I had to redesign my introductory psychology course in the fall semester of 2020 to teach remotely in response to the COVID-19 pandemic. It was an opportunity to integrate new elements into the course. I became more intentional in promoting the themes outlined in the SLOs, and I added activities on suicide prevention and the stigma surrounding psychological disorders and intellectual disability. These topics are far outside my specialization, but everyone teaches areas outside their specialization in introductory psychology. I felt these topics were especially relevant during the pandemic, and they also addressed both respect for diversity and using psychology to improve people's lives.

Course Models and Design

Samford offers a professional program for course development that incorporates backward design, although it also uses checklists for characteristics of high-quality courses. Faculty try to design courses that meet all the characteristics, which may be somewhat at odds with developing courses to accomplish learning outcomes, the basis of backward design. The program is voluntary, and faculty may develop courses in whatever way they wish.

There is no recognition of backward design as a best practice, and many faculty may be unfamiliar with it.

For introductory psychology, new faculty are often mentored by senior faculty in designing and teaching the course. They often share their syllabus and activities. There is no departmentally approved process for course development. A meeting of all instructors of introductory psychology to discuss backward course design and SLOs would be useful. We can use the recommendations from the IPI to initiate a departmental course review.

We are acutely aware of the need to make our teaching more inclusive and supportive of students who feel marginalized within the Samford context. Samford has an ongoing history of racially insensitive incidents, and the university has refused to give official recognition to a student organization that supports LGBTQ rights. As faculty, we try to be supportive of all students, especially ones that do not fit the typical Samford profile. Such groups would include first-generation students, veterans, and other nontraditional students.

Teacher Training and Development

Teacher development at Samford used to be guided by a teaching and learning center with a director who was active in pedagogical research and methods. The center has since been replaced by the Faculty Success Collaborative, which takes a more corporate approach to professional development. It is more teacher training than development, and its focus seems more on the use of technology than on effective teaching per se.

Student Success and Transformation

The recommendations from the Student Success and Transformation group have caused me to be more explicit and intentional in describing the value of introductory psychology to students. An underlying theme to my course is that psychology provides students with useful and valuable knowledge and skills to use now and in the future. The study skills module is a clear example of how psychology can make unique, important contributions to student success. Beyond study skills, I have modified my presentations to emphasize other relevant applications of psychological research. Memory processes can be distorted by misinformation. People can be pressured into making false confessions. Everyone is vulnerable to cognitive biases that affect judgment and problem solving. People may act differently as part of a crowd than when alone. We can discuss how the stigma of intellectual disability gave rise to eugenics and state-sanctioned sterilization or the prevalence of the misconception that people with psychological disorders are prone to violence. All of these applications are consistent with SLOs 1.3, 2.3, and 2.4 and the recommendations of the Student Success and Transformation group.

There are still areas that we need to improve on in our teaching of introductory psychology classes. The recommendations of the Student Success and Transformation group make these weaknesses clear. In particular, we clearly should do more to foster cultural competency among students, especially because we are a predominantly White institution with a homogeneous student body. The faculty have discussed this issue in the past, but national and local events have shown the need for taking immediate steps. Another area we need to address is using workplace examples in teaching to illustrate the career relevance of psychological concepts.

Overall, we do a good job of preparing students for academic success and transforming their thinking. The value of the IPI SLOs is that they help us clarify our goals and point out areas where we still need to improve.

REFERENCES

American Psychological Association. (2013). *APA guidelines for the undergraduate psychology major: Version 2.0*. https://www.apa.org/ed/precollege/about/psymajor-guidelines.pdf

American Psychological Association. (2020). *The APA Introductory Psychology Initiative*. https://www.apa.org/ed/precollege/undergrad/introductory-psychology-initiative

American Psychological Association. (2021). *APA Introductory Psychology Initiative (IPI) student learning outcomes for introductory psychology*. https://www.apa.org/ed/precollege/undergrad/introductory-psychology-initiative/student-learning-outcomes.pdf

14

TEACHING INTRODUCTORY PSYCHOLOGY IN A HISTORICALLY BLACK LIBERAL ARTS COLLEGE FOR WOMEN

Spelman College

SHANI N. HARRIS, KAI M. MCCORMACK,
ANGELA FARRIS-WATKINS,
JUANCHELLA GROOMS FRANCIS,
AND KAREN BRAKKE

- Context: Spelman College, Historically Black Liberal Arts College for Women
- Student Enrollment: 2,100 annually; on campus/full-time
- Average Student Age: 19–20
- Enrollment Type: Competitive
- Underrepresented Minoritized Students: 99.8%
- Term: Semester
- Introductory Psychology Class Sizes: 20–30 (2–3 sections per term)

CONTEXT

Spelman College is a private women's college and a Historically Black College/University (HBCU) located in Atlanta, Georgia. It is an internationally recognized liberal arts college for women with students from 43 states and

https://doi.org/10.1037/0000260-015
Transforming Introductory Psychology: Expert Advice on Teacher Training, Course Design, and Student Success, R. A. R. Gurung and G. Neufeld (Editors)

more than 10 countries. The majority of students are full-time, and approximately 65% live on campus.

Introductory psychology (Intro) is taught in three different formats. Nonmajors typically enroll in a 1-semester general psychology course, whereas majors are required to enroll in the 2-semester introduction to psychological science sequence with accompanying labs. Honors students, both majors and nonmajors, may alternatively enroll in the 1-semester, accelerated honors psychological science course. For this case study, we focus on the 2-semester introduction to psychological science I and II courses. Part I covers the history of psychology, research methods, biopsychology, stress and health, consciousness, sensation and perception, memory, learning, and intelligence. Part II covers developmental, personality, social, psychological disorders, and therapy. Each course is paired with a 1-hour weekly lab that allows students to apply the topics and theories to ministudies, which require students to write lab reports consisting of the four elements of a paper: introduction, methods, results, and discussion. All sections of the 2-semester course use the same textbook and require writing assignments that prepare students to complete a full research report.

The Intro courses are predominately, although not exclusively, taught by full-time faculty in face-to-face environments. Currently, two experienced tenured faculty members teach three sections of the course each semester. These faculty members work together to plan the course structure, select the textbook, and develop writing goals. The course has recently been taught in a hybrid and fully online setting, opening up this mode of teaching for future semesters. The course addresses the goals outlined in the *APA Guidelines for the Undergraduate Major: Version 2.0* (American Psychological Association [APA], 2013), particularly Goal 1: Knowledge Base in Psychology. The course also includes student learning outcomes (SLOs) related to written communication.

UNIQUE CHALLENGES OF TEACHING INTRODUCTORY PSYCHOLOGY

The Spelman psychology department primarily serves African American women. As such, it is important that students learn a curriculum that is inclusive of the unique perspectives of this population. The current textbook is authored by women and is intentionally inclusive of diverse research perspectives and diversity in researchers. Both women and African American psychological scientists are emphasized in the text. Instructors also include refereed literature and other sources (e.g., documentaries, book chapters) to teach about psychology from a framework that considers gender and race. For example, in fall 2020, when covering intelligence, one professor included an interview with Claude Steele discussing the development and testing of stereotype threat theory.

The current approach to including gender- and race-based frameworks is individually determined by the faculty member. Students taking one section of Intro may not review the same material related to race/gender as students taking another section taught by another faculty member. While it is important to allow faculty to emphasize material that relates to their areas of expertise and interest, it is also important that the student experience be somewhat consistent. Moving forward, we will discuss ways to create more standard learning experiences related to the psychology of women and African Americans.

CURRENT AND FUTURE IMPLEMENTATIONS OF THE INTRODUCTORY PSYCHOLOGY INITIATIVE RECOMMENDATIONS

The faculty of the Spelman College psychology department worked together to create an integrated, innovative, and culturally sound learning environment that is aligned with APA goals. The college supports this environment by providing faculty numerous opportunities for pedagogical growth and by supporting students in their transformation from a scholar-in-training to a professional in the field.

SLOs and Assessment

The psychology department at Spelman College currently assesses SLOs, as required by the Southeastern Association of Colleges and Schools Commission on Colleges (SACSOC), for a portion of all courses taught. The SLOs are informed by the *APA Guidelines for the Undergraduate Psychology Major* (2013) but are not directly related to the APA Introductory Psychology Initiative (IPI; APA, 2021) SLOs. At the start of each academic year, the faculty discusses SLOs on which to focus and identifies the courses most appropriate for administering relevant assessments.

Over the past 5 years, the department has assessed a variety of SLOs in the introductory psychology course. The majority of these SLOs relate to written and oral communication. For example, in 2017, our department assessed student performance related to reading and summarizing general ideas and conclusions from psychological sources, and demonstrating effective use of APA Style in a written report or a research project. This established practice of assessing SLOs has positioned the department to easily shift to incorporate the latest APA IPI SLOs. As we make this shift, we will also consider a variety of assignment types and data measures that can be used to assess those outcomes.

Course Models and Design

Our department has spent several years refining the traditional 2-semester sequence of our introductory psychology course. A team of faculty members revised the lab portion of the course to increase its alignment with course content and to infuse more writing assignments into the lab. These lab assignments are scaffolded across the 2 semesters, such that they first focus on the elements of APA Style, and then build into several scaffolded assignments focused on writing different sections of an APA Style report. This process culminates in the last two written assignments of the second-semester labs, including all elements of an APA Style research paper based on data collected in the lab. The lecture portion of the course was also revised to include scaffolded writing assignments based on the development of arguments, as opposed to a large, end-of-term literature review. Students start with small writing prompts making an assertion and supporting it with evidence from their textbook, and end the second semester with an argument that integrates five to eight pieces of primary peer-reviewed literature. Faculty members who teach the course and labs remain in close communication regarding course materials, major assignments, and teaching strategies. These changes to our writing requirements have resulted in a distributed and iterative process, which has greatly increased the quality of our students' writing skills.

The delivery of course material is centered on evidence-based, innovative teaching methods. Lectures are brief and are sometimes prerecorded to allow viewing before class. The majority of class time is used to apply the content to hands-on assignments or discussions, encouraging active learning and providing time to elaborate on relevant topics. Short online or in-class quizzes promote student engagement in course material and enable faculty to assess content mastery.

The introductory psychology course at Spelman meets many of the recommendations outlined in this volume. Faculty are rooted in evidence-based teaching methods, well-versed in assessing SLOs, and are passionate about maintaining a culturally informed and culturally inclusive learning environment. Our faculty have responded to recent public health challenges by shifting to an online learning environment, supported by extensive training in online teaching and campus-wide discussions about course structure and effectiveness in the online environment.

Moving forward, the faculty will work toward incorporating integrative themes to organize course material (see the recommendations in Chapter 2). This will enable faculty to personalize sections of the course and provide a path to seamlessly incorporate race- and gender-based frameworks. Faculty members also look forward to adopting a backward course design built around the latest IPI SLOs. This will create a logical feedback loop that allows faculty, students, and administration to have a roadmap that details learning goals and assessment modalities that are unique to the course.

Teacher Training and Development

Spelman College provides exceptional faculty training opportunities through its Teaching Resource and Research Center, which hosts talks and workshops related to best practices in the scholarship of teaching and learning (SoTL), and through annual faculty institutes focused on professional development. Psychology faculty are actively engaged in psychology SoTL and regularly participate in teaching conferences. The department currently hosts the annual Southeastern Teaching of Psychology conference. These activities create an intellectual climate that consistently examines best practices in teaching and teaching innovations.

Student Success and Transformation

Our students receive support to improve student learning and overall student success in a number of ways. The college offers all students access to academic coaching, peer tutoring and supplemental instruction via the Student Success Program. Psychology majors are also supported by the campus writing center which, along with one-to-one tutoring, provides workshops related to APA Style, drafting literature reviews, and preparing curriculum vitae for postgraduate experiences.

Within the department, our low faculty-to-student ratio ensures that all students have access to individual consultations with faculty during office hours and by appointment. Within the Intro course, tools for student learning are integrated into the curriculum. Early content focuses on study habits and evidence-based methods for improving learning and enhancing academic success. This content is reiterated when we cover stress and health (e.g., stress and its impact on academic functioning and health), memory (e.g., strategies to improve the storage and retrieval of information), learning (e.g., different methods of direct and indirect learning), and intelligence (e.g., impact of anxiety on performance, different types of intelligence).

Moving forward, we will employ additional IPI recommendations. For instance, we will work to create a more inclusive learning environment by ensuring that all students have equal access to course materials in both online and face-to-face environments. We will also increase discussions of health and wellness by expanding the topic beyond the single chapter presented in the textbook. Finally, we will incorporate more examples that are applicable to the workplace. While many of our students pursue graduate degrees, the majority enter the workforce after graduating. This increased emphasis should help them to better prepare for the workforce and should increase the relevance of the course material to their lived experiences.

REFERENCES

American Psychological Association. (2013). *APA guidelines for the undergraduate psychology major: Version 2.0.* https://www.apa.org/ed/precollege/about/psymajor-guidelines.pdf

American Psychological Association. (2021). *APA Introductory Psychology Initiative (IPI) student learning outcomes for introductory psychology.* https://www.apa.org/ed/precollege/undergrad/introductory-psychology-initiative/student-learning-outcomes.pdf

15

TEACHING INTRODUCTORY PSYCHOLOGY WHEN CLASSES HAVE UNEVEN ENROLLMENT

The University of Tennessee

ERIN E. HARDIN

- Context: Public doctoral granting institution
- Student Enrollment: ~24,000 annually; < 700 part-time
- Average Student Age: 21
- Underrepresented Minoritized Students: 18%
- Term: Semesters
- Introductory Psychology Class Sizes: 150–380

CONTEXT

The University of Tennessee, Knoxville (UTK) is the flagship public university in the state of Tennessee. Undergraduates come from across the United States and 130 other countries, but the majority (78%) of students are from Tennessee. UTK offers more than 360 undergraduate majors across

https://doi.org/10.1037/0000260-016
Transforming Introductory Psychology: Expert Advice on Teacher Training, Course Design, and Student Success, R. A. R. Gurung and G. Neufeld (Editors)

10 colleges. The department of psychology offers a bachelor of arts (BA) degree in psychology and bachelor of science (BS) degree in neuroscience. The BA in psychology is typically one of the two largest majors on campus.

General psychology is offered each semester and is designated as a social sciences course in the general education curriculum. As such, students from over 120 different majors complete the course each semester, with typically fewer than 10% of students being psychology majors at the time they complete the course.

Course sections are taught by doctoral students and two to three full-time faculty members. Graduate students teach sections of approximately 150 students each, which meet in a traditional lecture format two or three times a week. We typically offer one section (~380 students) that meets with a faculty instructor for two 50-minute sessions each week, followed by a 50-minute graduate student-facilitated discussion section with 25 to 30 students per section. In fall 2020, we piloted two large ($n > 270$) faculty-taught sections utilizing undergraduate teaching fellows to support the course. All sections typically have a graduate student teaching assistant (TA) for about 10 hours per week to support the course.

All sections use the same textbook and cover similar core content, which is informed by the Gurung et al. (2016) recommendations for a common core in introductory psychology. For some of the pillars (i.e., biological, cognitive, developmental) all instructors cover the same content. For the remaining pillars (i.e., social and personality, mental and physical health) individual instructors have some autonomy in content coverage. For example, all instructors cover social psychology, but then choose from among several other areas (e.g., emotion, personality) to complete the pillar. All students complete pre- and postdepartmental assessments and a research requirement for course credit. The departmental assessment includes multiple-choice measures of students' content knowledge and scientific and critical thinking, along with other program assessments. Beyond these common assessment and research requirements, individual instructors have autonomy to select and design course assessments, within some guidelines (e.g., no single assessment may be worth more than 20% of a student's overall grade).

UNIQUE CHALLENGES OF TEACHING INTRODUCTORY PSYCHOLOGY

Enrollment in the course is uneven, with nearly three times as many students (~1,900) enrolled each fall than in the spring (~700). This has meant that full-time faculty teach the course in fall only. It also means we cannot implement the small discussion section format consistently in the fall, because doing so would require more than 60 separate sections, for which we have neither sufficient staffing nor available classrooms. Thus, there are challenges in delivering active and engaged learning and a consistent course experience across sections. An additional challenge that complicates implementation of the American Psychological Association (APA) Introductory Psychology Initiative (IPI; APA, 2020) is a new general education course designation for which the department is striving to qualify in the near future. The *Engaged Inquiries* designation requires that students produce a significant creative or scholarly product and engage in self-reflective, applied, interdisciplinary, and/or collaborative learning.

CURRENT AND FUTURE IMPLEMENTATIONS OF THE INTRODUCTORY PSYCHOLOGY INITIATIVE RECOMMENDATIONS

Implementing the IPI recommendations offers potential solutions to many of these challenges. In addition, the introductory course at UTK has long been seen as a key component in the university's efforts to promote student success and the department's efforts to train graduate student instructors. The IPI recommendations enhance our ability to meet these goals, as well.

SLOs and Assessment

All course sections formally adopted all three broad goals from the APA IPI in fall 2020. Our standard departmental assessment does allow us to assess the first two goals related to content and scientific thinking. For example, we use items from the Test of Scientific Literacy Skills (TOSL; Gormally et al., 2012) to assess such skills as students' ability to evaluate a valid scientific argument or the use and misuse of scientific information. We also ask students to indicate concepts from the course that they found most important or personally relevant, which offers insight into the ways students *Apply psychological principles to personal growth and other aspects of everyday life* (Student Learning Outcome [SLO] 1.3).

We are also integrating the new SLOs into our efforts to achieve UTK's general education program *Engaged Inquiries* designation by engaging students in collaborative projects that highlight SLO Key Theme F: *Applying psychological principles can change our lives, organizations, and communities in positive ways.* For example, students have worked in groups to curate resources that highlight ways psychological science can address issues such as climate change or systemic racism.

Course Models and Design

Instructors are encouraged to organize content around key themes. Moving forward, more intentional efforts will be directed to identifying common themes across sections. There has been increased attention in recent years on an explicit skills focus, with all sections in fall 2020 having an early unit on using psychological science to promote academic and personal success (e.g., study skills, career exploration). We also continue to work intentionally toward increasing inclusiveness, including switching to free or very low-cost textbooks and examining data on course outcomes for equity gaps.

Teacher Training and Development

Graduate students engage in a structured and scaffolded multiyear training sequence that addresses the key recommendations of the IPI: (a) ongoing development, (b) explicit training in backward course design, and (c) opportunities for cohorts of newer instructors to build community and share ideas and strategies. Future goals are strengthening training in specific content and creating more formal communities of practice.

Student Success and Transformation

The new recommendations have inspired the requirement that every section now includes a stand-alone module around the theme of using psychology to be a more successful student. As part of an exploration of personality, many instructors require students to complete well-validated assessments through our career center and reflect on how an understanding of personality informs major and career choice. In addition, the course director creates fliers to promote the course with professional advisors. These fliers are college specific, pulling quotes from students in each college from our departmental assessment that highlight the significant learning they experienced in the course.

REFERENCES

American Psychological Association. (2020). *The APA Introductory Psychology Initiative.* https://www.apa.org/ed/precollege/undergrad/introductory-psychology-initiative

Gormally, C., Brickman, P., & Lutz, M. (2012). Developing a test of scientific literacy skills (TOSLS): Measuring undergraduates' evaluation of scientific information and arguments. *CBE-Life Sciences Education, 11*(4), 333–447. https://doi.org/10.1187/cbe.12-03-0026

Gurung, R. A. R., Hackathorn, J., Enns, C., Frantz, S., Cacioppo, J. T., Loop, T., & Freeman, J. E. (2016). Strengthening introductory psychology: A new model for teaching the introductory course. *American Psychologist, 71*(2), 112–124. https://doi.org/10.1037/a0040012

16 TEACHING INTRODUCTORY PSYCHOLOGY IN LARGE CLASSES

Missouri State University

DANAE L. HUDSON

- Context: Public Doctoral Granting Institution
- Student Enrollment: 26,000 annually; 24,000 on Springfield campus/full-time
- Average Student Age: 22 years
- Enrollment Type: Public
- Underrepresented Minoritized Students: 14%
- Term: Semesters
- Introductory Psychology Class Sizes: 330 (blended), 40 (online)

CONTEXT

Missouri State University (MSU) is a public university system with students from Missouri, the United States, and numerous countries around the world. The system has four physical campuses: three in Missouri and one in Dalian, China. The main campus, located in Springfield, Missouri, is home to more

https://doi.org/10.1037/0000260-017
Transforming Introductory Psychology: Expert Advice on Teacher Training, Course Design, and Student Success, R. A. R. Gurung and G. Neufeld (Editors)

than 24,000 students. MSU is divided into seven undergraduate colleges and one graduate college. The Department of Psychology, which includes gerontology, is housed within the McQueary College of Health and Human Services. Psychology is the most popular major on campus, with more than 900 undergraduate students. The department offers master's degrees in clinical psychology, experimental psychology, industrial–organizational psychology, and applied behavior analysis.

Introductory psychology (PSY 121) is a popular general education choice among students. Between 2,000 and 2,500 students enroll in PSY 121 annually. PSY 121 is a semester-long course that introduces students to 12 chapters of content that provide a broad overview of the field of psychology. The choice of content was guided by the American Psychological Association (APA) working group on strengthening the introductory psychology course (Gurung et al., 2016). At least two chapters of content are included from each of the five pillars: biological, cognitive, developmental, social and personality, and mental and physical health. Cross-cutting themes related to ethics, cultural and social diversity, application, and variations in human functioning are emphasized throughout the semester and addressed specifically in extra credit assignments.

A course coordinator manages the daytime teaching team and teaches one section of PSY 121 each semester. All daytime sections are offered in a blended format and taught primarily by full-time tenure-track faculty members in the department. All sections have a common syllabus; use the same digital, interactive textbook; have the same assignments; and take multiple-choice exams drawn from the same large pool of items curated by the teaching team. Online sections and evening face-to-face sections are taught by adjunct faculty and have more flexibility in terms of course delivery.

Daytime sections include 330 students, one faculty instructor, one senior learning assistant (SLA; a graduate assistant), and approximately six undergraduate learning assistants (ULAs). All ULAs are enrolled in a 3-credit, undergraduate course specifically focused on evidence-based teaching strategies. Furthermore, the SLAs and ULAs attend a 1-day training before the semester begins as well as weekly staff meetings with the faculty member leading their section. The SLA assists the instructor with managing grades and student emails. Each ULA is assigned a group of students who sit together during the class. The ULAs manage the attendance each week and email students who do not attend class. The ULAs' primary job is to lead small-group study sessions prior to each unit exam. PSY 121 was redesigned to this format in 2012 and since that time has demonstrated impressive improvements in learning outcomes and retention rates (for more information, see Hudson et al., 2014, 2015; Whisenhunt et al., 2019).

Students in all daytime sections of the course complete a multiple-choice pretest that measures important concepts related to the student learning outcomes (SLOs). The posttest is contained within the comprehensive multiple-choice final exam. In addition to the final, four unit exams, weekly quizzes, and other low-stakes assignments are spread out over the semester.

UNIQUE CHALLENGES OF TEACHING INTRODUCTORY PSYCHOLOGY

The introductory psychology course at MSU was originally redesigned in 2012; since that time, it has evolved based on course-specific empirical data and student feedback. Overall, the course is evidence based, uses active learning strategies when possible, and is responsive to student needs (all of which are Introductory Psychology Initiative [IPI; APA, 2020] recommendations; see Part I of this book). However, there are still a number of challenges, most of which are a result of the large class size. Establishing individual connections with students is difficult with a class size of 330. Furthermore, class discussions are limited, it is impossible to learn student names, and it is likely that the anonymity of a large class results in more time spent on devices rather than on actively engaging with the course content. In addition, even though each section of introductory psychology has a course staff of at least eight, it is not feasible to assign writing as part of assignments or exams. At MSU, undergraduates are not permitted to grade assignments or have access to student grades. As a result, the teaching teams feel limited in opportunities to develop critical thinking skills and assess learning outcomes through methods other than multiple-choice questions.

CURRENT AND FUTURE IMPLEMENTATIONS OF THE INTRODUCTORY PSYCHOLOGY INITIATIVE RECOMMENDATIONS

SLOs and Assessment

In fall 2019, one large section of introductory psychology adopted the first iteration of the APA IPI SLOs. Students were exposed to all recommended SLOs, but the primary focus for the semester involved psychology's integrative themes (see IPI recommendations in Part I of this book). The five integrative themes were introduced in the first class of the semester. In each subsequent class (i.e., once per week), the content for the day was explicitly connected to the most relevant integrative themes. In some cases, the faculty member presented the connections (e.g., the different approaches and theoretical perspectives in psychology = "Psychological, biological, social, and cultural factors influence mental processes and behavior"), and in other situations, the students were encouraged to find the most appropriate integrative theme for the content discussed that day (e.g., sensation and perception = "Our perceptions filter experience of the world through an imperfect lens").

At the end of the semester, the students in this section took a final exam that included the five integrative themes assessment questions provided by the IPI. The same five questions were also given to students in another section that was not using the new SLOs or exposed to the integrative themes. These two sections were equivalent in size, structure, and demographic composition. The only content difference involved the weekly discussion of integrative themes. Figure 16.1 presents the data comparing these classes' performance on the assessment questions. The section exposed to the integrative themes throughout the semester (i.e., pilot class) had significantly more students correctly answer three of the five assessment items than did the section that was not exposed to any of the new SLOs (i.e., control class).

FIGURE 16.1. Class Comparison of Correctly Answered Integrative Themes Assessment Questions

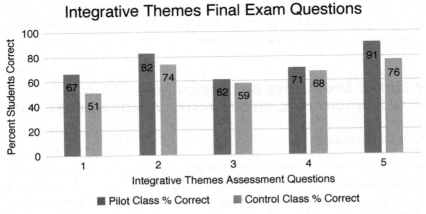

Note. Significantly more students answered three of the five assessment questions correctly in the pilot class compared with the control class (Q1, $p < .001$; Q2, $p < .05$; Q3, not significant; Q4, not significant; Q5, $p < .001$).

Course Models and Design

All three full-time, tenure-track faculty members who make up the majority of the teaching team have programs of research focused on the scholarship of teaching and learning. They are experts in course design and use many of the evidence-based strategies described in Part I of this book. PSY 121 is a blended course in which the online homework is due the day before the class meets. The instructors review the classwide data and use it to plan the lecture and class activities, focusing on the concepts the students appeared to struggle with the most. This just-in-time teaching is supplemented with interactive polling and peer instruction during the class (which is an IPI recommendation).

Student Success and Transformation

One of the overarching goals of the introductory psychology course at MSU is to teach students study skills informed by the science of learning and broad principles about human health and behavior that will remain with them long after the conclusion of the semester. One small but powerful syllabus change involved moving the chapter on memory to the first unit of material. Students are presented with information about memory in a way they can apply to their own studying behavior. Active-learning demonstrations are conducted in class to teach concepts such as deep processing and elaborative interrogation. In fact, after the first exam, an entire class is devoted to study skills. Students often remark, even years later, that this was one of the most helpful classes they attended while in college. A midterm wrapper assignment is completed midsemester. This assignment requires students to access the grades they have received by that point in the semester, calculate where they lost points, identify changes they can make to their studying behavior, and set goals for the last half of the class.

Teacher Training and Development

Teacher training and development is an important aspect of the introductory psychology course at MSU. Faculty model to SLAs, ULAs, and PSY 121 students what it means to be a lifelong learner. The teaching team is involved in regular professional development opportunities, both as participants and as presenters (which is an IPI recommendation). The scholarship of teaching and learning is evident in the course design, training of ULAs, and continual course refinement through ongoing assessment of the course (Hudson, 2021).

REFERENCES

American Psychological Association. (2020). *The APA Introductory Psychology Initiative*. https://www.apa.org/ed/precollege/undergrad/introductory-psychology-initiative

Gurung, R. A. R., Hackathorn, J., Enns, C., Frantz, S., Cacioppo, J. T., Loop, T., & Freeman, J. E. (2016). Strengthening introductory psychology: A new model for teaching the introductory course. *American Psychologist, 71*(2), 112–124. https://doi.org/10.1037/a0040012

Hudson, D. L. (2021). Evidence-based teaching and course design: Using data to develop, implement, and refine university courses. In S. A. Nolan, C. M. Hakala, & R. E. Landrum (Eds.), *Assessing undergraduate learning in psychology: Strategies for measuring and improving student performance* (pp. 127–139). American Psychological Association. https://doi.org/10.1037/0000183-010

Hudson, D. L., Whisenhunt, B. L., Shoptaugh, C. F., Rost, A. D., & Fondren-Happel, R. N. (2014). Redesigning a large enrollment course: The impact on academic performance, course completion and student perceptions in introductory psychology. *Psychology Learning & Teaching, 13*(2), 107–119. https://doi.org/10.2304/plat.2014.13.2.107

Hudson, D. L., Whisenhunt, B. L., Shoptaugh, C. F., Visio, M. E., Cathey, C., & Rost, A. D. (2015). Change takes time: Understanding and responding to culture change in course redesign. *Scholarship of Teaching and Learning in Psychology, 1*(4), 255–268. https://doi.org/10.1037/stl0000043

Whisenhunt, B. L., Cathey, C., Visio, M. E., Hudson, D. L., Shoptaugh, C. F., & Rost, A. D. (2019). Strategies to address challenges with large classes: Can we exceed student expectations for large class experiences? *Scholarship of Teaching and Learning in Psychology, 5*(2), 121–127. https://doi.org/10.1037/stl0000135

17

TEACHING INTRODUCTORY PSYCHOLOGY WHEN THE DEPARTMENT IS GROWING

Oregon State University

REGAN A. R. GURUNG

- Context: Public Doctoral Granting Institution
- Student Enrollment: 32,000 annually; 2,600 on campus/full-time
- Average Student Age: 19
- Enrollment Type: Open
- Underrepresented Minoritized Students: 18%
- Term: Quarters
- Introductory Psychology Class Sizes: 50–350

CONTEXT

Oregon State University (OSU) is a land, air, sea, and space grant public institution. An international public research university, OSU draws people from all 50 states and more than 100 countries. With two campuses (Corvallis and Bend, Oregon), OSU is divided into 11 colleges and has more than

https://doi.org/10.1037/0000260-018
Transforming Introductory Psychology: Expert Advice on Teacher Training, Course Design, and Student Success, R. A. R. Gurung and G. Neufeld (Editors)

200 academic programs. The School of Psychological Science is a unit in the College of Liberal Arts.

The introductory psychology course is divided into two parts. Both cover the history of psychology and research methods. In addition, Psych 201 covers biopsychology, consciousness, sensation and perception, memory, learning, and industrial–organizational psychology. Psych 202 covers personality, psychological disorders, therapy, and developmental, social, and health psychology. Content selection was guided by Gurung et al. (2016) and the report of the American Psychological Association (APA; 2014) working group on strengthening the introductory psychology course.

Sections of the course are taught by the director and coordinator of the general psychology program, graduate students, and tenured, tenure-track, and adjunct faculty. Courses are offered in both face-to-face and online formats. All sections use the same textbook, draw exams from a shared pool of questions, and have similar course components. All students have to complete a research requirement (1.5 hours), and extra credit opportunities are available.

Sections of the course, which are large (approximately 300), are supported by graduate teaching assistants (GTAs) and undergraduate learning assistants (LAs). All GTAs enroll in a teaching seminar run by the director, which prepares them to be instructors of record for the course. The seminar is a 2-credit course during the fall term and a 1-credit course during the winter and spring terms. GTAs also attend a 1- to 2-day summer bootcamp to prepare them to assist with the course. LAs have weekly meetings with the director and coordinator of the program and assist in classroom management and tutoring.

Students in all sections of the course complete a pretest gauging endorsement of the course student learning outcomes (SLOs). Each section of the course features three exams, all of which are cumulative. The multiple-choice exams are supplemented by weekly activities completed either individually (in online courses) or in groups (in in-person classes). After the final exam, students complete a posttest. The posttest features the SLOs again as well as measures of study skills and attitudes toward psychology and the class.

UNIQUE CHALLENGES OF TEACHING INTRODUCTORY PSYCHOLOGY

The general psychology program at OSU has gone through a few different iterations over the years given the infancy of the graduate program. As of this writing, there have been only four cohorts of graduate students in the program, which has made it difficult to establish a clear training sequence. In the new iteration, the program is hitting its stride: Graduate students first serve as GTAs for the course, then go on to teach their own face-to-face or online course. There are still times when staffing issues necessitate the hiring of ad hoc instructors for the course. Consequently, consistency of training and course delivery varies, although the existence of a coordinated program results in a higher level of coordination than would otherwise be attained. For example, all instructors have access to Canvas templates for the course, and all online sections of the course use the same course shell.

CURRENT AND FUTURE IMPLEMENTATIONS OF THE INTRODUCTORY PSYCHOLOGY INITIATIVE RECOMMENDATIONS

SLOs and Assessment

In fall 2019, all sections of introductory psychology adopted the first iteration of the APA Introductory Psychology Initiative (IPI; APA, 2020) SLOs. In fall 2020, all sections adopted the final set of SLOs. Although the course has a premeasure (Week 1) and a postmeasure (Week 11) of the extent to which students endorse the SLOs, future work is aimed toward the creation of activities and assessments of the learning outcomes.

The course currently has applied activities (e.g., watch a psychology TED Talk and critically analyze the video), but assessments do not tie in directly to the new APA (2021) IPI SLOs. None of the recommended assessments have been used to date, and work is afoot to create ways to assess the three SLOs and the themes in particular. Similar to many introductory psychology courses, the major assessment uses multiple choice, but since fall 2019, the program has had writing and testing assessments that climb to the higher rungs of Bloom's taxonomy as well as more directly tap into the new SLOs.

Course Models and Design

The introductory psychology course currently utilizes most of the main recommendations for course design presented in this book. Because the program has been managed for many years by faculty who are immersed in the scholarship of teaching and learning and who participate in activities that enhance their skills in teaching psychology, current practices are primarily evidence-informed. This notwithstanding, future work is directed toward more explicitly using themes to establish coherence, more explicitly building skills, and promoting inclusion (which are all IPI recommendations; see

Part I of this book). Course instructors are trained to share learning strategies (which is an IPI recommendation).

Teacher Training and Development

Oregon State provides a strong training program for graduate students (an IPI recommendation), who teach the course exemplifying the main IPI recommendations. In particular, the program uses evidence-based instructional methods and course design, is regularly assessed and modified, and provides sustained opportunities for development via communications (an IPI recommendation) from the director and coordinator to all instructors teaching the course. This communication also provides a sense of community for the group.

As part of training activities, graduate students in the applied cognition area also conduct research on learning in the introductory psychology course: implementation research (Soicher & Becker-Blease, 2020; Soicher et al., 2020) and assessments of teaching and learning (Gurung & Stone, 2020; Gurung et al., 2020).

Student Success and Transformation

Guided by the recommendations of the student success group, the general psychology program at OSU charges instructors to be as applied as possible in the discussion of content. In particular, we make available modules on key studying techniques (see Appendix C: Study Skills Lesson) and share chapters on how to study (Gurung & Dunlosky, 2021). In addition, we are working to better address the new SLOs, which, by virtue of being mostly content-agnostic, require some creative class planning. When discussing the memory chapter, instructors emphasize ways that students can improve their study skills by applying psychology concepts (which is an IPI recommendation). Our design of the structure of the course and requirements now requires students to use effective study techniques (an IPI recommendation), especially spaced and retrieval practice. We have instructors explain the connection between the course design and psychological principles. We have added a new chapter to the course—health psychology—which emphasizes the ways students can improve their health and wellness by applying psychology concepts (an IPI recommendation).

We continue to work on additional recommendations. For example, we are developing new material to foster students' cultural competency (an IPI recommendation) and modifying previous exercises designed to emphasize the ways students can overcome inaccuracies in their intuitions about psychology (an IPI recommendation). Finally, we continue to build on using workplace-relevant examples in course design and delivery (an IPI recommendation).

REFERENCES

American Psychological Association. (2014). *Strengthening the common core of the introductory psychology course.* https://www.apa.org/ed/governance/bea/intro-psych-report.pdf

American Psychological Association. (2020). *The APA Introductory Psychology Initiative.* https://www.apa.org/ed/precollege/undergrad/introductory-psychology-initiative

American Psychological Association. (2021). *APA Introductory Psychology Initiative (IPI) student learning outcomes for introductory psychology.* https://www.apa.org/ed/precollege/undergrad/introductory-psychology-initiative/student-learning-outcomes.pdf

Gurung, R. A. R., & Dunlosky, J. (2021). *The Worth expert guide to studying like a champion: Metacognition in action.* Worth.

Gurung, R. A. R., Hackathorn, J., Enns, C., Frantz, S., Cacioppo, J. T., Loop, T., & Freeman, J. E. (2016). Strengthening introductory psychology: A new model for teaching the introductory course. *American Psychologist, 71*(2), 112–124. https://doi.org/10.1037/a0040012

Gurung, R. A. R., Mai, T., Nelson, M., & Pruitt, S. (2020). Predicting learning: Comparing study techniques, perseverance, and metacognitive skill. *Teaching of Psychology.* Advance online publication. https://doi.org/10.1177/0098628320972332

Gurung, R. A. R., & Stone, A. R. (2020). You can't always get what you want and it hurts: Learning during a pandemic. *Scholarship of Teaching and Learning in Psychology.* Advance online publication. https://doi.org/10.1037/stl0000236

Soicher, R. N., & Becker-Blease, K. A. (2020). Utility value interventions: Why and how instructors should use them in college psychology courses. *Scholarship of Teaching and Learning in Psychology.* Advance online publication. https://doi.org/10.1037/stl0000240

Soicher, R. N., Becker-Blease, K. A., & Bostwick, K. C. P. (2020). Adapting implementation science for higher education research: The systematic study of implementing evidence-based practices in college classrooms. *Cognitive Research: Principles and Implications, 5,* Article 54. https://doi.org/10.1186/s41235-020-00255-0

CENSUS QUESTIONNAIRE

INTRODUCTORY PSYCHOLOGY INITIATIVE WORKING GROUP

What is your age (in years)?

What is your gender?

O Female

O Male

O Not listed

How would you classify your current institution type?

O Not classified

O Tribal college

O High school

O Special focus institution

O 2-year associate's degree–granting college

O Public 4-year baccalaureate college or university (i.e., no graduate degrees)

O Private 4-year baccalaureate college or university (i.e., no graduate degrees)

O Public master's university

O Private master's university

O Public doctorate university

O Private doctorate university

What best describes your role?

O High school teacher

O Graduate student

O Tenure-track faculty

O Non–tenure-track faculty (full time)

O Non–tenure-track faculty (part time)

O Professional staff or administrator

O Other (please specify) _____

If you are tenure-track, what is your rank?

O Assistant

O Associate

O Full

O Not applicable

What is your primary research area or area of training?

_____

Please answer the questions below about your course load	Fall	Winter	Spring	Summer
How many courses do you teach per term in total?				
How many sections of introductory psychology do you teach per term?				

What is the average size of an introductory psychology class for your most frequently taught modality (face-to-face, blended, online)?

	0 100 200 300 400 500 600 700 800 900 1000
Average number of students in your introductory psychology course.	▬▬▬▬▬▬▬█▬▬▬▬▬▬▬

Is your introductory psychology course offered in a semester or quarter format?

○ Semester

○ Quarter

○ Another format (please describe):

_____

Over how many terms is your introductory psychology course offered (i.e., is it a one-term or a two-term course)?

○ 1

○ 2

Is introductory psychology a general education course at your institution?

○ Yes

○ No

○ Not sure

Do students in your introductory psychology course serve as participants in research studies as a part of the course, either as a requirement or for extra credit?

☐ Yes

☐ No

☐ Not sure

To what extent do you address each of the five APA Learning Goals from the APA Guidelines 2.0 for the Undergraduate Psychology Major in your introductory psychology course syllabi?

Please check all that apply.

	None at all	A little	A moderate amount	A lot	A great deal
1. Knowledge Base of Psychology	O	O	O	O	O
2. Scientific Inquiry and Critical Thinking Skills	O	O	O	O	O
3. Ethical and Social Responsibility in a Diverse World	O	O	O	O	O
4. Communication	O	O	O	O	O
5. Professional Development	O	O	O	O	O

Which of the following best represent how introductory psychology is taught at your school?

Please select one option.

O All sections use the same student learning outcomes.

O Sections use some of the same student learning outcomes.

O Each instructor selects their own student learning outcomes.

O Each instructor has a selection of student learning outcomes to choose from.

Have you used the APA Guidelines for the Undergraduate Major 2.0 to develop learning goals and outcomes?

Please select one option.

O We have used the APA Guidelines for the Undergraduate Psychology Major 2.0 verbatim.

O We have used the APA Guidelines for the Undergraduate Psychology Major 2.0 with changes.

O We have not referenced or incorporated any of the recommendations included in the APA Guidelines for the Undergraduate Psychology Major 2.0.

O Other (please specify): _____

How many sections of introductory psychology do you teach per year in each of the following modalities? *Please enter the number in the box provided.*	Sections per Year
Face-to-face	
Online	
Hybrid/blended	

What format do you typically teach introductory psychology?

Please select the format that you typically teach.

O Face-to-face

O Online

O Hybrid/blended

What chapters/topics do you typically include in your introductory psychology course?

Please select all that apply.

☐ Biology (neuroscience)

☐ Sensation

☐ Consciousness

☐ Motivation

☐ Cognition

☐ Memory

☐ Perception

☐ Learning

☐ Lifespan development

☐ Language

☐ Social psychology

☐ Personality

☐ Intelligence

☐ Emotion

☐ Multiculturalism (cultural psychology)

☐ Gender (sexuality)

☐ Abnormal (psychological disorders)

☐ Health (stress)

☐ Therapies

☐ Other _____

How challenging is each of the following for you?

Please indicate how challenging each of the items is for you. If the item does not apply to your course, select NA.

	Extremely challenging	Very challenging	Moderately challenging	Slightly challenging	Not challenging at all	NA
Class size is too large	O	O	O	O	O	O
Covering required content	O	O	O	O	O	O
Engaging students	O	O	O	O	O	O
Class attendance	O	O	O	O	O	O
Getting students to read assignments	O	O	O	O	O	O
Getting students to think critically	O	O	O	O	O	O
Time to thoughtfully grade or provide feedback on writing	O	O	O	O	O	O
Managing graduate teaching assistants	O	O	O	O	O	O
Managing undergraduate teaching assistants	O	O	O	O	O	O
Running labs effectively	O	O	O	O	O	O
Making material more personally relevant	O	O	O	O	O	O

	Extremely challenging	Very challenging	Moderately challenging	Slightly challenging	Not challenging at all	NA
Managing wide range of student abilities, skills, and knowledge	O	O	O	O	O	O
Assessing higher level thinking	O	O	O	O	O	O
Lack of my expertise on the wide range of topics typically covered	O	O	O	O	O	O
Staying current regarding new findings (e.g., the replication crisis)	O	O	O	O	O	O
Administration or state official pressure to teach in a particular way	O	O	O	O	O	O
Administration or state official pressure to select particular course materials (e.g., low-cost, digital, open educational resources)	O	O	O	O	O	O
Other	O	O	O	O	O	O

How confident are you in your ability to effectively teach the content in introductory psychology?

Please indicate your confidence using the slider bar below.

0 10 20 30 40 50 60 70 80 90 100

% Confident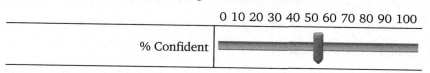

How confident are you in your teaching skills in introductory psychology?

Please indicate your confidence using the slider bar below.

0 10 20 30 40 50 60 70 80 90 100

% Confident

How confident are you in your ability to find evidence-based practices (e.g., teaching methods that have been demonstrated to be effective through research) to improve your teaching in introductory psychology?

Please indicate your confidence using the slider bar below.

0 10 20 30 40 50 60 70 80 90 100

% Confident

How confident are you in your ability to implement evidence-based practices to improve your teaching in introductory psychology?

Please indicate your confidence using the slider bar below.

0 10 20 30 40 50 60 70 80 90 100

% Confident

Where do you go to find resources to teach your classes?

Please select all that apply.

☐ Teaching journals such as *Teaching of Psychology, Scholarship of Teaching and Learning in Psychology,* or *Psychology Learning and Teaching*

☐ Teaching books

☐ Blogs/Internet

☐ Society for the Teaching of Psychology (APA Division 2) online resources

☐ Society for the Teaching of Psychology (APA Division 2) Facebook group

☐ Observe other teachers

☐ Attend teaching conferences

☐ Other _____

What types of professional development activities do you participate in to improve your teaching?

Please select all that apply.

◯ Publish research in Society for the Teaching of Psychology journals

◯ Present research at conferences

◯ Present teaching demonstrations and strategies at conferences

◯ Publish chapters on teaching

◯ Publish books on teaching

Please indicate how often you use these instructional methods when teaching introductory psychology.

	Often	Sometimes	Seldom	Never
Direct instruction (e.g., lecturing)	◯	◯	◯	◯
Active learning (e.g., students engage in higher order cognitive strategies)	◯	◯	◯	◯
Cooperative/collaborative learning (e.g., students working together in groups)	◯	◯	◯	◯
Just-in-time teaching (e.g., instructor tailors class using student performance data)	◯	◯	◯	◯
Inquiry-based learning (e.g., students research their topic, present to the class, and reflect)	◯	◯	◯	◯
Interteaching instruction (e.g., students complete instructor designed work before class)	◯	◯	◯	◯
Problem-based instruction (e.g., learning centered around complex problems)	◯	◯	◯	◯
Team-based instruction (e.g., students work in teams and follow a predictable learning process)	◯	◯	◯	◯

	Often	Sometimes	Seldom	Never
Socratic method (e.g., reflective questioning)	O	O	O	O
Experiential learning (e.g., students learn through engaging with content)	O	O	O	O
Other	O	O	O	O

Please indicate the level of autonomy you typically have in the following aspects of your introductory psychology course.

	Decision is completely up to me	I contribute to the decision	Decision is completely up to someone else
Textbook choice	O	O	O
Topics covered in your course	O	O	O
Course syllabus	O	O	O
Materials used in your course	O	O	O
Assignments and exams	O	O	O

Do you assign a textbook in your course?

O Yes/No

- -

Display This Question:

If "Do you assign a textbook in your course?" = Yes

Which textbook do you use for introductory psychology?

O Author(s) _____

O Title _____

Display This Question:

If "Do you assign a textbook in your course?" = Yes

How much do you rely on your textbook . . .

	Not at all	A little	A moderate amount	A lot	A great deal
to know what content to cover?	○	○	○	○	○
for current research?	○	○	○	○	○

Display This Question:

If "Do you assign a textbook in your course?" = Yes

How much do you rely on publisher-provided teaching resources or ancillaries for the following?

	Not at all	A little	A moderate amount	A lot	A great deal
Lecture notes	○	○	○	○	○
Slides or presentations	○	○	○	○	○
Quizzes	○	○	○	○	○
Homework or assignments	○	○	○	○	○
Exams	○	○	○	○	○

Please indicate:

1. **what type of training you received before you taught for the first time, and**
2. **what type of training you have ongoing access to in the past 5 years.**

(If you had no training before teaching for the first time, select "None of the Above" in the first column. If you have not had any training in the past 5 years, select "None of the above" for the second column.)

Please select all that apply.

	Before I taught	Have had access to within the past 5 years
A credit-bearing course or seminar on college teaching	☐	☐
Workshops on college teaching	☐	☐

	Before I taught	Have had access to within the past 5 years
An orientation program within an institution	◯	◯
Online courses, modules, or tutorials on teaching	◯	◯
Apprenticeship or mentoring, including being mentored while serving as a course assistant	◯	◯
Teaching observations by a supervisor or peer	◯	◯
A conference with a teaching component	◯	◯
None of the above	◯	◯

Considering all the types of training you received, which one of these did you find most valuable?

Please select only one.

◯ A credit-bearing course or seminar on college teaching

◯ Workshops on college teaching

◯ An orientation program within an institution

◯ Online courses, modules, or tutorials on teaching

◯ Apprenticeship or mentoring, including being mentored while serving as a course assistant

◯ Teaching observations by a supervisor or peer

◯ A conference with a teaching component

◯ None of the above

Considering all the types of training you received, which of these were specific to teaching introductory psychology?

Please select all that apply.

◻ A credit-bearing course or seminar on college teaching

◻ Workshops on college teaching

◻ An orientation program within an institution

◻ Online courses, modules, or tutorials on teaching

☐ Apprenticeship or mentoring, including being mentored while serving as a course assistant

☐ Teaching observations by a supervisor or peer

☐ A conference with a teaching component

☐ None of the above

Which of the following topics were covered in the types of training you received?

Please select all that apply for each type of training.

	Information relevant to course content	Pedagogy	Institutional policies/ practices (e.g., academic misconduct)	Departmental policies or practices (e.g., assessment)	Technology (e.g., learning management system)
A credit-bearing course or seminar on college teaching	☐	☐	☐	☐	☐
Workshops on college teaching	☐	☐	☐	☐	☐
An orientation program within an institution	☐	☐	☐	☐	☐
Online courses, modules, or tutorials on teaching	☐	☐	☐	☐	☐
Apprenticeship or mentoring, including being mentored while serving as a course assistant	☐	☐	☐	☐	☐
Teaching observations by a supervisor or peer	☐	☐	☐	☐	☐
A conference with a teaching component	☐	☐	☐	☐	☐
None of the above	☐	☐	☐	☐	☐

How much do you agree with the following statement?

I currently have adequate access to the training and support I need as a teacher of introductory psychology.

○ Strongly agree

○ Somewhat agree

○ Neither agree nor disagree

○ Somewhat disagree

○ Strongly disagree

Which of the following sources do you currently use for information to support or enhance your teaching?

Please select all that apply.

☐ Publishers or other commercial sources

☐ Open educational resources

☐ Research articles and books

☐ Colleagues or one's peer network

☐ A mentor on your institution

☐ A mentor outside of your institution

☐ Blogs or other online resources

☐ Listservs

☐ Professional organizations (e.g., STP, APA, APS, or others)

☐ Social media

☐ Conferences with a teaching component

☐ National teaching-specific conferences (e.g., ACT)

☐ None of these.

Does your current institution provide any of the following kinds of support for engaging in teacher training?

Please select all that apply.

☐ Promotion credit

☐ Release time

☐ Stipend or travel funding

☐ In-house training (e.g., Center for Teaching and Learning, etc.)

☐ Other: _____

☐ None of these.

Do you provide explicit instruction on the following study skills as part of your standard introductory psychology content?

Please select all that apply.

☐ **Spaced practice** (space out studying over time rather than cramming)

☐ **Interleaving** (switch between ideas/types of problems while studying)

☐ **Elaboration/deep processing** (explain and describe ideas with many details)

☐ **Retrieval practice/testing effect** (practice bringing information to mind)

☐ **Overlearning** (continuing to study after initial mastery)

☐ **Eliminating distractions** (focus on studying without multitasking)

☐ **Collaboration** (work with others to achieve and share knowledge)

☐ **Other** _____

What method(s) do you use for the instruction of study skills?

Please select all that apply.

☐ Assigned reading from the textbook

☐ Assigned materials outside of the textbook (e.g., video, website)

☐ Formal lecture

☐ Informal description or discussion

☐ Classroom demonstration

☐ Graded assignment

☐ Description in syllabus

☐ Make students aware of optional resources

☐ Other _____

What best describes how you incorporate study skills into the course?

Please select all that apply.

◯ They are included as one independent topic at the start of the course.

◯ They are included throughout the course as multiple independent topics.

◯ They are incorporated as part of other course topics (e.g., memory).

◯ Other _____

How do you address the following topics in your introductory psychology course?

Please indicate if you cover each topic not at all, indirectly (through activities, assignments, or course policies), or directly (it is a course topic).

	Do not address	Indirectly (through activities, assignments, or course policies)	Directly (it is a course topic)
Adaptability (e.g., adjusting to change, being flexible)	◯	◯	◯
Analytical thinking (e.g., problem-solving, planning, tolerating ambiguity)	◯	◯	◯
Collaborative skills (e.g., effectively cooperating with others, effectively working in groups)	◯	◯	◯
Critical thinking (e.g., research methods, statistics, evaluating research findings)	◯	◯	◯
Creativity (e.g., innovation, resourcefulness)	◯	◯	◯
Diversity (e.g., multicultural sensitivity, respecting individual differences)	◯	◯	◯
Hardware/software skills (e.g., troubleshooting technical problems, coding, create web pages)	◯	◯	◯

	Do not address	Indirectly (through activities, assignments, or course policies)	Directly (it is a course topic)
Information management (e.g., locating sources, evaluating information)	☐	☐	☐
Interaction with technology (e.g., computer platforms, software systems)	☐	☐	☐
Integrity and ethics (e.g., maintaining high levels of ethics, being honest)	☐	☐	☐
Judgment and decision making	☐	☐	☐
Leadership	☐	☐	☐
Oral communication skills (e.g., public speaking, conversational skills)	☐	☐	☐
Self-regulation (e.g., manage stress, complete assignments on time without prompting)	☐	☐	☐
Service orientation (e.g., helping others, empathy, community engagement)	☐	☐	☐
Writing skills	☐	☐	☐

We invite you to upload your introductory psychology syllabus. The syllabus will be stored separately from your responses.

(To upload your syllabus, click on the "Choose File" button and locate your syllabus on your hard drive.)

Become a part of a national network of intro psychology instructors: by providing your email you will receive census results and updates on the initiative and be eligible to participate in future IPI classroom studies.

Thank you for your participation.

Appendix B

CENSUS RESPONSE DATA

INTRODUCTORY PSYCHOLOGY INITIATIVE WORKING GROUP

TABLE B.1. Frequency Data for Demographic Variables

Variable	f (%)
Gender (n = 814)	
Female	530 (64.7)
Male	282 (34.4)
Not listed	2 (0.2)
Institution type (n = 817)	
High school	67 (8.2)
2-year associate's degree–granting college	217 (26.5)
Public baccalaureate college or university	53 (6.5)
Private baccalaureate college or university	145 (17.7)
Public master's university	69 (8.4)
Private master's university	71 (8.7)
Public doctorate university	132 (16.1)
Private doctorate university	59 (7.2)
Not classified	4 (0.5)
Teaching role (n = 818)	
Tenure-track faculty	448 (54.7)
Nontenure track faculty (full time)	135 (16.5)
Nontenure track faculty (part time)	100 (12.2)
Professional staff/administrator	14 (1.7)
Graduate student	22 (2.7)
High school teacher	64 (7.8)
Other	35 (4.3)
Tenure-track rank (n = 479)	
Assistant	122 (14.9)
Associate	139 (17.0)
Full	218 (26.6)

Note. Total n = 819; f = frequency.

TABLE B.2. Perceived Challenges in Teaching Introductory Psychology

Challenges	M (SD)	n
Time to thoughtfully grade or provide feedback on writing	3.50 (1.14)	750
Getting students to read assignments	3.39 (1.10)	785
Getting students to think critically	3.37 (0.95)	790
Assessing higher level learning	3.25 (0.98)	786
Managing wide range of student abilities, skills, and knowledge	3.14 (1.03)	784
Covering required content	2.92 (1.16)	774
Staying current regarding new findings (e.g., the replication crisis)	2.72 (1.02)	788
Running labs effectively	2.65 (1.05)	100
Engaging students	2.63 (0.99)	789
Class attendance	2.22 (0.97)	770
Lack of my expertise on the wide range of topics typically covered	2.11 (0.89)	778
Managing graduate teaching assistants	2.10 (1.06)	135
Making material more personally relevant	2.07 (0.90)	785
Class size is too large	2.01 (1.15)	706
Managing undergraduate teaching assistants	1.98 (0.99)	144
Administration or state official pressure to select particular course materials (e.g., low-cost, digital, open educational resources)	1.83 (1.14)	606
Administration or state official pressure to teach in a particular way	1.78 (1.12)	610
Other	3.80 (1.20)	45

Note. Participants could select the challenges that applied to their situation. Thus, there are different ns for each challenge. 1 = *not challenging at all*, 2 = *slightly challenging*, 3 = *moderately challenging*, 4 = *very challenging*, and 5 = *extremely challenging*.

TABLE B.3. Frequency of Instructional Methods Used in Introductory Psychology

Type of instructional method	M (SD)	n
Direct	3.77 (0.54)	773
Active learning	3.40 (0.62)	774
Cooperative or collaborative learning	2.98 (0.86)	775
Experiential learning	2.89 (0.86)	770
Socratic method	2.77 (0.96)	772
Interteaching	2.46 (1.00)	773
Problem based	2.24 (0.89)	773
Inquiry based	2.18 (1.01)	772
Just-in-time teaching	2.14 (0.92)	772
Team based	1.96 (0.95)	769

Note. Participants were allowed to select only the instructional methods that applied to them. Thus, there are different *ns* for each frequency of instructional method. 1 = *never*, 2 = *seldom*, 3 = *sometimes*, and 4 = *often*.

TABLE B.4. Frequency of Incorporating Career Skills Into Introductory Psychology

Skill	Directly address f (%)	Indirectly address f (%)	Do not address f (%)
Critical thinking	474 (63.0)	341 (45.3)	13 (1.7)
Diversity	317 (42.2)	409 (54.4)	58 (7.7)
Integrity and ethics	311 (41.4)	406 (54.3)	75 (10.0)
Self-regulation	289 (38.4)	419 (55.7)	82 (10.9)
Judgment and decision-making	288 (38.3)	354 (47.1)	125 (16.6)
Analytical thinking	277 (36.8)	471 (62.6)	47 (6.3)
Written communication	195 (25.9)	444 (59.00)	119 (15.8)
Information management	176 (23.4)	446 (59.3)	146 (19.4)
Creativity	123 (16.4)	396 (52.7)	232 (30.9)
Collaboration	111 (14.8)	468 (62.2)	178 (23.7)
Adaptability	106 (14.1)	397 (52.8)	252 (33.5)
Service orientation	98 (13.0)	329 (43.8)	320 (42.6)
Interaction with technology	94 (12.5)	504 (67.0)	156 (20.7)
Oral communication	86 (38.4)	361 (48.0)	301 (40.0)
Leadership	33 (4.4)	226 (30.1)	467 (62.1)
Hardware/software skills	23 (3.1)	280 (37.2)	432 (57.4)

Note. f = frequency. These skills are from the *Skillful Psychology Student* (Naufel et al., 2018).

TABLE B.5. Percentage of Introductory Psychology (IP) Instructors Reporting Characteristics of Sources of Teaching Training

Training characteristic	Course for credit f (%)	Workshops f (%)	Orientation program f (%)	Online training f (%)	Mentoring f (%)	Being observed f (%)	Conference f (%)	None f (%)
Availability								
Had access before teaching	332 (43.2)	215 (28.0)	254 (33.0)	117 (15.2)	325 (42.3)	289 (37.6)	122 (15.9)	156 (20.3)
Had access in past 5 years	107 (13.9)	491 (63.8)	215 (28.0)	366 (47.6)	132 (17.2)	473 (61.5)	427 (55.5)	52 (6.8)
Topics covered								
Course content	218 (28.6)	160 (21.0)	34 (4.5)	116 (15.2)	228 (29.9)	218 (28.6)	294 (38.5)	26 (3.4)
Pedagogy	395 (51.8)	431 (56.5)	131 (17.2)	248 (32.5)	261 (34.2)	395 (51.8)	365 (47.8)	9 (1.2)
Institutional policies	139 (18.2)	140 (18.3)	290 (38.0)	79 (10.4)	123 (16.1)	99 (13.0)	27 (3.5)	15 (2.0)
Departmental policies	114 (14.9)	90 (11.8)	188 (24.6)	44 (5.8)	148 (19.4)	139 (18.2)	32 (4.2)	20 (2.6)
Technology	128 (16.8)	308 (40.4)	212 (27.8)	242 (31.7)	101 (13.2)	77 (10.1)	177 (23.2)	16 (2.1)
Source was specific to IP	104 (13.6)	143 (18.7)	47 (6.2)	96 (12.6)	125 (16.4)	205 (26.9)	219 (28.7)	91 (11.9)
Most valuable training type	115 (15.6)	180 (24.5)	26 (3.5)	43 (5.8)	122 (16.6)	62 (8.4)	125 (17.0)	63 (8.6)

Note. n = 763; f = frequency.

FIGURE B.1. Extent of American Psychological Association Learning Outcomes 2.0 Use in Introductory Psychology

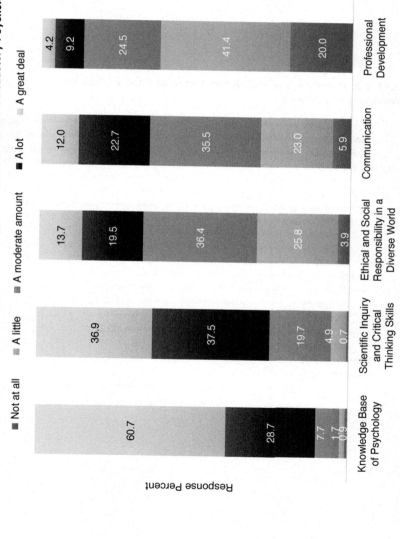

Note. Percentage indicating how much each learning outcome is addressed in introductory psychology course.

FIGURE B.2. Percentage of Instructors Including Chapter Type in Introductory Psychology

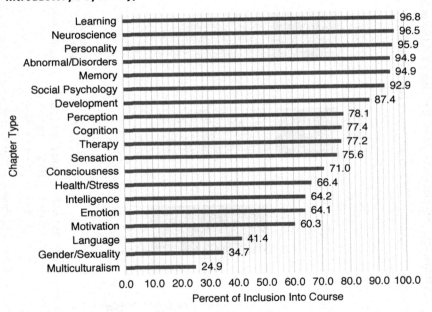

Appendix C

STUDY SKILLS LESSON

STEPHEN L. CHEW AND GUY A. BOYSEN

DESCRIPTION

This lesson plan outlines an introduction to effective study skills that can be integrated into your introductory psychology course. It can be covered in one class or over a longer period. It also includes a selection of optional activities for each section of the lesson, formative and summative assessments of learning, and supplementary resources. A set of presentation slides to accompany this lesson plan can be found at http://bit.ly/StudySkills_IPI.

Learning Goals for This Module

- Identify the components of effective studying (attention, multitasking, working memory, learning strategies, metacognition)
- Design a study plan using effective study strategies

Presentation Outline

This is an outline of major points in the lesson. Additional information about effective study skills and supporting research are located in the Resources and References section.

- Studying in ways that effectively promote learning is a critical academic skill, but it is also a critical career and life skill. People need to learn new things throughout their life.
  - Instructors can conduct the Study Strategy Poll here (**Activity 1**).
  - Research shows that some of the most popular study strategies that students use are also the least effective for learning. For example,

rereading and highlighting are not effective learning techniques by themselves.

- If a student uses poor study strategies, the student can study long and hard but still fail.

• The content of introductory psychology includes concepts that are necessary for effective studying.

- Attention: People, and that includes students, cannot multitask. Students often believe that they are expert multitaskers because they do it a lot. Trying to multitask causes people to constantly switch the focus of their attention. Research shows people miss a lot of information outside of their focus of attention, and they are not aware of what they have missed (i.e., inattentional blindness). Students must eliminate distractions and study with full focus. Instructors can conduct the Inattentional Blindness activity here (**Activity 2**) and the Cost of Multitasking activity here (**Activity 3**).

- Short-term or working memory: Short-term memory, also known as working memory, is what students use when actively thinking about study materials. This memory is limited in capacity. Effective studying involves transferring information through this limited-capacity memory to long-term memory, which has an enormous capacity. Using short-term memory for this transfer can take time and effort.

- There are six key learning strategies in this lesson. Instructors should introduce the strategies to students. For example, instructors may have students view the *How to Study* videos by Stephen Chew (**Activity 4**), or they may assign Miyatsu, Nguyen, and McDaniel (2018) as a reading (**Activity 5**). These activities might occur before class or during class time. Instructors may also assign other readings or lecture to introduce the strategies. For more information about each strategy plus downloadable teaching resources, instructors can go to https://www.learningscientists.org and https://www.retrievalpractice.org. They can also refer to the books listed under Resources and References.

  o Distributed or spaced practice: Learning takes time. Students should distribute studying across multiple sessions rather than massing it in one session. Cramming is ineffective for long-term retention of information.

  o Interleaving: Students should mix up the content that they are studying rather than studying just one type of content (e.g., rather than studying for one course in one block of time, study for two courses during that one block of time, going back and forth from one to the other).

- ○ Chunking: Group ideas together into meaningful chunks of information. Organize facts into meaningful categories that go together. So, if someone has to remember to buy lettuce, cheese, cucumber, tomatoes, dressing, and croutons, this grocery list is easier to recall if they group all of these ingredients into one chunk called "salad."

- ○ Elaboration: Elaboration occurs when students make meaningful associations with what they are studying. Deep thinking might include connecting material to things that they already know, producing examples, and asking questions. The Depth of Processing activity can occur here to introduce elaboration (**Activity 6**).

- ○ Retrieval practice: To help learning, students should practice recalling and using information. Rather than just reexposing oneself to information by repeatedly looking over material, students should test their ability to explain information or produce answers to questions without looking at notes or the textbook.

- ○ Overlearning: Students should keep studying well after it feels like they have mastered the material. Once students have correctly answered a question, they should not quit studying that topic. The more students correctly retrieve and apply information, the easier it becomes to do so.

- – Metacognition: In the context of learning, metacognition has to do with student awareness of their own level of understanding of a concept.

- ○ Successful students have an accurate sense of metacognition. They know when they have mastered material. Struggling students have poor metacognition because they are overconfident. They think they have a good understanding when their understanding is shallow and has gaps and misconceptions. As a result, they start studying too late and stop studying too early. They think they do well on exams and are surprised to find out they have done poorly.

- ○ Introductory students struggle the most with metacognition. Those who know the least about a field are the least prepared to grasp what they do not know.

- ○ Bad study strategies increase confidence without increasing learning. For example, textbook material will feel familiar and easy after reading it several times, but that feeling does not mean that a student will be able to recall the material on a test. Don't confuse familiarity with learning.

o The best way students can combat poor metacognition is to test their understanding and get feedback about accuracy. Practice tests and review questions work well for evaluating understanding. Students can also explain the material to someone else or write down what they know and check it against the textbook. In introductory courses, it is best for students to assume that they have poor metacognition and simply study more than they think is necessary.

- To summarize, effective studying involves multiple components:
  - Study with full focus and minimize distractions.
  - Study using effective learning strategies.
  - Assess one's level of understanding to identify confusions, gaps, and misconceptions.
- Conclusion: Effective studying is more than the amount of time spent studying, it is the quality of study, which takes time and effort.
  - Instructors can use the Study Plan discussion activity (**Activity 7**) or the Distributing Study Time activity (**Activity 8**) here. Activity 7 can also be used as an assessment. Instructors can also discuss the Intense Study Session as an example of structuring an effective study session (**Activity 9**).

List of Activities and Assignments for Students

1. Activity 1: Study strategy poll (see Activity C.1)

2. Activity 2: Inattentional blindness demonstration (see Activity C.2)

3. Activity 3: Cost of multitasking demonstration (see Activity C.3)

4. Activity 4: View *How to Get the Most Out of Studying* videos by Stephen Chew (see Resources)

5. Activity 5: Read study skills article by Miyatsu, Nguyen, and McDaniel (see Resources)

6. Activity 6: Depth of processing activity (see Resources listed as Chew, 2010)

7. Activity 7: Discussion of study plan essay (see Assessment 1)
   - The scoring rubric for the essay is in Table C.1.

8. Activity 8: Discussion of distributing study time (see Activity C.4)

9. Activity 9: Discussion of intense study sessions (see Activity C.5)

Formative and Summative Assessments

- Concept Checks for Formative Assessment

(These questions can be used to gauge student understanding at key points during the lesson. They may be used as a think-pair-share or a clicker question for peer instruction.)

1. Which of the following statements on how people learn is supported by research?
   a. People are worse at multitasking than focusing on one task at a time.
   b. Effective learning is a matter of the amount of time spent studying.
   c. Effective learning is a matter of how many times a student has read the material.
   d. People learn best when the learning material matches their specific learning style.

2. Which of the following is most likely to lead to long-term learning?
   a. Highlighting key terms and phrases
   b. Closing your book and notes and writing down everything you can remember about a topic
   c. Reading over the textbook multiple times
   d. Concentrating on only one course or topic during a block of study time

3. Which of the following is an example of poor metacognition?
   a. Joe failed an exam because he memorized definitions, but his professor tested him over comprehension.
   b. Amy felt confident she did well on the exam but was stunned to find out she barely made a D grade.
   c. Cindy studied by reading her notes and her textbook over and over again, but she still made a bad grade.
   d. Sam thought he could learn the material well enough if he just read the chapter summaries, but he ended up failing the exam.

Answers: 1. A; 2. B (a form of retrieval practice); 3. B but also D (the students show poor awareness of what they learned and how to effectively learn).

- Formative or Summative Assessments

Assessment 1: Study Plan Essay

- Consider your academic schedule for the upcoming weeks. Design a study plan that will allow you to learn effectively. The plan should do the following things:

  o Describe specific ways that you account for limitations of attention and working memory.

  o Describe specific plans to apply at least two effective learning strategies.

  o Describe ways that you will use metacognition to become aware of your level of understanding.

  o Identify potential obstacles and describe methods for overcoming them.

- Instructors can find a scoring rubric in Table C.1.

TABLE C.1. Rubric for Assessment 1, Study Plan Essay Question

Performance domain	Effective (2)	Needs improvement (1)	Missing (0)
Attention	The plan makes specific mention of methods for eliminating distractions and the need to maintain focus based on limited attention and working memory capacity.	The plan mentions distractions and limited attention or working memory, but it is not specific.	The plan does not address distractions, attention, or working memory.
Learning strategies	The plan contains accurate and practical application of two or more learning strategies (e.g., distribution, interleaving, chunking, elaboration, overlearning).	The plan contains accurate and practical application of one learning strategy.	The plan includes no accurate or practical applications of learning strategies.
Metacognition	The plan includes a specific strategy for gaining accurate feedback on comprehension.	The plan mentions feedback on comprehension.	The plan includes no means of feedback on comprehension.

TABLE C.1. Rubric for Assessment 1, Study Plan Essay Question (*Continued*)

Performance domain	Effective (2)	Needs improvement (1)	Missing (0)
Practicality	The plan is practical and could be realistically implemented. The plan identifies obstacles and effective methods for overcoming them.	The plan could be implemented. The plan identifies obstacles and possible methods for overcoming them.	The plan could not be implemented. The plan identifies no obstacles.

Assessment 2: Multiple Choice Questions

1. Many first-year students have poor metacognition. This could result in which of the following?

   a. They are likely to stop studying before they truly understand a concept.

   b. They believe they have a complete understanding of a concept when really their understanding is shallow, with both gaps and misconceptions.

   c. They will overestimate how well they do on exams.

   d. All of the above are consequences of poor metacognition.

2. Which of the following statements is TRUE about multitasking?

   a. People have a pretty accurate sense of how good they are at multitasking.

   b. You become better at multitasking the more you do it.

   c. Younger people who have been raised with technology are good at multitasking.

   d. Multitasking virtually always hurts performance compared with focusing on one task at a time.

3. Which of the following statements is true?

   a. Attention allows us to notice most anything going on in our environment.

   b. Students who are more motivated to learn will learn more.

   c. A major challenge of studying effectively is getting information through the limited capacity of working memory.

   d. Any study strategy will lead to learning.

4. In an evening study session, Joan first studies a section from her psychology course. Then she switches to study a section of art history. Then she studies more psychology. Finally, she goes back and studies more art history. Joan is using the study strategy of

   a. Spacing

   b. Interleaving

   c. Retrieval practice

   d. Chunking

5. Instead of studying the properties of cornea, lens, rods, cones, and fovea separately, Astrid studies them all together as parts of the eye for vision. Astrid is using the learning strategy of

   a. Spacing

   b. Interleaving

   c. Retrieval practice

   d. Chunking

Answers: 1. D; 2. D; 3. C; 4. B; 5. D

RESOURCES AND REFERENCES

Agarwal, P. K., & Bains, P. M. (2019). *Powerful teaching: Unleash the science of learning*. Jossey-Bass.

Benassi, V. A., Overson, C. E., & Hakala, C. M. (2014). *Applying science of learning in education: Infusing psychological science into the curriculum*. http://teachpsych.org/ebooks/asle2014/index.php

Brown, P. C., Roediger, H. L., & McDaniel, M. A. (2014). *Make it stick: The science of successful learning*. The Belknap Press of Harvard University Press.

Chew, S. L. (2010). Improving classroom performance by challenging student misconceptions about learning. *APS Observer, 23*, 51–54. http://bit.ly/oFEkRu and available in summary form here: https://bit.ly/32FFhqZ

Chew, S. *How to get the most out of studying* [video]. A series of five videos (with optional introduction) created by Stephen Chew on how to study based on cognitive principles. https://www.samford.edu/departments/academic-success-center/how-to-study

Learning Scientists.org. A website comprising summaries and blog posts about learning science written by learning scientists, including downloadable activities and posters. https://www.learningscientists.org

Miyatsu, T., Nguyen, K., & McDaniel, M. A. (2018). Five popular study strategies: Their optimal implementation and pitfalls. *Perspectives on Psychological Science, 13*(3), 390–407. https://doi.org/10.1177/1745691617710510

Retrievalpractice.org. A website of blogs, summaries, and downloadable resources related to the study strategy of retrieval practice. https://www.retrievalpractice.org

Weinstein, Y., Sumeracki, M., & Caviglioli, O. (2019). *Understanding how we learn: A visual guide*. Routledge.

ACTIVITY C.1: CLASS POLL ON STUDY STRATEGIES

- Description
  - Instructors can conduct an informal poll at the start of the module using clickers or votes by hand to illustrate how frequently students use various study strategies. Instructors can point out when the results suggest that students are using ineffective strategies.
  - A variation on this activity would be to ask students to vote whether each method is effective or ineffective.
- Sample script
  - I am going to list off a number of strategies for studying. Vote for the methods that you typically use when studying for your classes.
    1. Reading the material over and over
    2. Spreading out your studying over many days
    3. Staying up late the night before to pull an all-nighter
    4. Using flashcards to test your knowledge
    5. Cramming right before the test
    6. Mixing up material from different classes rather than studying for just one class at a time
    7. Rewriting your notes
    8. Coming up with questions to test your understanding
    9. Memorizing definitions of key terms
    10. Applying the information to your own life
    11. Making the material fit your personal learning style
    12. Studying in a quiet place with no distractions

ACTIVITY C.2: INATTENTIONAL BLINDNESS

There are many good examples of inattentional blindness on YouTube. Here are two:

1. *The Monkey Business Illusion* by Dan Simons: https://youtu.be/IGQmdoK_ZfY

2. *Test Your Awareness: Whodunnit?* A Public Service Announcement commercial for bicycle awareness: https://youtu.be/ubNF9QNEQLA

ACTIVITY C.3: THE COST OF MULTITASKING

The following demonstration shows the cost of multitasking. The class carries out this task in pairs. A group of three is acceptable for odd numbers. One member of the pair will act as the timer as the other carries out the task. Then the two members switch roles. Each member should have his or her time for each task.

1. Partner up; you will need a stopwatch.

2. Time each other doing the following:

   a. As quick as you can, count down from 10 to 0, then immediately say the alphabet out loud from A to K.

   b. Now, alternate between the alphabet and counting down, 10-A, 9-B, . . .

3. Divide your second task time by your first task time.

   - Everyone should have their times and their ratio from Step 3.

   - If their ratio is 1 or less, they are good at multitasking.

   - If their ratio is greater than 1, it indicates how much slower they were at multitasking. For example, a 3.0 means they were 3 times slower multitasking than focusing on one task at a time. Ask which task was easier to see if their experience matches their times.

   - Have students consider how much more inefficient they are while multitasking than focusing on one topic and then another. Note that these are familiar, highly overlearned tasks. Multitasking is likely worse when doing complex, unfamiliar tasks such as studying.

   - Ask how the students plan to reduce the effects of multitasking and have them share with each other or the class.

ACTIVITY C.4: DISTRIBUTING STUDY TIME

Table C.2 shows three plans for study time.

Discussion Questions

1. What do you think are the strengths and weaknesses of each plan?

2. Which of the plans do you think would be most effective and least effective for learning? Explain your reasoning.

TABLE C.2. Distributing Study Time

It's Monday. You have an exam on Friday over four chapters. What is your study plan?

Plan A	Plan B	Plan C
Monday: Read Ch. 1	**Monday**: Do other stuff	**Monday**: Read Ch. 1 & 2 (at least)
Tuesday: Read Ch. 2	**Tuesday**: Do other stuff	**Tuesday**: Test self over Ch. 1 & 2; read Ch. 3 & 4
Wednesday: Read Ch. 3	**Wednesday**: Start reading	**Wednesday**: Test self over Ch. 3 & 4; review Ch. 1 & 2 based on self-test
Thursday: Read Ch. 4 and review all chapters	**Thursday**: Finish reading and review	**Thursday**: Review Ch. 3 & 4 based on self-test; review and self-test all chapters
Friday: Take exam	**Friday**: Take exam	**Friday**: Take exam

3. Which plan do you think you should follow? Which plan do you think you would likely follow (or what plan of your own would you follow)? Explain your choices.

Instructor Discussion Guide for "Distributing Study Time" Activity

Plan A represents a methodical approach to studying. Every chapter is read once. Students may see this as a good study plan because it is thorough, but reading a chapter only once is not sufficient for learning new, complex concepts. There is no mechanism for feedback about proper understanding (metacognition) or misconceptions. In addition, chapters read early in the week are likely to be forgotten by the exam. Students need to have an opportunity to read the chapter, reflect on it, get answers to any questions about it, get feedback about their understanding, and review the material. Although comprehensive, this is not a good study plan for long-term learning.

Plan B represents cramming, concentrating study time immediately before the exam. Although cramming can be an effective study strategy for immediate recall, it is a poor study strategy for long-term recall because forgetting is rapid from massed studying. It is also a highly risky strategy. If it turns out that the material is more complex than the student anticipates, there is no additional time that the student can allocate for studying. If the student cannot grasp the material quickly or has questions, there is no opportunity to get help. If the student has misconceptions from the reading, there is no way to discover these before the exam. Students, especially struggling students and those who are aiming just to pass the exam, may easily fail the exam using this strategy.

Plan C requires the most effort to carry out but will lead to the most enduring learning and gives the student the best chance of developing a deep, accurate understanding of the material. By reading, self-testing, then reviewing, students have a chance to reflect on the material, discover gaps and misconceptions, formulate questions, and get answers to those questions. This plan incorporates spacing, interleaving, and retrieval practice—all highly effective long-term learning strategies. This method requires more planning and self-discipline than the other plans.

ACTIVITY C.5: INTENSE STUDY SESSIONS (ISS)

Originally from the Louisiana State Website and adapted for use here (https://www.depauw.edu/files/resources/cook2013.pdf).

1. Set a Goal (1–2 min)
   - Decide what you want to accomplish in your study session
2. Study With Focus (30–50 min)
   - Eliminate all distractions and temptations
   - Use deep processing
3. Reward Yourself (5–10 min)
   - Take a break—call a friend, play a short game, get a snack—but keep it short.
4. Review (5 min)
   - Go over what you just studied
   - Recall without looking

Index

A

Academic integrity, 150
Academic momentum, 16–17
Academic self-efficacy, 146–148
Academic skills, 140–148
  academic self-efficacy, 146–148
  self-regulation, 143–146
  study skills, 140–143
  taught in introductory psychology, 10
Academic success, 16–17. *See also* Student
  Success and Transformation
  and application of psychological
    principles, 76
  teaching necessary skills for, 10
Accessibility tools, 45
Action (stage of change), 96
Active learning, 116, 119
Active learning classrooms (ALCs), 119
Administration, of assessments, 101
Adoption (in stages of change), 97
Advanced Placement (AP) Psychology
  exam, 14, 59
Affordability, of course materials, 45–46
Afful, S. E., 117
Ages, students of varying, 211–215
Aging, as diversity topic, 152
American Association of Colleges and
  Universities, 83
American Psychological Association (APA)
  APA Dictionary of Psychology, 9
  *APA Guidelines for the Undergraduate
    Psychology Major*, 13, 17, 61, 64, 84,
    213, 231, 243
  APA IPI introductory psychology student
    learning outcomes, 64–68

  Board of Educational Affairs, xiii–xiv, 3,
    84, 219
  Committee on Associate and
    Baccalaureate Education, 17, 84–85
  divisions of, 32
  *Ethical Principles for Psychologists and
    Code of Conduct*, 150
  *National Standards for High School
    Psychology Curricula*, 61, 84, 206–207
  Project Assessment, 127, 226
  Skillful Psychology Student, 18
  Society for Teaching of Psychology, 115,
    124, 193, 208, 221
  *Strengthening the Common Core of the
    Introductory Psychology Course*, 84
  Summit on High School Psychology
    Education, 71
  Summit on National Assessment of
    Psychology, xiv, 84–85
  Teachers of Psychology Secondary
    Schools, 208
American Psychologist, xiv
Anderson, J. R., 38
Angelo, T., 83
Annual Conference on Teaching, 193, 208
APA. *See* American Psychological
  Association
APA Dictionary of Psychology, 9
*APA Guidelines for the Undergraduate
  Psychology Major*, 13, 17, 61, 64, 84,
  213, 231, 243
APA IPI introductory psychology student
  learning outcomes, 64–68
Appleby, D. C., 156

T

Teacher education, 12
Teachers of Psychology Secondary Schools
(TOPSS), 208
Teacher Training and Development (TTD),
5, 171–196
challenges for introductory psychology,
181–189
departmental changes context study,
262
formal training, 189–192
in high school elective context study,
208
historically Black liberal arts college for
women context study, 245
lack of consistency in, 173–174
large classes context study, 257
and nature of paradigm shifts, 176
new approach to, 174–175
ongoing support following, 192–195
operationalizing recommendations
context studies, 232, 239
proposed model for, 176–181
recommendations, 171–172
standardization of teaching context
study, 221
students of varying ages context study,
214–215
students with varying degrees of
readiness context study, 227
uneven enrollment context study,
249–250
Teaching conferences, 193
Teaching Introductory Psychology (Griggs
& Jackson), 117
Teaching of Psychology, 226
Teaching Resource and Research Center,
245
Technological skills, 37
Technology(-ies)
choosing to adopt, 123–124
classroom use of, 119
Test anxiety, 145–146
Test-enhanced learning, 39
Testing effect, 39
Test of Scientific Literacy Skills (TOSL),
249
Themes
in core content, 62, 63
integrative, 33–34
in large classes context study, 255–256

in selection of assessments, 102–103
student learning outcomes for, 67–68,
72–77
teacher training on, 182
Timing, of assessments, 99–100
TOPSS (Teachers of Psychology Secondary
Schools), 208
TOSL (Test of Scientific Literacy Skills), 249
Transformative, introductory psychology
as, 15–19
Transformative skills. *See* Student Success
and Transformation
Transtheoretical model of stages of
change, 96
TTD. *See* Teacher Training and
Development

U

Unconscious mental processes, 153–154
Universal design for learning, 44
University of Tennessee, Knoxville (UTK),
247–250
Utah, 206–207
Utah State Office of Education (USOE),
206
Utah Teachers of Psychology in Secondary
Schools, 208

V

Verbal messages, from instructors and
peers, 147
Veterans, 122

W

Walker, J., 150
Wang, X., 10, 16
Warchal, J., 151
Weiten, W., 61
Wellness, skills related to, 148–149
Western, educated, industrialized,
rich, and democratic (WEIRD)
populations, 47–48
Wiggins, G. P., 30, 126, 127
Wilson, J. H., 49
Working memory, 290

Y

Yu, M. C., 15

About the Editors

Regan A. R. Gurung, PhD, is Associate Vice Provost and Executive Director of the Center for Teaching and Learning, professor of psychological science, and director of the General Psychology program at Oregon State University. His Applied Social Cognition lab studies factors influencing teaching and learning. A recipient of the American Psychological Foundation Charles L. Brewer Distinguished Teaching of Psychology Award, he is the author, coauthor, or editor of 15 books and more than 100 peer-reviewed articles. He was founding coeditor of the American Psychological Association's (APA's) journal *Scholarship of Teaching and Learning in Psychology* and past president of both the Society for the Teaching of Psychology (STP; APA Division 2) and Psi Chi, the International Honor Society in Psychology.

Garth Neufeld, MA, is a professor of psychology at Cascadia College, founder of Teaching Introductory Psychology Northwest and the Teaching of Psychology Incubator workshop, and cofounder of the *PsychSessions* podcast. He has served the national teaching of psychology community through the Society for the Teaching of Psychology, the Advanced Placement Psychology Reading, and APA's Education Directorate. In 2018, he was awarded a Citizen Psychologist presidential citation from APA for cofounding Shared Space for All (https://www.sharedspaceforall.com), an organization that educates and mentors at-risk Thai children toward the prevention of prostitution. He is also the recipient of the 2019 STP Wayne Weiten Teaching Excellence Award.